PENGUIN HANDBOOKS

The Knitwear Revolution

Suzy Menkes is Fashion Editor of *The Times*. Her interest in clothes started, appropriately enough, with knitting – when she cast on the stitches of a flamboyant pink scarf at the age of six. She went on to make and create her own clothes and ultimately to become a leading authority in fashion. She studied English at Cambridge and dress design in Paris before joining the London *Evening Standard* as Fashion Editor and later becoming Woman's Editor of the *Daily Express*. She has always taken a particular interest in the creative designers in the fashion world and has continued to knit for herself and her three sons. She is married to a journalist and lives in London.

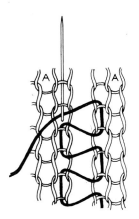

Suzy Menkes

The Knitwear Revolution

Designer Patterns to Make

Penguin Books

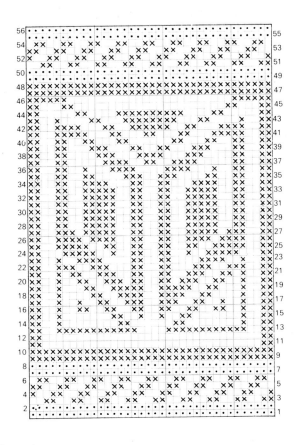

Penguin Books Ltd, Harmondsworth, Middlesex, England
Viking Penguin Inc., 40 West 23rd Street, New York, New York 10010, U.S.A.
Penguin Books Australia Ltd, Ringwood, Victoria, Australia
Penguin Books Canada Ltd, 2801 John Street, Markham, Ontario, Canada L3R 1B4
Penguin Books (N.Z.) Ltd, 182–190 Wairau Road, Auckland 10, New Zealand

First published by Bell and Hyman 1983
Published in Penguin Books 1985

Printed and bound in Great Britain by
Hazell Watson & Viney Limited,
Member of the BPCC Group,
Aylesbury, Bucks
Typeset in Photina

Acknowledgements

My especial thanks to Christine Painell for all her unflagging hard work, her research and for her inspiration and help with styling.

To Elenka for the hair and make-up in all the model shots.

To Elizabeth Aitken of Lister-Lee for her patience and technical skill.

To Liz Specterman at the International Wool Secretariat.

To Chattels, 53 Chalk Farm Road, London NW1 for their dried flowers.

To the following designers and shops:

Giorgio Armani
Sheridan Barnett
Browns
Detail
Joseph
Kenzo
Liberty
Mulberry
Michaela Frey
N. Peal
Pineapple Dance Centre
Practical Styling
Stephanel
Whistles

Contents

Introduction: Knitting for Victory

Knitting is women's work. I prefer to call it women's art. For the best hand-knitting is a pleasure to look at and a skilful craft as well as something warm and comfortable to wear.

The current renaissance of knitting reflects absolutely the changing status of women. From subservient wife knitting balaclavas for the troops (and later knitting for victory), we now have a creative flowering of hand-knitting that has become high fashion and a serious commercial business.

This book is about the people behind the knitwear revolution. To be more precise, it is a book about women, for the designers who have transformed knitwear from the dull necessities of winter woollies to imaginative, elegant and even amusing garments, are almost entirely female. They are also British, for knitting is one fashion area where Britain unequivocally leads the world, partly because of our traditional skill with the needles, passed down from the generation of Fair Isle knitters, partly because of art school training which has encouraged students to stretch the boundaries of knitting beyond slipovers and stocking stitch.

We also have a British tradition of small businesses that makes us receptive to the idea of a hand-knit company which can never reach factory production levels because it is about people – about 'the little old ladies out there' as one yarn manufacturer ignorantly defined for me Britain's six million hand-knitters.

Knitting today is no longer granny's preserve. Now needles are in the hands of the young, who have confounded predictions by taking up the more rustic crafts in defiance of technology. The role of the older generation has been to pass on its crafts and skills. Nearly three quarters of the designers in this book picked up stitches on their grandmothers' knees, rather than learning from their own mothers.

The idea of knitting as an old lady's occupation is as old as this century. While sewing has historically been a suitable occupation for a young lady (and an endless drudge for maids and mothers until the sewing machine was invented), knitting, by contrast, was a contracting industry. In Tudor times, Queen Elizabeth I set up a knitted hose business in England (with the work carried out by men). By the last century, the machine frame had driven hand-knitting out into the remote rural and fishing communities and into the parlours of old ladies with time on their hands.

Ernest Shepard, the illustrator of *Winnie the Pooh*, paints a vivid picture of the maiden lady knitter in this gentle autobiography of his late Victorian Childhood:

'The Aunts rested or knitted garments for the people of Algoma. Aunt Emily had her own special activity, which was in aid of the Deep Sea fishermen. The garments she knitted, which were of fearful and wonderful proportions, were often tried on Father, who was inclined to make derogatory remarks, while Emily, with puzzled looks, and a knitting needle in her mouth, would say "Tut-t-t, very odd, I know I followed the pattern most carefully".'

The 'Aunts' were not knitting for the pleasure of creating, and seldom knitting for themselves. They were, significantly, knitting for worthy causes.

The War Effort has been a motivating force that runs like a row of purl stitches through twentieth century knitting. Young, middle class women often took up knitting for the first time to make the eponymous 'Balaclava'. Knitting for Our Brave Boys in the First World War became a poignant symbol of the futility of woman's role, and at the same time an emotional gesture of solidarity. Rose Macaulay expresses vividly the frustration of the woman left behind in *Poems of Today 1915*:

'In a trench you are sitting, while I am knitting
A hopeless sock that never gets done.'

By the time of the Second World War, women were knitting out of necessity as they had not done since well before the industrial revolution. With two ounces of wool rationed at one precious coupon, (the year's total clothing allowance in 1941 was just 66 coupons per person), knitting was the business of Make Do and Mend, as the worthy wartime slogan put it. 'Why not turn that old bedsock into a snazzy little hat?' asked a

Sunday Pictorial article. Government propaganda introduced Mrs. Sew-and-Sew, whose cosy hints were supposed to help the housewife kit out her family by showing women how to unpick two old-fashioned dishcloths and turn them into a sweater. (With the irony of history, Suzanne Russell of Rococo was knitting this same dishcloth yarn into a high fashion hand-knit sweater thirty years later.)

The need to use thrift and imagination for survival in time of war is not new. What ring so oddly to modern ears are the cloying phrases which ladled out advice. 'Here's a grand job for black-out evenings...' cooed *Weldon Ladies' Journal* over their knitting patterns in 1939. Did the women who joined the WAAF, worked as Land Army girls and faced death for their country deserve the bathetic advice to knit the Victory Jumper (V-neck, V-motif and make it as a waistcoat if you were short of wool) to greet their men as they came home?

No wonder that the earliest thrust of the women's movement was designed to free woman from her role as domestic dormouse and to challenge the women's magazines which had interpreted the German 'kinder, kirche, kuche' as 'children, kitchen and knitting'.

The bad name of knitting as a domestic tie that binds, stems from the thirties, when unemployment and the Depression drove the Establishment to stifle women's burgeoning expectations of their prospects. Women were pushed back into the home and their role as housewife to 'hubby' was glorified. A close study of knitting patterns alone in women's magazines of the thirties, tells us a great deal about the society's view of women.

'He's sporting the woollen lumber jacket which his wife's clever fingers have knitted for him,' reads the introduction to a man's jacket pattern in *Wife and Home* of July 1936. Appropriately enough, the pattern for this clinging 'little woman' to knit is worked in moss stitch.

Here is woman knitting not for personal satisfaction or creative pleasure, but for male approval. *Wife and Home* of October 1933 offered 'A Pullover He'll Appreciate': 'Hubby will be only too pleased to discard his waistcoat and instead sport the comfortable garment his little wife has knitted for him.' 'The Man of the Family,' says the *Farmer's Home* of November 1935, 'Will be sure to welcome a Gift Like This'.

The idea of a woman knitting for her man has a fine historical pedigree. Traditional knitting in the fishing communities was always done in this way and ritualised the woman's role: she stayed at home by the fireside to knit while man the hunter went to sea. The finest folk art of the Fair Isles, the so-called 'Robes of Glory', were specifically knitted by older women for their grandsons to mark their arrival on the threshold of manhood. Into the intricate knitting were woven symbols of the waters and flower of life, the star of Bethlehem to follow and the crown of glory as a reward for a good life. These adolescent dreamcoats are now prized as museum pieces.

Knitting in our own time is as much a reflection of society as it has been in the past. Emancipated women design not for men, but for themselves or other women. Designers now have the confidence to regard themselves as professionals and to turn their knitting skills into a business. Sociologists would probably note that many of the women designers in this book have male back-up (husband, partner, brother) on the business side of their companies. Woman as creative force and breadwinner with man in the supporting role is a neat contrast with the past.

The renaissance of hand-knitting dates from the revolt against mass production and the revival of interest in craft and handwork which affected all the decorative arts in the late sixties and early seventies. The search for the Good Life, the back-to-nature enthusiasm for wholesome food and for goods which had been made with love and personal attention, made people appreciate hand-knitting as never before. It also inspired fashion students who might otherwise have been absorbed into mass production, to set up a cottage industry.

These students also had the opportunity to study textiles and to absorb patterns from different ethnic cultures into their work, in a way that had been done quite naturally in the earliest history of knitting, when the Vikings introduced Berber rug patterns to Nordic knitters.

One of the most effective design springs of the new knitting has been the use of pattern drawn from the kelims, the antique textiles and the paisley shawls with which the knitting designers tend to surround themselves. With the exception of a very few designers (notably Patricia Roberts who believes strongly in stitchcraft and significantly has a plain white home with not an oriental rug in sight), today's knitting is visual: that is, it relies for its effect on colour and pattern. At its most extreme, this leads weaver and painter Kaffe Fassett to claim that knitting patterns are unnecessary, that garments should be one size and unisexual, and that experimenting with colour and texture is the essential of good knitting.

This view is now being challenged by the new wave of student knitters who are influenced by the graphic patterns and geometric shapes of Japanese knitwear.

Changes in the shape and proportions of fashion must be an important part of modern knitting. I make a distinction in my own mind (if not directly in this book) between knitters who are fashion designers with knitting as part of their total style, and those who are first and foremost knitters. Fashion designers like Zandra Rhodes will cut a shape in toile and then knit it up. Sandy Black, a one-time maths student, works out her patterns according to the behaviour of the stitches.

Since the history of twentieth century fashion is all about the development of casual wear, the fashion role of knitting is important. But within the recent hand-knit revolution, various design strands are interwoven. The chapter headings are designed to unravel them.

This is a Fashion Editor's book and I believe that a garment that is designed to be worn must fulfil its function, however attractive its pattern or stunning its combination of colour or texture. Knitwear is made to be worn – even if the idea of the sweater as an art form reached its height in the sixties when David Hockney designed a picture sweater that was framed to hang on the wall.

The thirty patterns featured illustrate aptly the design strength of hand-knitting and provide a wardrobe for all reasons and seasons. They give to any competent knitter the chance to make a designer original. I hope they will also inspire knitters to make up their own designs and provide them with a source of innocent and creative pleasure.

Abbreviations and Notes

Abbreviations

A, B, C, etc.	contrast yarns
alt	alternate
BC	back cross: slip the next st onto c.n. and leave at back of work, K the next 2 sts, then P the st from c.n.
beg	beginning
C3b	cable 3 back: slip the next 3 sts onto c.n. and leave at back of work. K the next 3 sts from left hand ndl. Then K the 3 from c.n.
C3f	cable 3 front: as C3b above, but hold the 3 sts on c.n. at *front* instead of back of work.
c.n.	cable needle
cont	continue
dec	decrease
FC	front cross: slip the next 2 sts onto c.n. and hold at front of work. P the next st then K the 2 sts from c.n.
foll	following
g	gramme
K	knit
m1	make one
MY	main yarn
ndl(s)	needle(s)
P	purl
patt	pattern
PSSO	pass slip stitch(es) over
single rib	K1, P1 alternately
SKPO	slip 1, knit 1, pass slip stitch over
sl	slip
st(s)	stitch(es)
st.st	stocking stitch
T2L	twist 2 left: knit into the back of the 2nd st on left hand ndl, then knit into the 1st st and slip both off ndl together
T2R	twist 2 right: knit into the front of the 2nd st on left hand ndl, then knit the 1st st and slip both off ndl together
tbl	through back loop
tog	together
YB	yarn back
YFD	yarn forward
yon	yarn over needle
yrn	yarn round needle

Tension

It is *essential* to test out your tension before beginning any garment. Knit a sample using the needle size and stitch specified in the pattern. Pin out your sample carefully without stretching it and compare the number of rows and stitches to a 10cm (4in) square with that given. If you have fewer rows and stitches than the pattern states, try again using smaller needles. If you have more, change to larger needles.

Notes

N.B. Some of the patterns are more complicated than others. You should read through any pattern carefully before starting on it to check how much knitting experience it requires.

Instructions in brackets are repeated the number of times stated after the brackets.

In patterns with more than one size, instructions for the different sizes are separated by oblique lines.

Buttonholes: To make buttonholes cast off 1 st (or more for larger buttonholes). Then cast back on on the following row.

In the Fair Isle charts, each square represents one stitch. Odd numbered (knit) rows are read right to left and even numbered (purl) rows left to right.

Yarn stockists

Addresses for suppliers of specialist yarns are given with the relevant patterns. The other yarns are commonly available from local retailers but, in case of difficulty, lists of stockists can be obtained from the manufacturers at the following addresses:

Lister-Lee, 11 Harley Street, Cavendish Square, London W1N 1DA.
Patons & Baldwins Ltd, PO Box, Darlington, Co. Durham, DR1 1YQ.
Georges Picaud Coton Cannele, Priory Yarns Ltd, 48 Station Road, Osset, W. Yorkshire.
Pingouin, 7–11 Lexington Street, London W1.
Sirdar Ltd, PO Box 31, Wakefield, W. Yorkshire, WF2 9ND.
Twilleys, 52 Westmoreland Terrace, London SW1.

Susan Walmsley: Sea-Faring Guernsey

[See photograph previous page]

Sweaters were the workwear of the sea. Centuries before the nylon anorak and the steel hull were invented, sailors and fishermen discovered the ideal garment to keep them warm and comfortable as they worked, in a material that breathed in the salt spray and exhaled the sweat of heavy toil.

The sea-faring sweater is knitted into the history of all countries with a shoreline and a fleet, and especially into the island communities who drew their livelihood from the surrounding sea. Although nobody has been able to unravel the history of knitting, it is believed to have originated in the East and been brought to the Northern countries by the trade routes.

The sea-faring life was ritualised in wool, so that stitches were symbols of every day life or patterns became woven emblems to ward off disaster. In the case of Fair Isle and Nordic sweaters, tribal totems and community interests were worked into the wool, as well as designs from more far-flung cultures like the Berber carpets and Nomad rugs. In Arans, jerseys and most especially Guernseys, the stitches became a complex web of pattern reflecting the islanders' everyday life and surroundings. From the sea came anchors and waves, sand and shingle, the thick ropes and naval knots and the diamond weave of fishing nets. Guernseys were made by women for their menfolk, the patterns passed down from mother to daughter within one small parish, and they wove into their work more domestic symbols like the familiar marriage lines.

The traditional Guernsey is constructed like a tube, the body knitted in one piece to give warmth and strength, as these traditional sweaters were for centuries a fisherman's uniform. The decorative stitches were often only on the yoke and many of the patterns disappeared as the industrial revolution brought wider possibilities of work and of clothing.

Our current interest in the art of crafts has brought a revival of interest in the traditional knitting and extinct Guernseys have even been recreated from Victorian photographs.

Susan Walmsley was a fashion student at the influential Royal College of Art when she first studied the history and especially the stitchcraft of the Guernsey. Long before that time, she had been fascinated by the sea and by its restless changing patterns. She was brought up in Lancashire 12 miles from the coast and in her local towns and villages she saw the tradition of knitting carried on by the women who worked at the Mills. As a fashion student the two ideas meshed in her mind.

After Sue left Preston Polytechnic and won her place at the Royal College of Art, she became increasingly involved with knitting and her degree collection was a series of sea sweaters using both colour and stitches to recreate the movement of waves and the patterns of light on water.

'I had a strong feeling that I wanted to use the sea and its environment' she says. 'It came to me as an idea because I had read and looked at the historic tradition of Guernseys and I studied the patterns so that I understood about the combination of stitches. But I decided to move right away from the traditional shapes and introduce a different concept of the sweater as fashionable outerwear.'

In particular, Sue developed the idea of the gusset into a complete side panel and made her oversweater big enough to substitute for a jacket or coat (see photograph).

Although her stitchcraft is very precise, she cut the body shapes out of calico to give a fashion cut. The result is an effective fusion of fashion with an age-old craft.

Susan Walmsley's imaginative interpretation of the sea-faring sweater inspired by her study of traditional guernseys. It is knitted in a cable wave pattern in Icelandic wool with inserts of other yarns to give texture interest and sea blue colour splashed in a random pattern to give the effect of water. The idea of the guernsey gusset is developed into bold underarm panels to make a loose oversweater that is warm enough to wear as a jacket.

Size: One size.

Yarn:
MY: 1500g Icelandic Softspun, shade 18 (Light Brown) by T. Forsell & Sons from Ries Wools, Holborn, London WC2, and all good wool shops.
A: 2 × 50g balls Patons Clansman, shade 11 (Navy).
B: 2 × 50g balls Sirdar Astrakhan, shade 348, (Bright Blue).
C: 1 × 50g ball Patons Clansman, shade 2481, (Rust).
D: 1 ball Twilleys loosely spun cotton (Natural).

Needles: 6mm (no. 4) and cable needle.

Tension: 24 sts and 24 rows worked in cable pattern on 6mm (no. 4) ndls to 11.5cm (4½in) square.

Note: The contrast colours in this garment were placed at random using the judgement of the eye, making the front, back and sleeves totally individual. It is advisable to work a sample square using MY and a length of one of the contrast yarns to experiment, following these hints:

Yarns A and B are the main contrast colours with yarns C and D used as highlights. The highlights should not be used frequently and are placed sporadically where necessary.

The coloured shapes are all knitted individually with separate lengths of yarn, i.e. the contrast colour yarn is not carried across the work to form each new shape, only the MY is constant, being 'knitted in' on the wrong side of the work when a contrast colour is used. This produces a neat wrong side free from floating yarn, which makes it less likely to snag.

The contrast colour lengths can vary from approx. 46–90cm (18–36in) which determines the size of the coloured shape. As it is a random pattern, lengths can be cut as required without using a tape measure.

To achieve a random effect

1. Bring the contrast colours in gradually by working 1–4 sts only. e.g. if using A on a knit row, K3A. Any more than 4 sts would create a definite line.
2. Make the shapes irregular by increasing and/or decreasing the number of stitches worked in that colour on each row.
3. Finish the shapes subtly by ending with 1–4 sts in that contrast colour.
4. When a contrast colour shape has been completed, work at least 8 rows in MY above that shape before beginning another contrast length. It is important that MY remains dominant and surrounds each coloured shape.
5. Avoid placing the same contrast colour too much in one area.

6. Use yarns A and B as alternately as possible. e.g. across one row may read: 12MY, 3A, 5MY, 2B, 30MY, 2A, 29MY, 3B, 10MY.

As this is a random design any given examples are only suggestions. The cables will help to create the shapes.

Back panel
Using 6mm (no. 4) ndls and MY cast on (preferably using thumb method) 72 sts.
Purl 6 rows.
Next row: K1, inc into next st, * K2, inc into next st, rep from * to last st, K1 (96 sts).
Cable pattern:
Row 1 and every alt row: P to end.
Row 2: * C3f, K6, rep from * to end.
Row 4: K to end.
Row 6: * K6, C3b, rep from * to end.
Row 8: K to end.
Rows 1 to 8 form the cable pattern. Repeat throughout, adding the contrast colours at random until 135 rows in cable pattern have been worked and work measures 66cm (26in) from cast on row.
Now using MY cast off 24 sts for shoulder, break MY. Rejoin MY to remaining sts and cast off 48 sts for back neck, break MY. Rejoin to remaining sts and cast off for shoulder, break yarn.

Front panel
Work as for back panel until 123 rows in cable pattern have been worked and work measures 61cm (24in) from cast on edge.
Neck shaping: Keeping cable pattern correct work 24 sts, turn. Continue on these 24 sts until 12 rows have been worked. Cast off in MY.
Rejoin MY to remaining sts and cast off next 48 sts. Work remaining sts keeping cable pattern correct for 12 rows. Cast off these sts in MY.

Sleeves
Using 6mm (no. 4) ndls and MY cast on (as before) 58 sts.
Purl 5 rows.
Next row: P, inc 1 st into the first and every following 3rd st across the row ending with an inc into last st (78 sts).
Next row: K, inc 1 st into first and last st.
The sleeves are worked in the cable pattern as for the front and back panels but on the centre 36 sts only, throughout. The remaining sts are worked in st.st. Use the contrast yarns at random as before.
Row 1: P to end.
Row 2: K22, (C3f, K6) 3 times, K22.
Row 3: P to end.
Row 4: K to end.
Row 5: P to end.
Row 6: K22, (K6, C3b) 3 times, K22.
Row 7: P inc 1 st into first and last st.
Row 8: K to end.
Row 9: P to end.
Row 10: K23, (C3f, K6) 3 times, K23.
Row 11: P to end.
Row 12: K to end.

Row 13: P to end.
Row 14: K23, (K6, C3b) 3 times, K23.
Row 15: As 7.
Row 16: K to end.
Row 17: P to end.
Row 18: K24, (C3f, K6) 3 times, K24.
Row 19: P to end.
Row 20: K to end.
Row 21: P to end.
Row 22: K24, (K6, C3b) 3 times, K24.
Row 23: As 7.
Row 24: K to end.
Row 25: P to end.
Row 26: K25, (C3f, K6) 3 times, K25.
Row 27: P to end.
Row 28: K to end.
Row 29: P to end.
Row 30: K25, (K6, C3b) 3 times, K25.
Row 31: As 7.
Row 32: K to end.
Row 33: P to end.
Row 34: K26, (C3f, K6) 3 times, K26.
Row 35: P to end.
Row 36: K to end.
Row 37: P to end.
Row 38: K26, (K6, C3b) 3 times, K26.
Row 39: As 7.
Row 40: K to end.
Row 41: P to end.
Row 42: K27, (C3f, K6) 3 times, K27.
Row 43: P to end.
Row 44: K to end.
Row 45: P to end.
Row 46: K27, (K6, C3b) 3 times, K27.
Row 47: As 7.
Row 48: K to end.
Row 49: P to end.
Row 50: K28, (C3f, K6) 3 times, K28.
Row 51: P to end.
Row 52: K to end.
Row 53: P to end.
Row 54: K28, (K6, C3b) 3 times, K28.
Row 55: P to end.
Row 56: K to end.
Row 57: P to end.
Continue without shaping repeating rows 51 to 57 inclusive for 28 rows, cast off using MY.
Repeat these instructions for 2nd sleeve.

Side panels

Using 6mm (no. 4) ndls and MY, cast on (as for sleeves) 44 sts.
Purl 6 rows.
Row 1: Join in D (using from ball), K2MY, P2D, rep to end, break D.
Row 2: P to end in MY.
Row 3: K to end in MY.
Row 4: P to end in MY.
Row 5: Join in B (using from ball), P2B, K2MY, rep to end, break B.
Rows 6 to 8: Rep rows 2 to 4 once.

Row 9: Join in A (using from ball), K2MY, P2A, rep to end, break A.
Row 10: P to end in MY.
Row 11: K to end in MY.
Rows 12 to 33: Rep rows 10 and 11 eleven times.
Row 34: P to end in MY.
Row 35: Join in C (using from ball), P2C, K2MY, rep to end, break C.
Rows 36 to 38: Rep rows 2, 3 and 4 once.
Row 39: Join in A, K2MY, P2A, rep to end, break A.
Rows 40 to 42: Rep rows 2, 3 and 4 once.
Row 43: Join in B, P2B, K2MY, rep to end, break B.
Row 44: P to end in MY.
Row 45: K to end in MY.
Rows 46 to 67: Rep rows 44 and 45 eleven times.
Row 68: Join in A, K2MY, P2A, rep to end, break A.
Rows 69 to 71: Rep rows 2, 3 and 4 once.
Row 72: Join in D, P2D, K2MY, rep to end, break D.
Rows 73 to 75: Rep rows 2, 3 and 4 once.
Row 76: Join in B, K2MY, P2B, rep to end, break B.
Row 77: P to end in MY.
Cast off in MY.
Repeat these instructions for 2nd side panel.

Side edge trims

SIDE PANELS
Using 6mm (no. 4) ndls and MY and with right side facing, pick up along the right-hand edge (starting at the cast on end and up to the bottom of the first P2C, K2MY row) 24 sts and K 5 rows. Cast off purlwise. This is now the right-hand side panel.
Using 6mm (no. 4) ndls and MY and with right side facing, pick up along the left-hand edge (starting at bottom of the P2C, K2MY row and ending at the cast on edge) 24 sts and K 5 rows. Cast off purlwise. This is now the left-hand side panel.

FRONT PANEL
Using 6mm (no. 4) ndls and MY and with right side facing, pick up along the left-hand edge (to the bottom of the 5th cable curve) 24 sts and K 5 rows. Cast off purlwise. Repeat for right-hand edge starting at bottom of the 5th cable curve.

Neckband
Neatly stitch right-hand shoulder seam. Using 6mm (no. 4) ndls and MY used single, and with right side facing, pick up evenly along front neck edge 60 sts, then pick up evenly along back neck edge 46 sts. Now continue, joining in another end of MY to make it double thickness, in K1, P1 rib for 7 rows.
Next row: Join in A, used single, and keeping rib correct P1A, K1MY to the end keeping the yarn not being used at the back of the work. Break A.
Continue using MY double and rib 7 more rows. Cast off ribwise.

Finishing
Join shoulder seam as before and neckband opening. Fold neckband in half with the cast off edge on the right side of the garment, and pin or tack into place keeping the ribs vertical. Using MY slip stitch each K1 rib at cast

Kaffe Fassett's richly coloured Moghul gardens jacket (page 39)

off edge on neckband to the row below pick-up line on the garment.

Lay garment open and flat, put centre of sleeve 'head' (i.e. centre of cabling on sleeve) to shoulder seam.

Count down from shoulder seam on front and back panels 7 cable edge curves, and pin the cast off edge of the sleeve to this mark. Sew the sleevehead following the curve of the cables.

Sew sleeve seam from cast on edge to 4th row after the increases have finished.

Sew the side panels to the front panel, overlapping the front edge trims over the side panel edge trims at each side, and leave these free. Then pin each front edge trim onto the actual side panel and neatly stitch the top end. Pin the side panel edge trim to the inside of the front panel and neatly stitch the top end. Sew back panel to side panels.

Put top of sleeve seam to centre of cast off edge on side panel. Neatly stitch together.

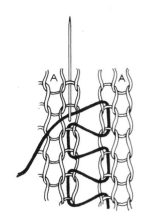

Mattress stitch can be used when joining the back and front panels to the side panels. This form of stitching is worked on the right side of the garment. If the edge is not very neat, use the second channel marked A.

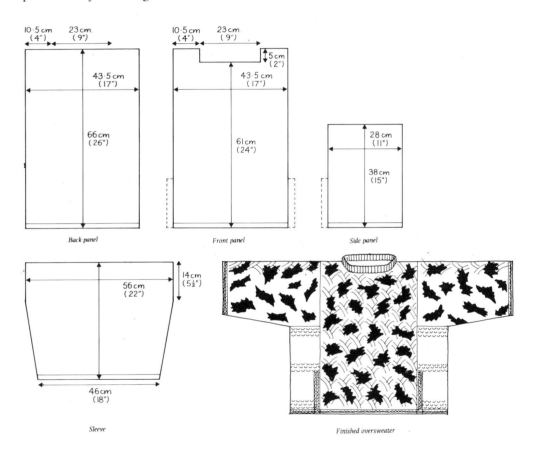

Back panel

Front panel

Side panel

Sleeve

Finished oversweater

PRESSING

Turn garment inside out and lay flat on a padded board. Push pins through front and back seams to hold in place. Do not pull out of shape. Pin the bottom edge into place allowing it to flute if necessary thus keeping the seams straight. Using a hot iron with a damp cloth and without letting either touch the garment, lightly steam seams and bottom edge, gently tapping with the flat of the hand to help flatten the seams and remove any excess fullness which may occur at the bottom edge. Leave to dry completely once steaming is finished.

Jane Wheeler wearing her Persian medallion coat (page 43) watches the Norfolk lambs with her daughter Lucy in her Fair Isle cardigan (page 46)

17

Edina Ronay: Fair Isles for the Family

[*See also colour photograph on back of jacket*]

Fair Isle was beached on the tiny Scottish island of that name when a stray ship from the Spanish Armada was wrecked offshore in 1558. The brightly coloured, richly patterned sweaters worn by the Spanish sailors wove a new strand of knitting into Nordic folklore, and many of the symbols of Catholic Europe – the star of Bethlehem, the sacred heart and the 'Armada' cross – were incorporated into Fair Isle sweaters.

In contrast to the textured, celtic patterns of Arans, Fair Isle knitting is worked in flat stocking stitch, but takes its life from patterns and colours. Traditionally, the background is neutral, mostly the natural creamy beige of shetland wool, but the intricate patterns are worked in strong colour.

Edina Ronay says that her bright, fresh, unexpected use of colour owes a lot to her Hungarian background. Her home (where she is pictured with her children) is filled with the vivid red and green and the flat, stylised flowers of Hungarian folk art, and these are translated into embroidered flowers on a Tyrolean cardigan or bold bright colours in cotton Fair Isles. 'I love putting colours together that don't conventionally mix,' she explains. 'But I also love the quiet and muted colours in traditional Fair Isles. I started collecting original twenties and thirties Fair Isles 16 years ago. I would see one and fall in love with it.'

While Edina was at St. Martin's School of Art, she saw the potential of buying beautiful old clothes, made with the attention and in the high quality fabrics that were no longer attainable. She made her magpie purchases throughout her career as an actress and fashion model, and finally decided to set up an antique clothes stall in Chelsea's Antiquarius with a model colleague Lena Stengard.

A pretty, puff-sleeved thirties cardigan put Edina and Lena on the fashion map and encouraged them to recreate classic knits in delicate lacy stitches.

'But it was never a question of finding old patterns and getting them knitted up,' says Edina. 'The designs are never quite right for today; the waists are too high and the body shapes odd. We used the stitches and ideas from the thirties patterns to give a modern interpretation of traditional knits.'

Edina's fashion background helped her to introduce a new ethnic/romantic style of dressing to Britain in the nineteen seventies. The embroidered cardigans and Fair Isles were put with antique petticoats and old lace, with jeans and khaki shorts, with sparkling paste necklaces and plain tee-shirts. Edina and Lena grew into a big business, with 800 hand-knitters, mostly in the West country, collated by a series of local agents, a booming export business and a shop in Los Angeles as well as in the King's Road, Chelsea.

'I still find it quite surprising that there is such a big fashion interest in hand-knits,' says Edina, who has recently discovered a voracious new market in Japan. 'I personally like wearing knits. I find it practical clothing because it is casual wear. More and more people – both men and women – wear the same things through the day and out in the evenings and my sweaters are basically fashion garments.'

Edina now runs the business on her own, but with the support of her photographer husband. Her two children, Shebah and Max, both already have a wardrobe of knitted heirlooms to hand down to their own children like the family Fair Isles that Edina designed for this book.

'I still love old clothes because of the cut, the style and the amount of work that went into them,' says Edina. 'Even the top British designers today can't put in that much craftsmanship. I know just what goes into our hand-knits. I would compare the Fair Isles with Kelim rugs. And I believe that future generations will prize them in that way.'

Adult waistcoat

Edina Ronay's family Fair Isles re-coloured in the vivid shades that reflect her Hungarian background. She started by collecting traditional Fair Isles from the 1920s and re-interpreted the patterns in modern shapes and colours and even in summer-weight cotton. Her slipover with poster paint red border edging is knitted in cotton according to the chart.

Sizes: To fit bust: 85/90/95/100/105cm (34/36/38/40/42in).

Yarn: Any 4-ply cotton yarn.
MY: 4 balls Red.
E: 1 ball Emerald Green.
Y: 1 ball Yellow.
B: 2 balls Mid-Blue.
P: 1 ball Pale Pink.
G: 2 balls Gold.
BP: 1 ball Bright Pink.
T: 2 balls Dark Turquoise.

Needles: $3\frac{1}{4}$mm (no. 10) and a set of (or circular) $2\frac{1}{4}$mm (no. 13).

Tension: 32 sts knitted over Fair Isle pattern, to 10cm (4in).

Body

Using $2\frac{1}{4}$mm (no. 13) needles and MY cast on 249/259/269/279/289 sts and work in K1, P1 rib for 10cm (4in). Increase evenly on last row to 299/313/329/345/361 sts. Change to $3\frac{1}{4}$mm (no. 10) needles and work from pattern (see below and chart) working rows 1 to 33, then rows 2 to 33 throughout until work measures 34/36/37/38/41cm ($13\frac{1}{2}$/14/$14\frac{1}{2}$/15/16in) from beginning.

SHAPE ARMHOLE AND RIGHT FRONT
With right side facing pattern 74/78/82/86/90 sts. Turn. Cast off 8/8/9/10/11 sts, patt to last 2 sts, K2 tog.
Continue to decrease at neck edge on every alternate row, *at the same time* decrease at armhole edge on *every row* until 40/42/44/46/48 sts rem. Continue to decrease at *neck edge* as before until 30/32/34/36/38 sts remain. Continue to work in pattern until armhole measures 19/19/20/22/23cm ($7\frac{1}{2}$/$7\frac{1}{2}$/8/$8\frac{1}{2}$/9in).

SHAPE SHOULDER
With wrong side facing cast off 10/10/11/12/12 sts at beginning of next and following alt row. Work 1 row. Then cast off remaining stitches.

Back

With right side facing rejoin yarn to remaining stitches. Cast off 8/8/9/10/11 sts, pattern across 143/149/156/163/170 including cast off stitch. *Turn.* Cast off 8/8/9/10/11 sts, patt to end. Then K2 tog both ends of every row until 107/113/119/125/131 sts remain. Continue until armhole is same as front to shoulder shaping.

SHAPE SHOULDER
With right side facing cast off 10/10/11/12/12) sts at beginning of next 4 rows. Then cast off 10/12/12/12/14 sts at beginning of next 2 rows. Cast off remaining stitches.

Left front

Rejoin yarn to remaining stitches and complete to match first side reversing all shapings.

Front band

Using $2\frac{1}{4}$mm (no. 13) needles and MY cast on 9 sts and work 4 rows in K1, P1 rib.
Make a buttonhole: rib 4, cast off 2 sts, rib 3.
Next row: rib 3, cast on 2 sts, rib 4.
Continue in rib making further buttonholes 6 to 6.5cm ($2\frac{1}{4}$ to $2\frac{1}{2}$in) apart evenly spaced, the last one to come 13mm ($\frac{1}{2}$in) below beginning of neck shaping. Now continue in rib until band is long enough to reach all round fronts and back neck when slightly stretched. Attach to fronts neatly using a small neat flat stitch. Remember to stretch band at back of neck to ensure a neat fit. Sew on buttons.

Armbands

Join shoulder seams using a small neat backstitch as near to edge of work as possible. Using a set of $2\frac{1}{4}$mm (no. 13) (or circular) and MY and with right side facing, pick up evenly round armholes 138/146/152/160/ 168 sts and work in K1, P1 rib for 6 rows. Cast off evenly in rib.

Pattern rows

1ST SIZE
Row 1 and every following odd numbered row knit, row 2 and every following even numbered row purl.
Row 1: Knit in MY.
Row 2: Purl in MY.
Row 3: * 1MY, 1E, rep from * to last st, 1MY.
Row 4: Purl in MY.
Row 5: 1MY, * 1Y, 3MY, rep from * to last 2 sts, 1Y, 1MY.
Row 6: * 3Y, 1MY, rep from * to last 3 sts, 3Y.
Row 7: 1B, * 1P, 3B, rep from * to last 2 sts, 1P, 1B.
Row 8: * 3P, 1B, rep from * to last 3 sts, 3P.
Row 9: 3E, 1G, 1E, * 1G, 1E, 1G, 3E, 1G, 3E, 1G, 1E, rep from * to last 6 sts, 1G, 1E, 1G, 3E.
Row 10: 1E, * 3G, 3E, rep from * to last 4 sts, 3G, 1E.
Row 11: * 5G, 1Y, rep from * to last 5 sts, 5G.
Rows 12 to 20: As rows 10 back to 2.
Row 21: 1MY, * 1B, 3MY rep from * to last 2 sts, 1B, 1MY.
Row 22: * 3B, 1MY, rep from * to last 3 sts, 3B.
Row 23: 1G, * 1BP, 3G, rep from * to last 2 sts, 1BP, 1G.
Row 24: * 3BP, 1G, rep from * to last 3 sts, 3BP.
Row 25: 3P, 1T, 1P, * 1T, 1P, 1T, 3P, 1T, 3P, 1T, 1P, rep from * to last 6 sts, 1T, 1P, 1T, 3P.
Row 26: 1P, 3T, * 3P, 3T, rep from * to last st, 1P.
Row 27: * 5T, 1Y rep from * to last 5 sts, 5T.
Rows 28 to 33: As rows 26 back to 21.
Repeat rows 2 to 33 throughout.

2ND AND 5TH SIZES

Row 1 and every following odd numbered row, knit.
Row 2 and every following even numbered row, purl.
Row 1: Knit in MY.
Row 2: Purl in MY.
Row 3: * 1MY, 1E, rep from * to last st, 1MY.
Row 4: Purl in MY.
Row 5: 1Y, * 3MY, 1Y, rep from * to end.
Row 6: * 2Y, 1MY, 1Y, rep from * to last st, 1Y.
Row 7: * 1P, 3B, rep from * to last st, 1P.
Row 8: * 2P, 1B, 1P rep from * to last st, 1P.
Row 9: * 1G, 1E, 1G, 3E, 1G, 3E, 1G, 1E, rep from * to last st, 1G.
Row 10: 1E, * 1E, 3G, 2E, rep from * to end.
Row 11: * 1Y, 5G rep from * to last st, 1Y.
Rows 12 to 20: As rows 10 back to 2.
Row 21: * 1B, 3MY, rep from * to last st, 1B.
Row 22: 1B, * 1B, 1MY, 2B, rep from * to end.
Row 23: * 1BP, 3G, rep from * to last st, 1BP.
Row 24: 1BP, * 1BP, 1G, 2BP, rep from * to end.
Row 25: * 1T, 1P, 1T, 3P, 1T, 3P, 1T, 1P, rep from * to last st, 1T.
Row 26: 1P, * 1P, 3T, 2P, rep from * to end.
Row 27: * 1Y, 5T, rep from * to last st, 1Y.
Rows 28 to 33: As rows 26 back to 21.
Repeat rows 2 to 33 throughout.

3RD SIZE

Row 1 and every following odd numbered row knit.
Row 2 and every following even numbered row purl.
Row 1: Knit in MY.
Row 2: Purl in MY.
Row 3: * 1MY, 1E, rep from * to last st, 1MY.
Row 4: Purl in MY.
Row 5: 2MY, * 1Y, 3MY, rep from * to last 3 sts, 1Y, 2MY.

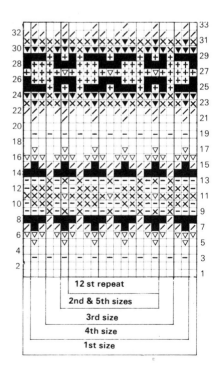

□ MY (Red)
⊟ E (Emerald)
▽ Y (Yellow)
◺ B (Mid Blue)
■ P (Pale Pink)
⊠ G (Gold)
▼ BP (Bright Pink)
⊞ T (Dark Turquoise)

Row 6: 1MY, * 3Y, 1MY, rep from * to end.
Row 7: 2B, * 1P, 3B, rep from * to last 3 sts, 1P, 2B.
Row 8: 1B, * 3P, 1B, rep from * to end.
Row 9: 1G, 1E, * 1G, 1E, 1G, 3E, 1G, 3E. 1G, 1E, rep from * to last 3 sts, 1G, 1E, 1G.
Row 10: 1G, * 3E, 3G, rep from * to last 4 sts, 3E, 1G
Row 11: 2G, * 1Y, 5G, rep from * to last 3 sts, 1Y, 3G.
Rows 12 to 20: As rows 10 back to 2.
Row 21: 2MY, * 1B, 3MY, rep from * to last 3 sts, 1B, 2MY.
Row 22: 1MY, * 3B, 1MY, rep from * to end.
Row 23: 2G, * 1BP, 3G, rep from * to last 3 sts, 1BP, 2G.
Row 24: 1G, * 3BP, 1G rep from * to end.
Row 25: 1T, 1P, * 1T, 1P, 1T, 3P, 1T, 3P, 1T, 1P rep from * to last 3 sts, 1T, 1P, 1T.
Row 26: 1T, * 3P, 3T, rep from * to last 4 sts, 3P, 1T.
Row 27: 2T, * 1Y, 5T, rep from * to last 3 sts, 1Y, 2T.
Rows 28 to 33: As rows 26 back to 21.
Repeat rows 2 to 33 throughout.

4TH SIZE

Row 1 and every following odd numbered row knit.
Row 2 and every following even numbered row purl.
Row 1: Knit in MY.
Row 2: Purl in MY.
Row 3: * 1MY, 1E, rep from * to last st, 1MY.
Row 4: Purl in MY.
Row 5: * 1Y, 3MY, rep from * to last st, 1Y.
Row 6: * 2Y, 1MY, 1Y, rep from * to last st, 1Y.
Row 7: * 1P, 3B, rep from * to last st, 1P.
Row 8: * 2P, 1B, 1P, rep from * to last st, 1P.
Row 9: 2E, 1G, 1E * 1G, 1E, 1G, 3E, 1G, 3E, 1G, 1E, rep from * to last 5 sts, 1G, 1E, 1G, 2E.
Row 10: * 3G, 3E, rep from * to last 3 sts, 3G.
Row 11: * 4G, 1Y, 1G, rep from * to last 3 sts, 3G.
Rows 12 to 20: As rows 10 back to 2.
Row 21: * 1B, 3MY, rep from * to last st, 1B.
Row 22: * 2B, 1MY, 1B, rep from * to last st, 1B.
Row 23: * 1BP, 3G, rep from * to last st, 1BP.
Row 24: * 2BP, 1G, 1BP, rep from * to last st, 1BP.
Row 25: 2P, 1T, 1P, * 1T, 1P, 1T, 3P, 1T, 3P, 1T, 1P, rep from * to last 5 sts, 1T, 1P, 1T, 2P.
Row 26: 3T, * 3P, 3T, rep from * to end.
Row 27: * 4T, 1Y, 1T, rep from * to last 3 sts, 3T.
Rows 28 to 33: As rows 26 back to 21.
Repeat rows 2 to 33 throughout.

21

Child's waistcoat

Edina's Fair Isle waistcoats designed for her children using eight colours and knitted according to the chart. They can be knitted up in any 4-ply yarn for children from toddlers to twelve-year-olds.

Sizes: To fit child aged 2/4/6/8/10/12 years. Chest: 56/61/66/71/76/81cm (22/24/26/28/30/32in).

Yarn: Any 4-ply wool
MY: 3–4 balls Blue.

Contrasts:
1 ball Ecru.
1 ball Marble Green.
1 ball Pale Pink.
1 ball Lilac.
1 ball Crimson.
1 ball Bright Pink.
1 ball Primrose Yellow..

Needles: 3¾mm (no. 9) and a set of (or circular) 2½mm (no. 12).

Tension: 30 sts knitted over Fair Isle pattern to 10cm (4in).

Body

Using 2½mm (no. 12) needles cast on 140/156/170/180/190/210 sts and work in K1, P1 rib for 5/5/6.5//7.5/8/9cm (2/2/2½/3/3¼/3½in). Increase evenly on last row to 165/181/197/213/227/243 sts. Change to 3¾mm (no. 9) needles and commence pattern as chart, working rows 1 to 33. Then work rows 2 to 33 throughout. Continue in pattern until work measures 18/20/23/25/28/30cm (7/8/9/10/11/12in) from beginning.

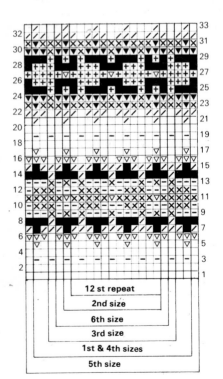

SHAPE ARMHOLE AND RIGHT FRONT

With right side facing, pattern across 41/45/49/53/56/60 sts. *Turn.* Cast off 6 sts, pattern to last 2 sts, K2 tog. Continue to decrease at *neck edge* on every alternate row and on every row at *armhole edge* until 22/24/26/28/30/32 sts remain. Now keeping armhole edge straight continue to decrease at neck edge until 18/20/22/23/24/26 sts remain. Continue until armhole is 13/13/14/15/16.5/18cm (5/5/5½/6/6½/7in) from beginning.

SHAPE SHOULDER

With wrong side facing cast off 6/6/7/7/8/8 sts at beginning of next and following alternate row. Work 1 row. Cast off.

Back

Rejoin wool to remaining sts. Cast off 6 sts. Pattern across next 77/85/93/101/109/117 sts including cast off stitch. *Turn.* Cast off 6 sts, patt to end. Continue to decrease both ends of every row until 59/63/67/73/79/85 sts remain. Continue until armholes are same as front to shoulder shaping.

SHAPE SHOULDER

With right side facing cast off 6/6/7/7/8/8 sts at beginning of next 4 rows. Then cast off 6/8/8/9/8/10 sts at beginning of next 2 rows. Cast off remaining stitches.

Left front

Rejoin wool to remaining stitches and complete to match first side reversing all shapings.

Buttonband

Using MY and 2½mm (no. 12) needles cast on 9 sts, and work in K1, P1 rib for 4 rows.
Make a buttonhole: rib 4, cast off 2, rib to end.
Next row: rib 3, cast on 2, rib to end. Continue in rib making more buttonholes 5cm (2in) apart, the last one to come 13mm (½in) below beginning of neck shaping. Continue in rib until band is long enough to reach all round neck and down the front when slightly stretched. Cast off in rib.

Armbands

Join shoulder seams and using set of (or circular) 2½mm (no. 12) ndls and MY pick up evenly around armhole 100/106/112/118/124/130 sts and work in K1, P1, rib for 2/2.5/2.5/2.5/2.5/2.5 cm (¾/1/1/1/1/1in). Cast off in rib.

Finishing

Join front band to fronts and back neck using a small neat flat seam. Press lightly. Sew on buttons.

Chart legend

- ☐ MY (Blue)
- ⊟ Ecru
- ▽ Marble Green
- ☑ Pale Pink
- ■ Lilac
- ☒ Crimson
- ▼ Bright Pink
- ⊞ Primrose Yellow

12 st repeat
2nd size
6th size
3rd size
1st & 4th sizes
5th size

Alison Robson: Asymmetric Aran

Ireland calls its most insistent knitwear pattern the 'trinity' stitch. But the origins of the richly textured Aran knits go back earlier than the deep-rooted Irish Catholicism.

It is the intricate pagan patternings, moulded out of metal and carved in stone by the celts, which are woven into the Aran sweaters of today.

The trinity stitch (often called 'blackberry' in England) is so named because you work three stitches into one and one into three. It is just part of the extraordinary interlacing patterns, which criss-cross the rough cream ground like fields and furrows ploughed out of the harsh and stony landscape of the Isles of Aran, on Ireland's wild West coast.

Today, cables and bobbles, diamonds and chevrons are all combined into interesting patterns. But the traditional Arans, like the other folk weave Guernseys and Fair Isles, recorded the life of the close communities who wore them. The diamond is the mesh of the mackerel nets, the cables are the ship's ropes, the squares and trellises and ridged surfaces represent the neat fields of a farmer's world.

Arans are found in Scotland too, as part of their own celtic heritage, although no-one has been able to trace the exact origins of a folk art which was nearly lost in the last century to mass manufacture.

The first recorded Aran-style design is found in the Book of Kells in a picture of Daniel feeding the Dragon, in an interlaced knitted garment and hose. The Book of Kells was begun on the Isle of Iona off the West coast of Scotland in 820 AD, which makes the Aran tradition more than a thousand years young.

Alison Robson steeped herself in the history of Aran stitchcraft when she was a fashion student at Harrow College of Art. She experimented with stitches, practised inventive knitting when she worked with Patricia Roberts (see page 63) in a vacation job. She began to realise how much the use of stitches could change the shape and texture of a garment, and she started to emphasise the pattern of the stitches by decorating the criss-cross weaves with beads.

'I'm interested in stitches and especially in the textures you can achieve,' she explains. 'I study stitch books, then I experiment myself and react to the way the stitches look.'

Significantly, Alison's family ancestry is in Scotland and Ireland and her mother feels strong ties with her Scottish background. But it was Alison's grandmother who first taught her the mechanics of knitting. 'When I go to Scotland now, I find that only a very small proportion of knitters know the traditional stitches,' says Alison. 'It really only lives on now in the fishing communities.'

But Alison was surprised to find that there are still expert knitters able to undertake her most complex patterns. After she left College in 1982, retailers from small London boutiques and from the giant Macy's in the United States took an interest in her work. Alison advertised for knitters in a Northern paper, and the sample patterns she got back proved that the art of Aran patternings is still very much alive.

Although Alison Robson's stitches are authentic, the strong, square shapes of her diploma collection were not. She worked out the loose Aran smock for this book from a toile to get the shape and swing so contrary to the conventional round-necked Aran sweater.

Alison Robson's interesting new way of working an Aran yarn, using the century old stitches that are rooted in celtic tradition. The cable and bobble pattern stands out against moss stitch in relief like stone carvings. The cap-sleeved waistcoat falls in a smock shape from a square neck and is worn as an oversweater.

Sizes: One size. Back width 63cm (25in). Each front width (including moss st band) 44cm (17½in).

Yarn: 27 × 50g balls of Lister Lee Aran yarn.

Needles: 3¾mm (no. 9) and 4½mm (no. 7); cable needle.

Tension: Using 4½mm (no. 7) ndls, one repeat of the pattern should measure 14cm (5¾in) across when pressed.

Notions: 4 buttons.

Special abbreviations:

mb = make bobble thus: K1, yrn, K1 all into next st, turn, P3, turn, K3, turn, P3, turn, Sl 1, K2 tog, PSSO.

mlb = make large bobble thus: K1, yrn, K1, yrn, K1 all into next st, turn P5, turn, K5, turn, P2 tog, P1, P2 tog, turn, Sl 1, K2 tog, PSSO.

Back

Using 3¾mm (no. 9) ndls, cast on 148 sts and work in single moss st for 6cm (2½in).
Now change to 4½mm (no. 7) ndls and work in pattern as follows. For the first 29cm (11½in) work a 4 st panel of moss st at each end. This is because the sides are split to this point.
Row 1 (wrong side row): moss st 4, * K2, P9, K4, P1, K8, P2, K1, P2, K6. Rep from * 3 times more, moss st 4.
Row 2: moss st 4, * P6, Sl next 3 sts onto c.n. and hold at back, K2, then Sl the P st from c.n. back onto left ndl and purl it, then K2 from c.n., P8, mlb, P4, K9, P2, rep from * 3 times more, moss st 4.
Row 3: As row 1.
Row 4: moss st 4, * P5, BC, P1, FC, P7, K1, P4, C3f, K3, P2. Rep from * 3 times more, moss st 4.
Row 5: moss st 4, * K2, P9, K4, P1, K7, P2, K3, P2, K5. Rep from * 3 times more, moss st 4.
Row 6: moss st 4, * P4, BC, P1, mb, P1, FC, P6, mlb, P4, K9, P2. Rep from * 3 times more, moss st 4.
Row 7: moss st 4, * K2, P9, K4, P1, K6, P2, K2, P1, K2, P2, K4. Rep from * 3 times more, moss st 4.
Row 8: moss st 4, * P3, BC, P5, FC, P5, K1, P4, K3, C3b, P2. Rep from * 3 times more, moss st 4.
Row 9: moss st 4, * K2, P9, K4, P1, K5, P2, K7, P2, K3. Rep from * 3 times more, moss st 4.
Row 10: moss st 4, * P2, BC, P1, mb, P3, mb, P1, FC, P4, mlb, P4, K9, P2. Rep from * 3 times more, moss st 4.
Row 11: moss st 4, * K2, P9, K4, P1, K4, P2, K2, P1, K3, P1, K2, P2, K2. Rep from * 3 times more, moss st 4.
Row 12: moss st 4, * P2, K2, P9, K2, P4, K1, P4, C3f, K3, P2. Rep from * 3 times more, moss st 4.
Row 13: moss st 4, * K2, P9, K4, P1, K4, P2, K9, P2, K2. Rep from * 3 times more.
Row 14: moss st 4, * P2, K2, P2, mb, P3, mb, P2, K2, P4, mlb, P4, K9, P2. Rep from * 3 times more, moss st 4.
Row 15: As row 11.
Row 16: moss st 4, * P2, FC, P7, BC, P4, K1, P4, K3, C3b, P2. Rep from * 3 times more, moss st 4.
Row 17: moss st 4, * K2, P9, K4, P1, K5, P2, K7, P2, K3. Rep from * 3 times more, moss st 4.
Row 18: moss st 4, * P3, FC, P2, mb, P2, BC, P5, mlb, P4, K9, P2. Rep from * 3 times more, moss st 4.
Row 19: moss st 4, * K6, P1, K8, P1, K6, P2, K2, P1, K2, P2, K4. Rep from * 3 times more, moss st 4.
Row 20: moss st 4, * P4, FC, P3, BC, P6, K1, P8, mb, P6. Rep from * 3 times more, moss st 4.
Row 21: moss st 4, * K6, P1, K8, P1, K7, P2, K3, P2, K5. Rep from * 3 times more, moss st 4.
Row 22: moss st 4, * P5, FC, P1, BC, P7, K1, P7, mb, P1, mb, P5. Rep from * 3 times more, moss st 4.
Row 23: moss st 4, * K5, P1, K1, P1, K7, P1, K8, P2, K1, P2, K6. Rep from * 3 times more, moss st 4.
Row 24: moss st 4, * P6, Sl next 3 sts onto c.n. and hold at back, K2, then Sl the P st from c.n. back onto left ndl and purl it, then K2 from c.n., P8, K1, P6; mb, P1, mb, P1, mb, P4. Rep from * 3 times more, moss st 4.
Row 25: moss st 4, * K4, P1, K1, P1, K1, P1, K6, P1, K8, P2, K1, P2, K6. Rep from * 3 times more, moss st 4.
Row 26: moss st 4, * P5, BC, P1, FC, P7, K1, P8, K1, P6. Rep from * 3 times more, moss st 4.
Row 27: moss st 4, * K6, P1, K8, P1, K7, P2, K3, P2, K5. Rep from * 3 times more, moss st 4.
Row 28: moss st 4, * P4, BC, P3, FC, P6, K1, P8, mb, P6. Rep from * 3 times more, moss st 4.
Row 29: moss st 4, * K6, P1, K8, P1, K6, P2, K5, P2, K4. Rep from * 3 times more, moss st 4.
Row 30: moss st 4, * P4, K2, P2, mb, P2, K2, P6, K1, P7, mb, P1, mb, P5. Rep from * 3 times more, moss st 4.
Row 31: moss st 4, * K5, P1, K1, P1, K7, P1, K6, P2, K2, P1, K2, P2, K4. Rep from * 3 times more, moss st 4.
Row 32: moss st 4, * P4, FC, P3, BC, P6, K1, P6, mb, P1, mb, P1, mb, P4. Rep from * 3 times more, moss st 4.
Row 33: moss st 4, * K4, P1, K1, P1, K1, P1, K6, P1, K7, P2, K3, P2, K5. Rep from * 3 times more, moss st 4.
Row 34: moss st 4, * P5, FC, P1, BC, P7, K1, P8, K1, P6. Rep from * 3 times more, moss st 4.

These 34 rows form the pattern. Repeat them until work measures 29cm (11½in) from the cast on edge. Now continue in pattern for a further 24cm (9½in), but omitting moss stitch edging and in its place working K2, P2 at beginning and P2, K2 at the end of every right side row. On wrong side rows begin with P2, K2 and end with K2, P2.

Sleeveband shaping: When work measures 52.5cm (21in) from cast on edge, cast off 4 sts at the beg of the next 2 rows. Continue in pattern for a further 25cm (10in). Work should now measure 77.5cm (31in) from cast on edge.
Next row: Work one repeat of the pattern, then moss st for 70 sts, continue in pattern for another repeat.
This forms a moss st panel across the centre back for the back neckband.
N.B. When working moss st panel try to knit as tightly as possible for a better fit around the neck.

Work in this pattern (35 sts pattern, 70 sts moss st, 35 sts pattern) for another 9 rows.
Shape shoulder: Cast off 8 sts at the beginning of the next 12 rows. Cast off remaining 44 sts in moss st.

Pocket back
(One only for right front)
Using 4½mm (no. 7) ndls, cast on 35 sts and work in reverse st.st for 12.5cm (5in). Leave on a spare ndl until required.

Right front
Using 3¾mm (no. 9) ndls cast on 103 sts and work in single moss st for 6cm (2½in).
Now change to 4½mm (no 7) ndls and work as follows:
Row 1 (wrong side row): moss st 4, * K6, P2, K1, P2, K8, P1, K4, P9, K2. Rep from * once, then work one more cable and bobble panel as follows: K6, P2, K1, P2, K6, Sl the last 12 sts onto a safety pin and leave until required for front band.
Row 2: P6, Sl the next 3 sts onto c.n. and hold at back, K2, then Sl the P st from c.n. back onto left ndl and purl it, then K2 from c.n., P6, * P2, K9, P4, mlb, P8, Sl the next 3 sts onto c.n. and hold at back, K2, then Sl the P st from c.n. back onto left ndl purl it, then K2 from c.n., P6. Rep from * once more, moss st 4.
Row 3: As row 1.
Row 4: P5, BC, P1, FC, P5, * P2, C3f, K3, P4, K1, P7, BC, P1, FC, P5. Rep from * once more, moss st 4.
These 4 rows set the position of the pattern which you will note has now changed. The cable with bobbles inside is now on the outside edge, with the ear of wheat pattern next to it, then the plaited cable and grapes next to that. This alteration is made so that the shoulders will match at right back and right front. Continue in new pattern until work measures 26cm (10½in) from cast on edge, ending at side seam.
Next row (pocket): Moss st 4, pattern 17, Sl the next 35 sts onto a stitch holder and leave at front of work, work the sts from pocket back in pattern, then continue to end of row.
Continue in pattern until work measures 29cm (11½in) from cast on edge. Now continue in pattern for a further 24cm (9½in) to match the back, but omitting the 4 sts of moss st at the side seam and working P2, K2 at this edge on a wrong side row, or K2, P2 on a right side row in its place. The last of these rows should finish at the side seam.
Work should now measure 53cm (21in) from cast on edge.
Shape sleeveband: Cast off 4 sts at the beginning of the next row. Continue in pattern for a further 9cm (3½in) ending at front band edge.
Next row: Cast off 48 sts, pattern to end of row.
Continue on these 35 sts until work measures 29cm (11½in) from beginning of armhole shaping.
Cast off the remaining 35 sts.

POCKET TOP
Using 3¾mm (no. 9) ndls with right side of work facing pick up 35 sts from stitch holder and work in moss st for 2.5cm (1in). Cast off in moss st.

Left front
Using 3¾mm (no. 9) ndls, cast on 99 sts and work in single moss st for 6cm (2½in) to match right front.
Now change to 4½mm (no. 7) ndls and work as follows:
Row 1 (wrong side row): moss st 12, then leave these 12 sts on a safety pin until required for front band, K37, P9, K8, P2, K1, P2, K8, P1, K4, P9, K2, moss st 4.
Row 2: Moss st 4, P2, K9, P4, mlb, P8, Sl next 3 sts onto c.n. and hold at back, K2, then Sl the P st from c.n. back onto left ndl and purl it, then K2 from c.n., P8, K9, P37.
Row 3: as row 1.
Row 4: moss st 4, P2, C3f, K3, P4, K1, P7, BC, P1, FC, P7, C3f, K3, P37.
These 4 rows set the position of the pattern, which you will note has now changed again. The inside 35-stitch panel is now worked entirely in reverse stocking stitch, and the cable with bobbles inside and ear of wheat patterns are reversed, so the left front and back match at the shoulders.
In this new pattern, complete the left front as the right front, omitting the pocket and reversing the shapings.

Right front band
Using 3¾mm (no. 9) ndls pick up the 12 sts on a safety pin at the base of the right front, and work in moss st until work measures 32.5cm (13in) from cast on edge, ending at inside edge.
1st buttonhole row: moss st 3, cast off 4 sts, moss st 5.
2nd buttonhole row: moss st 5, cast on 4, moss st 3.
Work in moss st for a further 14cm (5½in), ending at inside edge.
Cast on 40 sts, so there are now 52 sts on ndl.
Work in moss st for 2.5cm (1in) ending at armhole edge.
Next row: moss st 3, cast off 4, moss st 36, cast off 4, moss st 3.
Next row: moss st 5, cast on 4, moss st 36, cast on 4, moss st 3.
Work in moss st for 2.5cm (1in) more, ending at front edge.
Cast off 40 sts, then continue in moss st on the remaining 12 sts for 12.5cm (5in).
Cast off the remaining 12 sts in moss st.

Left front band
Work as for right front band, but omitting buttonholes.

Sleevebands
(2 alike)
Using 3¾mm (no. 9) ndls cast on 95 sts and work in moss st for 6cm (2½in), then cast off in moss st.

Finishing
Pin out and press lightly with a warm iron under a damp cloth. *Take great care not to overpress.*
Attach the front bands to the two fronts, using a flat stitch (they will have to be slightly stretched on).
Join the shoulder seams.
Attach sleevebands, using a flat stitch again and stretching them slightly into position.
Join the side seam as far as the moss st band.
Sew pocket on wrong side of right front.
Sew on buttons.

Jasper Conran: Aran Style

[*See colour photograph opposite page 65*]

Jasper Conran's heroine is the legendary Mademoiselle Chanel – who although she was French, drew her designs from the tradition of the English country gentleman's wardrobe. He himself has delved back into that trunk of classic good taste, working sharply tailored clothes in cashmere and wool, in fine colonial linens and simple silks that are redolent of days of the Grand Tour.

Coco Chanel was the designer who brought knitwear out of the country and off the sports field, into the sophisticated salons of Paris. Her first design thoughts were for using the hand-knits of her own peasants culture to recreate the knitted shirts and sweaters that her aristocratic English friends wore on the polo field. But in 1916 when she was designing her first Paris collection, wool was scarce and nimble needles were working to knit balaclavas for troops in the first World War. Out of necessity, she turned to jersey, the nearest machine-made equivalent of knitting. It was because she brought this lowly material (it had been destined for men's underclothes) into the orbit of high fashion, that she began the popularity of the sweater.

Jasper Conran is of a different generation. He is the son of Terence Conran, the founding father of Britain's design revolution in the sixties, and a product not of the British Art College system, but of Parson's Fashion School in New York.

Knitwear for Jasper Conran is the essential accessory to his streamlined clothes. He himself wears crunchy Aran-style knits from his first major design project in wool. He produces cotton knits too for summer, always in colours co-ordinating with his other designs and in simple shapes that still have an edge of style.

Both colour and shape lift the Conran knits out of the realm of classic knitwear as we understand it: V-neck or round-necked sweaters that have not changed their body shapes for thirty years.

He believes primarily in cut and tailoring, which means for him making clothes that reveal the body shape, while apparently concealing it: 'There is something about the English mentality which makes us appear rather staid, while actually underneath we are rather naughty,' he explains. 'That is the look that I like to think that I have captured in my clothes.'

Since Aran knitwear is part of the mainstream of celtic culture (see Alison Robson, page 23) it might seem too rough in style, too essentially folkloric to go with the quiet, understated and very English style of Conran's collection.

His feeling is much more for the texture and shape of knits than for re-creating the interlaced and symbolic celtic patterns in any serious way. He dyes the wool jewel bright or dark colours (his own favourite is black) as a deliberate fashion statement to shock against the traditional natural Aran colours. You can see the pink sweater I chose in the photograph opposite page 65.

Jasper's mother, Shirley ('Superwoman') Conran is on record as saying that the best way to deal with domestic crafts like sewing is to eliminate them. So it is not surprising to find that it was his grandmother, not his mother, who taught him to knit. He does not make up his own designs, but he understands the principles of hand-knitting and how to make knit shapes as though he were working with cloth.

Jasper Conran takes the flavour of Aran – its texture and stitchcraft – for a sophisticated and shapely sweater. The body is in blackberry/trinity stitch, knitted three in one. The sleeves are in diamond mesh puffed by setting in with two box pleats.

Sizes: 10/12/14. To fit bust 88/93/98cm (35/37/39in).

Yarn: 14/15/16 × 50g balls Standard Aran yarn.

Needles: 5mm (no. 6), 4mm (no. 8).

Tension: 27 sts and 24 rows knitted in blackberry st on 5mm (no. 6) ndls to 10cm (4in) square. 20 sts and 24 rows knitted in diamond pattern on 5mm (no. 6) ndls to 10cm (4in) square.

Notions: 3 buttons.

Back

With 4mm (no. 8) ndls, cast on 75/80/85 sts and work 10cm (4in) single rib. Change to 5mm (no. 6) ndls and inc evenly across row to 112/116/124 sts. Work in blackberry stitch as follows:

BLACKBERRY STITCH
Row 1 (right side): Purl.
Row 2: * (K1, P1, K1) all into next st, P3 tog, rep from * to end.
Row 3: Purl.
Row 4: * P3 tog, (K1, P1, K1) all into next stitch, rep from * to end.
Continue in this way until work measures 36/37.5/39cm (14½/15/15½in) from beg.
Cast off 4 sts at beg next 2 rows then dec 1 st at both ends following 7/8/9 alt rows.
Cont without shaping until work measures 56/58/60cm (22½/23/23½in) from beg. Shape shoulder:
Cast off 10/11/12 sts at beg of next 4 rows, knitting first 3 sts tog. Then cast off 10 sts at beg next 2 rows knitting first 3 sts tog as before. Cast off rem sts for back neck.

Front

Work as for back until work measures 49/50/51cm (19½/20/20½in) from beg.

SHAPE NECK
Work 35/37/39 sts, cast off 20, work 35/37/39. Cont on last set of sts, dec 1 st at neck edge of the following 8 rows. Cont without shaping until work measures 56/58/60cm (22½/23/23½in) from beg.
Shape shoulder as for back.
Rejoin yarn to rem sts and complete other side to match.

Sleeves

(2 alike)
With 4mm (no. 8) ndls cast on 38 sts and work 7.5cm (3in) single rib.
Change to 5mm (no. 6) ndls and inc to 58 sts. Work in diamond pattern as follows:

DIAMOND PATTERN
Row 1: * T2R, K12, rep from * to last 2 sts, T2R.
Row 2 and every following even row: Purl.
Row 3: K1, * T2L, K10, T2R, rep from * to last st, K1.
Row 5: * K2, T2L, K8, T2R, rep from * to last 2 sts, K2.
Cont in this way working 2 sts fewer between twists until diamond pattern is formed. Work in pattern increasing 1 st at each end of every 5th row until there are 90 sts. Cont without shaping until work measures 43/45/46cm (17/17½/18 in) from beg.

SHAPE SLEEVE TOP
Cast off 4 sts at beg next 2 rows. Dec 1 st at each end of every alt row until 38 sts remain. Cast off knitting 3 sts tog at beg and end of row.

Finishing

Join right shoulder seam. Using 4mm (no. 8) ndls, pick up sts round neck (approx 86 sts) and work 3cm (1¼in) single rib. Cast off ribwise. Join side seams. Join sleeve seams. Leave left shoulder seam open. With right sides facing, pin sleeves into armholes matching underarm seams and taking in excess with two box pleats (see diagram).
Finish with backstitch seam.

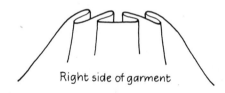

Fold to wrong side

Right side of garment

NECK FASTENING
Join left shoulder seam for about two thirds of its length, starting at armhole edge. Finish opening with double crochet, making buttonholes at top and bottom of neck rib and half way along remaining opening of front of garment. Sew buttons to back.

Pattern compiled by Sue Griffin for Jasper Conran.

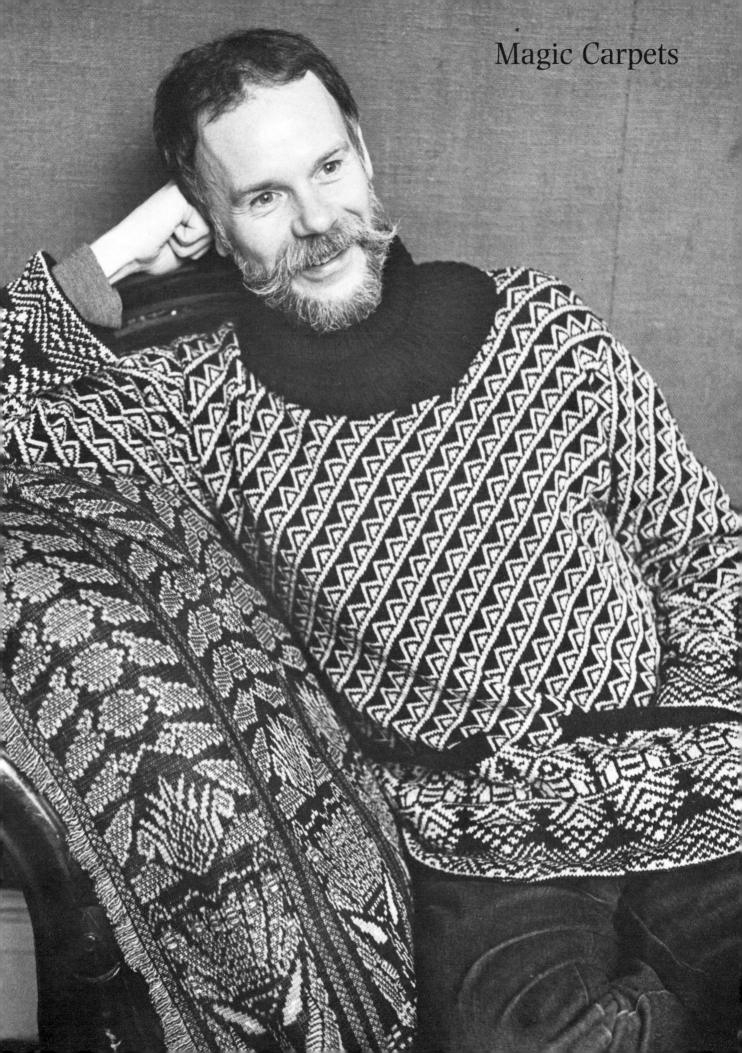

Bill Gibb: Artist's Smock Sweater and Magic Carpet Coat

[For sweater see photograph previous page. For coat see photographs on pages 33 and 34.]

Bill Gibb makes sweet harmony out of the most unlikely unions of pattern, texture and colour.

His background is Scottish and rural. But although he may have drawn a feeling for wool from the family farm in Aberdeen where he was brought up, his cloths have never been natural or rustic.

Instead they have an historical and theatrical feel, like his great collections inspired by Byzantine art or by the fragmented colour and pattern of stained glass windows. His earliest inspiration for fashion was the drawings he copied from a history book at the age of twelve, and throughout his training, first at St. Martin's and then at the Royal College of Art, he kept a dimension of history in his work.

The earliest Bill Gibb knits were done with Kaffe Fassett (see page 39) and were a mirror to the intricate assemblages of pattern found in his embroideries. From the first there was also the Bee. It started as 'B' for Bill and developed as a motif, a logo for his company and an ongoing source of design inspiration. You can see the bees buzzing across the pockets of the oversweater he wears in the picture. He designed the richly patterned sweater for this book, using one of his own favourite working pullovers in plain slate grey, re-drawing it with diagonals of pattern but keeping it generous in cut.

'I find it an easy shape to wear,' he explains. 'It is a development of the idea of the fisherman's smock with the two pockets that are so useful to me when I am doing a fitting and need to carry pins and a tape measure.'

Bill Gibb now works partly as a couturier, making to order fantastic and exotic gowns, especially wedding dresses. His own three sisters, solidly married in Scotland (he is one of seven children) wore fairy tale bridal creations he designed for them.

Bill Gibb also continues to work as a knitwear designer for factory production, using his rich textures and patterns. He currently favours animal markings, what he calls a 'feline feelng', although they are used in such an original way that no-one but the designer can trace the markings on a tiger's head through the print on his knits.

His designs have been worn by some of the world's most glamourous women and by anyone who appreciates his sense of romance. Film star Liz Taylor and actress Twiggy have always loved his clothes, and they have been worn too by Margaret Thatcher and by Princess Alexandra, a diverse group of celebrities.

Bill Gibb feels that his knitwear appeals because it is wearable as well as colourful and interesting. The cardigan coat he designed for this book (see page 32) in muted shades of grey and beige, combines three different scales of pattern which give depth to an apparently simple shape. The matching leg warmers add a sporty touch and are fun to wear on their own.

If the chevron patterns and quieter colours begin to look more like country tweeds than Byzantine court costumes, maybe it is a sign that Bill Gibb has gone back to his Scottish roots.

Artist's Smock Sweater

Bill Gibb uses pattern to create a three dimensional effect of rich texture even on quite simple shapes. His generously cut smock (for both sexes) is Fair Isle knitted in just two colours, with the bolder and more intricately patterned Bees (the Bill Gibb signature) on the pocket area. He is wearing it himself in the photograph. For added warmth, this loose fitting sweater is knitted in a thermal yarn.

Size: 95–105cm (38–42in). Length: 78cm (30½in).
Note: This garment is very loose fitting.

Yarn: Lister-Lee Thermo-Knit 4-ply.
MY: 7 × 50g balls Black
A: 5 × 50g balls Grey

Needles: 2¾mm (no. 12) and 3¾mm (no. 9).

Tension: 31 sts and 28 rows knitted over Fair Isle pattern on 3¾mm (no. 9) needles to 10cm (4in) square.

Back

Using 2¾mm (no. 12) ndls and MY cast on 189 sts and work 10 rows st.st.
Change to 3¾mm (no. 9) ndls and work from Chart 1 for 60 rows increasing 3 sts on final row (192 sts).
Now work from Chart 2 throughout remainder of Back.
Work straight until Back measures 48cm (19in) from start of Chart 1.

SHAPE ARMHOLE
(Keep pattern correct.)
Cast off 10 sts at beg of next 2 rows.
Dec 1 st each end of every alt row (156 sts).
Work straight until Back measures 75cm (29½in).

SHAPE SHOULDERS
Cast off 10 sts at beg of next 8 rows.
Leave rem 76 sts on thread for neckband.

Front

As Back until Front measures 65cm (25½in).

SHAPE NECK
Pattern 58 sts, turn, leave rem sts on a thread.
Dec 1 st at neck edge on next 18 rows (40 sts).
Continue straight to 75cm (29½in).

SHAPE SHOULDER
Cast off 10 sts on next 4 alternate rows. Fasten off.
Slip centre 40 sts onto thread.
Rejoin yarn to rem sts at neck edge and work to match, reversing all shapings.

Sleeves

Using 2¾mm (no. 12) needles and MY cast on 105 sts and work 10 rows st.st.
Change to 3¾mm (no. 9) needles and work 60 rows from Chart 1.
Now work from Chart 2 throughout remainder of sleeve.
Increase 1 st at each end of next and every 3rd row until there are 163 sts.

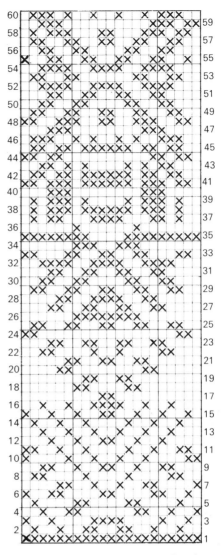

Chart 1

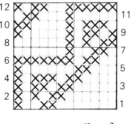

Chart 2

☐ MY
☒ A

31

Cast off 10 sts beg next 2 rows.
Dec 1 st each end every other row 8 times.
Cast off rem 127 sts loosely.

Pockets

2 alike.
Using 3¾mm (no. 9) needles and MY cast on 63 sts and
work 60 rows from Chart 1, increasing 1 st on last row.
Change to 2¾mm (no. 12) ndls and work 8 rows in K2,
P2 rib.
Cast off loosely in rib.

Polo collar

Join right shoulder seam.
With right side facing using 2¾mm (no. 12) ndls and
MY pick up and knit 24 sts down left front.
Knit across 40 sts at centre front. Pick up and knit
24 sts up right front and knit across 76 sts of back
(164 sts).
Work in K2, P2 rib for 14cm (5½in).
Change to 3¾mm (no. 9) ndls and work a further 14cm
(5½in) in rib.
Cast off loosely in rib.

Finishing

Follow pressing instructions on ball band.
Join left shoulder seam and polo collar seam.
Sew st.st facings to inside.
Sew in sleeve, matching centre of sleeve head to
shoulder seam.
Sew side and sleeve seams.
Sew on patch pockets carefully matching pattern to
pattern on fronts and placing them one pattern repeat
apart.

Magic Carpet Coat

An elongated cardigan that doubles up as a coat – and
with snazzy matching leg warmers – is the practical and
stylish theme of this Bill Gibb outfit. The strong cable
pattern on sleeves and neckband contrasts with the
quieter chevron Fair Isle and strong border print that
comes too on the leg warmers. The coat, with sporty
toggle fastenings, is knitted in a four-ply thermal yarn
in three natural colours.

Size: One size (medium).

Yarn: Lister-Lee Thermo-Knit 4-ply.
MY: 9 × 50g balls Cream.
A: 6 × 50g balls French Grey.
B: 5 × 50g balls Natural.

Needles: 2¾mm (no. 12), 3¼mm (no. 10) and 3¾mm
(no. 9).

Tension: 31 sts and 28 rows knitted on 3¾mm (no. 9)
needles in st.st over the Fair Isle pattern to 10cm (4in)
square. (28 sts and 36 rows using 3¾mm (no. 9) ndls).

Notions: 6 toggles.

Note: When working Fair-Isle *do not* weave in yarn but
strand *loosely* across back of work.

☒ Grey
⊡ Natural
☐ MY

Chart 1

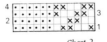

Chart 2

*Patricia Roberts wearing her patchwork jacket (page 63) at home
with daughter Amy in her grapes and cherries cardigan (page 68)*

Back

Using 2¾mm (no. 12) needles and MY cast on 180 sts and work 10 rows st.st.

Change to 3¾mm (no. 9) needles and commence Fair Isle pattern working from chart I setting row 1 as follows:

sts 19–36; sts 1–36 (4 times); sts 1–18.

Work 56 rows from chart I.

Now work from Chart 2 throughout remainder of Back, and decrease 1 st each end of every 10th row 10 times (160 sts).

Work straight until Back measures 90cm (35½in) from start of Chart I.

SHAPE ARMHOLE

Right side facing

Cast off 6 sts at beginning of next 2 rows.

Decrease 1 st at each end of next and every following 4th row 12 times in all (124 sts).

Continue straight until Back measures 118cm (46½in) from start of Chart I.

SHAPE NECK

Right side facing.

Work 46 sts, turn.

Decrease 1 st at neck edge on next 6 rows.

Cast off remaining 40 sts.

Slip centre 32 sts onto spare needle.

Rejoin yarn at neck edge and work 1 row.

Decrease 1 st at neck edge on next 6 rows.

Cast off remaining 40 sts.

Left front

Using 2¾mm (no. 12) needles cast on 100 sts and work 10 rows st.st.

Change to 3¾mm (no. 9) needles and work 56 rows of Chart 1 as follows, and *keeping last 10 sts in st.st in main colour for facing*:

Row 1: sts 19–36, sts 1–36 twice, K10 sts.

Now work from Chart 2 throughout remainder of Front.

Dec 1 st at side edge on every 10th row 10 times (90 sts).

Work straight until Front measures 90cm (35½in) from start of Chart 1.

SHAPE ARMHOLE

Right side facing.

Cast off 6 sts at beg of next row.

Dec 1 st at side edge of next and every following 4th row 12 times in all (72 sts).

Continue straight until front measures 115cm (45in) from start of Chart 1.

SHAPE NECK

Wrong side facing.

Cast off 26 sts, work to end.

Dec 1 st at neck edge on next 6 rows.

Work straight to match Back.

Cast off remaining 40 sts.

Right front

Work as for Left Front reversing all shaping and setting 1st row of Chart I as follows:

K10, sts 1–36 twice, sts 1–18.

Neckband

Join shoulder seams. With right side facing and using 2¾mm (no. 12) needles, with MY pick up and K 32 sts up right front neck band (excluding the 10 sts for facing), 44 sts across Back (excluding 10 sts for facing), and 32 sts down left front band (108 sts).

Work 13cm (5 in) in st.st., ending with a P row.

Next row: K5, YFD, K2 tog, K94, YFD, K2 tog, K5.

Work further 15cm (6in) in st.st.

Cast off loosely.

Cable neckband

Using 3¾mm (no. 9) needles and MY cast on 110 sts and work as follows:

Row 1: P2, K6, P2.

Row 2: K2, P6, K2.

Continue in this manner, but crossing cables on 5th and every following 10th row as follows:

Cable row: P2, C3f, P2.

Work cable trim to fit all round neck excluding facing.

Sleeves

Using 2¾mm (no. 12) needles and MY cast on 80 sts and work 10 rows st.st.

Change to 3¾mm (no. 9) needles and commence Fair Isle pattern working from Chart I and setting row 1 as follows:

sts 33–36, sts 1–36 twice, sts 1–4.

Work 56 rows of Chart, inc 16 sts evenly across last row (96 sts).

Change to 3¼mm (no. 10) needles and work in cable pattern, crossing cable on 5th and every following 10th row (C3f), and setting as follows:

Row 1: K3, * P2, K6, P2, K10, repeat from * to last 13 sts, P2, K6, P2, K3.

Row 2: P3 * K2, P6, K2, P10, repeat from * to last 13 sts, K2, P6, K2, P3.

Alternate each 6 st cable panel with yarns A and B, using separate balls of yarn and twisting yarns when changing colour to avoid making a hole.

At the same time, inc 1 st at each end of every 4th row to 168 sts.

SHAPE SLEEVE HEAD

Cast off 6 sts at beg of next 2 rows.

Dec 1 st at each end of next and every following 4th row 13 times in all.

Cast off remaining sts *loosely.*

Finishing

Turn in and stitch down all facings.

Sew in sleeves making 3 pleats between cable sections on each side of centre of sleeve head.

Join sleeve and side seams. Turn neckband to inside, and stitch down carefully.

Twist 2 strands of all colours to form cord. Trim end to form tassels and thread through top of neckband.

Attach cable neckband trim to base of neckband.

Leg warmers

Using 2¾mm (no. 12) needles and yarn B cast on 82 sts and work 10 rows st. st. ** inc 4 sts on last row. (86 sts).

Change to 3¼mm (no. 10) needles and commence pattern as follows:

Row 1: K8 * P2, K6, P2, K10, repeat from * to last 18 sts, P2, K6, P2, K8.

Row 2: P8 * K2, P6, K2, P10, repeat from * to last 18 sts, K2, P6, K2, P8.

Alternate each 6 st cable panel with yarns A and B, using separate balls of yarn, and twisting yarns when changing colour to avoid making a hole.

Cross cables on 5th and every following 10th row leaving cable needle on front of work. (C3f).

Continue in pattern until work measures 38cm (15in) from ** at the same time increasing 1 st at each end of every 4th row.

Change to Fair Isle from chart I and work 56 rows continuing to increase as before to 144 sts.

At the same time on row 55 of chart I work holes for cord ties on sts 68, 69, 76 and 77 as follows:

YFD, K2 tog. Work 10 rows st.st using 2¾mm (no. 12) needles. Cast off.

MAKE CORD

Twist two strands of all colours to form cord. Trim ends to form tassels and thread through top of leg warmers. Join back seam.

Veronica Franklin: Tapestry Knit

Rich, dark Jacobean colours glowing like knitted tapestries or the russet pheasant's plumage of an English autumn is the inspiration for Veronica Franklin. She likes to fuse colour and texture into high fashion – as befits a designer who started her career as a Fashion Assistant on a glossy magazine.

She started knitting because she 'got bored watching T.V.' and the delicate Fair Isle bags and cushions she produced began to turn a hobby into an embryonic business. During the seventies, Veronica was a model, making up specially commissioned clothes for friends in her spare time. With her partner Caroline Cardew, a textile graduate from the Camberwell College of Art, she produced the first Franklin Cardew collection in 1977. The individual and stylish sweaters were soon selling to important shops in Britain and especially in America.

'We could always have sold more. And I just love creating the things,' says Veronica, who decided to go back to one-off orders when she was expecting her first baby.

Her designs start always with interesting yarns and colours. The pattern and shape evolves from that point, and Veronica believes in designing with her needles, not a pencil.

'It is easy to make up designs if you have got yarns with a good texture,' she says. 'English women rely too much on patterns. You have to be adventurous and have the courage to go ahead. If you pick something with a lurex thread or other surface interest, a plain straight up and down sweater will look good.'

The Franklin Cardew partnership was a particularly good marriage of craft with fashion. Caroline Cardew's experience with printing and weaving knitted up well with Veronica Franklin's fashion know-how.

But one thing Veronica is adamant about: no knitter should start without working out a tension square to make sure that the finished garment will have the right shape and fit.

During her pregnancy, Veronica started on her first baby clothes, tactfully choosing a stripe of pink and blue to suit either sex. Even when her own shape was model thin rather than expanding, Veronica favoured big, simple shapes for sweaters and especially for cardigan jackets that she knits up in a cloud-soft marbled mohair to give the warmth of a coat without the weight, as in the pattern given here, which she is wearing herself in the picture.

But her own favourite creations are still the small sampler bags, knitted as a pastime and woven on to neat wooden handles.

'Knitting for me has always been a hobby,' she explains. 'But I like to turn my own pleasure into a business.'

Veronica Franklin and Caroline Cardew like yarns with rich texture and colour. This chunky tweed jacket is a bold, strong shape, with raglan shoulders, a stand-up collar and side pockets. It is worked in a triangle pattern for both body and sleeves with ribbed collar and front bands.

Size: One size.
Yarn: approx. 1200g Extra Chunky Polair mohair/wool, exclusive to Woolies, 32 Lower Richmond Road, Putney, London SW15. Plus 50g 4-ply for pockets.
Needles: 4mm (no. 8), 4½mm (no. 7) and 7½mm (no. 1).
Tension: 12 sts and 18 rows knitted on 7½mm (no. 1) to 10cm (4in) square.

Pattern

Row 1 (right side): K1 * P7, K1, rep from * to end.
Row 2: sts as set (i.e. P1 * K7, P1, rep from * to end).
Row 3: K2 * P5, K3, rep from * ending last repeat with K2.
Row 4: sts as set.
Row 5: K3 * P3, K5, rep from * ending K3.
Row 6: sts as set.
Row 7: K4 * P1, K7, rep from * ending K4.
Row 8: sts as set.
Rows 9 to 12: Knit.
These 12 rows form one triangle.
Row 13: P4 * K1, P7, rep from * ending P4.
Row 14: sts as set.
Row 15: P3 * K3, P5, rep from * ending P3.
Row 16: sts as set.
Row 17: P2 * K5, P3, rep from * ending P2.
Row 18: sts as set.
Row 19: P1 * K7, P1, rep from * to end.
Row 20: sts as set.
Rows 21 to 24: Knit.
These second 12 rows form one triangle.

Back

Using 4½mm (no. 7) ndls cast on 65 sts and K1, P1 rib for 9cm (3½in). Change to 7½mm (no. 1) ndls and knit one row, then continue in pattern from row 1. Work until the back is 5 triangles and 3 rows.

SHAPE RAGLAN
Cast off 3 sts beginning of the next 2 rows, then * dec 1 st at each end of the next 2 rows, work 1 row. Rep from * until 19 sts remain. Work 1 row more (8 triangles have been worked). Cast off.

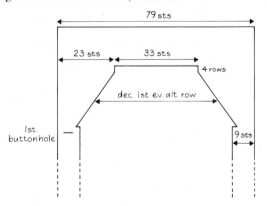

Fronts

Using 4½mm (no. 7) ndls cast on 33 sts and K1, P1 rib for 9cm (3½in). Change to 7½mm (no. 1) ndls and knit 1 row. Continue in pattern from row 1. Work until the front is 5 triangles and 3 rows.

SHAPE RAGLAN
Cast off 3 sts beginning of next row. Work 1 row. At arm edge * dec 1 st next 2 rows, work 1 row, rep from *.
Neck shaping: Whilst *continuing* with raglan shapings, when work measures 6 triangles dec 1 st at neck edge every alternate row until 1 st remains. Fasten off. Do the same for the other front, reversing all shapings.

Sleeves

Using 4½mm (no. 7) ndls, cast on 32 sts and K1, P1 rib for 6cm (2½in). Change to 7½mm (no. 1) ndls, knit 1 row increasing 15 sts evenly across row (47 sts). Work in pattern (row 1: P7, K1, rep across row ending P7), increasing 1 st at each end of every 6th row until there are 65 sts. Continue until work measures 5 triangles and 3 rows.

SHAPE RAGLAN
Cast off 3 sts at the beginning of the next 2 rows.
* Dec 1 st each end of the next 2 rows, work 1 row. Rep from * until 21 sts remain (7 triangles and 9 rows have been worked.)
Next row: K1, K2 tog across row (11 sts).
Next row: K3 tog across row, ending K2 tog, *casting off as you go along.*

Collar

Using 4mm (no. 8) ndls, cast on 79 sts and K1, P1 rib for 9cm (3½in).
Next row: Rib 23 sts, cast off the centre 33 sts, rib 23sts. On last set of 23 sts rib 4 rows, then dec 1 st at neck edge every alternate row 15 times (8 sts). Increase 1 st at the neck edge for the seam (9 sts). Rib on 9 sts for approx. 50cm (20in). Make sure that band fits well by pinning it onto the front before finally casting off. On the other side (23 sts) do the same collar shapings and 5 buttonholes on the band as follows:
From front edge work in rib 4 sts then yarn over needle and K (or P) the next 2 sts together. Make first buttonhole after increasing the 1 st for the seam, then remaining buttonholes approx. 10cm (4in) apart.

Pocket linings
(Knit 2)
Knit a rectangle 36 × 18cm (14 × 7in) in stocking stitch, using 4-ply yarn. Sew over to make square, leaving one side open.

Finishing
Sew together all the raglan seams.
Sew the sleeve seams. Sew the side seams, leaving a gap from the top of the 1st triangle to the top of the 3rd triangle for pocket opening.
Sew on collar and bands. Sew in pocket linings.
Sew on buttons.

Kaffe Fassett: Moghul Gardens Jacket

[*See colour photograph opposite page 16*]

Kaffe Fassett has a magical touch with colour, whether he is designing bold knitwear, working on a detailed needlepoint mural or painting his vivid still lives on canvas.

He comes from a family of artist/craftsmen in Big Sur, California, where the waves crash against the rugged coastline north of San Francisco and the light is particularly luminous.

'But in England there is so much hidden colour,' he says. 'There is something about the quality of the light here that has developed my eye for colour.'

Kaffe Fassett came to England in the sixties and it was a chance encounter on a train journey to Scotland which encouraged him to knit. After his first hesitant attempts at knitting, he visited a mill with a newly graduated fashion student by the name of Bill Gibb. They went to buy tweeds, but Kaffe was seduced by the rainbow of different coloured Shetland wools. Since that time he has become an expert on knitting and weaving, with teaching seminars where he exhorts his own students to experiment with colour and texture rather than follow a pre-set scheme.

'I don't do any fancy stitches,' he explains. 'Everything I do is simple and anyone can do it. I'll use all sorts of different materials, anything that helps me get on with the job. I like to see what the stitches evolve into.'

As you drive up the road to Kaffe's North London flat, you can see the concentration of colour, pattern and texture glowing through the window like multi-coloured embers. He collects kelims and scatters them on floor, walls and furniture, among his finely wrought tapestries and his paintings that reflect colour and pattern.

Ten years ago, Kaffe Fassett worked in Italy with the Missonis, whose richly woven knits have become classics of style. He himself insists that it is the complexities of colour (he often uses three to one row and a dozen different tones overall) that are significant to fashion. He does not believe in major changes of shape and style, and insists that his coats and jackets are unisexual.

Pulling his favourite sweaters, cardigans and magic carpet coats from a trunk in the corner of the studio, he demonstrates his belief in one-for-all garments by putting a round-collared jacket made in a mosaic of colour on his own gangling frame.

Because Kaffe works at and teaches weaving, he has always used the most subtle colours for his work. He feels strongly that knitters should have a choice of good textures and colours, and he advised Rowan Yarns of Yorkshire on a range of rich tweedy Woolmark yarns that you see made up into the Moghul Gardens jacket in the colour photograph. It was inspired by a postcard on an Indian miniature showing a formal garden.

Although his personal colour spectrum is very wide, his designs tend to be made up in the jewel colours of antique textiles, especially the deep madder red and Persian blue of the old rugs and the terracotta reds and rich browns of India, spiced with more exotic shades.

Some of his earlier work incorporated the movement of the sea from his native shoreline, and used shells and starfish as motifs. The flowers – very sweet, soft and plucked from an English cottage garden – that appear in so many of his paintings, are also translated into knitting.

'My world is colour,' Kaffe Fassett says simply. 'I will make anything that has to do with amazing colour.'

Kaffe Fassett's Moghul gardens jacket shows his use of rich colour and pattern, inspired by an Indian miniature painting. The drop shoulder edge-to-edge jacket with a lozenge-patterned border is knitted in an all over flower design. Front and back are worked in one piece with no shoulder seams.

Sizes: small/medium/large. Width between side seams: 53/60/66cm (21/23½/26). Length: 72.5cm (28½in).

Yarn: Pure new wool (Chunky Tweed for yarn A and Stranded Persian for the contrast.)
A: 600g Grey-Blue chunky tweed.
B: 40g Dark Green (91).
C: 40g Light Green (89).
D: 180g Pale Blue (63).
E: 50g Pale Pink (68).
F: 200g Medium Pink (69).
G: 30g Dark Pink (93).
H: 180g Purple (94).
J: 50g Orange (26).
L: 50g Magenta (96).
M: 25g Red (46).
N: 50g Sky Blue (50).
Q: 40g Cornflower Blue (501).
R: 50g Slate Blue (65).
S: 50g Black (62).
T: 25g Apricot (78).
U: 40g Rust (27).

Yarn available in knitting kit form from Rowan Yarns, Green Lane Mill, Washpit, Holmfirth, Huddersfield, West Yorkshire, HD7 1RW. Also from Yarncraft, 112a Westbourne Grove, London, W2.

Needles: circular needles, 1 metre long, sizes 4½mm (no. 7), 5½mm (no. 5) and 6½mm (no. 3). The circular needles are used in the same way as ordinary pins by knitting sts from left to right point, turning and repeating.

Tension: 17 sts and 18 rows knitted in pattern on 6½mm (no. 3) ndls to 10cm (4in) square.

Note: The body of the jacket is made in one piece starting at the bottom of the back, working up to the shoulder and down the fronts. The sleeves are added on afterwards. The pattern consists of 15 rows of flowers, 3 rows each of pink, red, blue, orange and magenta flowers. Each flower head has four colours. The sleeves have the same flowers but in a different order (orange, blue, pink), and have a check border at the cuffs and shoulders. The sleeves are the same length for all sizes because when the body is knitted to the larger sizes the sleeves get longer due to the dropped shoulders.

Body
Using yarn H and 4½mm (no. 7) ndl, cast on 91/101/111 sts and work 7 rows st.st. Then with wrong side facing, work a knit row to form turn-over edge. Change to 6½mm (no. 3) ndl. Work in st.st as follows:
Row 1 and every following odd numbered row, knit.
Row 2 and every following even numbered row, purl.

Row 1: A.
Row 2: 5A (1B, 9A) to last 6 sts, 1B, 5A.
Row 3: 5A (1B, 9A) to last 6 sts, 1B, 5A.
Row 4: 4A (3C, 7A) to last 7 sts, 3C, 4A.
Row 5: 3A (1C, 1A, 1C, 1A, 1C, 5A) to last 8 sts, 1C, 1A, 1C, 1A, 1C, 3A.
Row 6: 2A, (2C, 1A, 1C, 1A, 2C, 3A) to last 9 sts, 2C, 1A, 1C, 1A, 2C, 2A.
Row 7: 1A, (1C, 2A, 3C, 2A, 1C, 1A) to end.
Row 8: 3A (1D, 1A, 1D, 1A, 1D, 5A) to last 8 sts, 1D, 1A, 1D, 1A, 1D, 3A.
Row 9: 2A, (2D, 1A, 1D, 1A, 2D, 3A) to last 9 sts, 2D, 1A, 1D, 1A, 2D, 2A.
Row 10: 1A (1D, 2A, 3D, 2A, 1D, 1A) to end.
Row 11: 3A, (1D, 1A, 1D, 1A, 1D, 5A) to last 8 sts, 1D, 1A, 1D, 1A, 1D, 3A.
Row 12: 2A (2D, 1A, 1D, 1A, 2D, 3A) to last 9 sts, 2D, 1A, 1D, 1A, 2D, 2A.
Row 13: 1A (1D, 2A, 3D, 2A, 1D, 1A) to end.
Row 14: 3A (1D, 1A, 1D, 1A, 1D, 5A) to last 8 sts, 1D, 1A, 1D, 1A, 1D, 3A.
Row 15: 2A (1D, 1A, 3E, 1A, 1D, 3A) to last 9 sts, 1D, 1A, 3E, 1A, 1D, 2A.
Row 16: 1A (1D, 1A, 5E, 1A, 1D, 1A) to end.
Row 17: 2A (7F, 3A) to last 9 sts, 7F, 2A.
Row 18: 1D (1A, 7G, 1A, 1D) to end.
Row 19: 1D (2A, 5H, 2A, 1D) to end.
Row 20: 2D (7A, 3D) to last 9 sts, 7A, 2D. Mark each end of this row for bottom of pocket.
Row 21: 2E (7A, 3E) to last 9 sts, 7A, 2E.
Row 22: 3E (5A, 5E) to last 8 sts, 5A, 3E.
Row 23: 4F (3A, 7F) to last 7 sts, 3A, 4F.
Row 24: 4G (1A, 1D, 1A, 7G) to last 7 sts, 1A, 1D, 1A, 4G.
Row 25: 3H, (2A, 1D, 2A, 5H) to last 8 sts, 2A, 1D, 2A, 3H.
Row 26: 4A (3D, 7A) to last 7 sts, 3D, 4A.
Row 27: 4A (3E, 7A) to last 7 sts, 3E, 4A.
Row 28: 3A (5E, 5A) to last 8 sts, 5E, 3A.
Row 29: 2A (7F, 3A) to last 9 sts, 7F, 2A.
Row 30: 1B (1A, 7G, 1A, 1B) to end.
Row 31: 1B (2A, 5H, 2A, 1B) to end.
Row 32: 2C (7A, 3C) to last 9 sts, 7A, 2C.
Row 33: 1C, 1A, 1C (5A, 1C, 1A, 1C, 1A, 1C) to last 8 sts, 5A, 1C, 1A, 1C.
Row 34: 1D, 1A, 2D (3A, 2D, 1A, 1D, 1A, 2D) to last 7 sts, 3A, 2D, 1A, 1D.
Row 35: 2D, 2A, 1D (1A, 1D, 2A, 3D, 2A, 1D) to last 6 sts, 1A, 1D, 2A, 2D.
Row 36: 1D, 1A, 1D (5A, 1D, 1A, 1D, 1A, 1D) to last 8 sts, 5A, 1D, 1A, 1D.
Row 37: 2J, 1A, 1D (3A, 1D, 1A, 3J, 1A, 1D) to last 7 sts, 3A, 1D, 1A, 2J.
Row 38: 3J (5A, 5J) to last 8 sts, 5A, 3J.
Row 39: 4L (3A, 7L) to last 7 sts, 3A, 4L.
Row 40: 4M (1A, 1D, 1A, 7M) to last 7 sts, 1A, 1D, 1A, 4M.
Row 41: 3H (2A, 1D, 2A, 5H) to last 8 sts, 2A, 1D, 2A, 3H.
Row 42: 4A (3D, 7A) to last 7 sts, 3D, 4A.
Row 43: 4A (3J, 7A) to last 7 sts, 3J, 4A.
Row 44: 3A (5J, 5A) to last 8 sts, 5J, 3A.

Row 45: 2A (7L, 3A) to last 9 sts, 7L, 2A.

Row 46: 1D, 1A (7M, 1A, 1D, 1A) to last 9 sts, 7M, 1A, 1D.

Row 47: 1D, 2A (5H, 2A, 1D, 2A) to last 8 sts, 5H, 2A, 1D.

Row 48: 2D (7A, 3D) to last 9 sts, 7A, 2D.

Row 49: 2J (7A, 3J) to last 9 sts, 7A, 2J.

Row 50: 3J (5A, 5J) to last 8 sts, 5A, 3J.

Row 51: 4L (3A, 7L) to last 7 sts, 3A, 4L.

Row 52: 4M (1A, 1B, 1A, 7M) to last 7 sts, 1A, 1B, 1A, 4M.

Row 53: 3H (2A, 1B, 2A, 5H) to last 8 sts, 2A, 1B, 2A, 3H.

Row 54: 4A (3C, 7A) to last 7 sts, 3C, 4A.

Row 55: 3A (1C, 1A, 1C, 1A, 1C, 5A) to last 8 sts, 1C, 1A, 1C, 1A, 1C, 3A.

Row 56: 2A (2D, 1A, 1D, 1A, 2D, 3A) to last 9 sts, 2D, 1A, 1D, 1A, 2D, 2A.

Row 57: 1A (1D, 2A, 3D, 2A, 1D, 1A) to end.

Row 58: 3A (1D, 1A, 1D, 1A, 1D, 5A) to last 8 sts, 1D, 1A, 1D, 1A, 1D, 3A. Mark each end of this row for top of pocket.

Row 59: 2A (1D, 1A, 3N, 1A, 1D, 3A) to last 9 sts, 1D, 1A, 3N, 1A, 1D, 2A.

Row 60: 3A (5N, 5A) to last 8 sts, 5N, 3A.

Row 61: 2A (7Q, 3A) to last 9 sts, 7Q, 2A.

Row 62: 1D, 1A (7R, 1A, 1D, 1A) to last 9 sts, 7R, 1A, 1D.

Row 63: 1D, 2A, (5S, 2A, 1D, 2A) to last 8 sts, 5S, 2A, 1D.

Row 64: 2D (7A, 3D) to last 9 sts, 7A, 2D.

Row 65: 2N (7A, 3N) to last 9 sts, 7A, 2N.

Row 66: 3N, (5A, 5N) to last 8 sts, 5A, 3N.

Row 67: 4Q (3A, 7Q) to last 7 sts, 3A, 4Q.

Row 68: 4R (1A, 1D, 1A, 7R) to last 7 sts, 1A, 1D, 1A, 4R.

Row 69: 3S (2A, 1D, 2A, 5S) to last 8 sts, 2A, 1D, 2A, 3S.

Row 70: 4A (3D, 7A) to last 7 sts, 3D, 4A.

Row 71: 4A (3N, 7A) to last 7 sts, 3N, 4A.

Row 72: 3A (5N, 5A) to last 8 sts, 5N, 3A.

Row 73: 2A (7Q, 3A) to last 9 sts, 7Q, 2A.

Row 74: 1B, 1A (7R, 1A, 1B, 1A) to last 9 sts, 7R, 1A, 1B.

Row 75: 1B, 2A (5S, 2A, 1B, 2A) to last 8 sts, 5S, 2A, 1B.

Rows 76 to 97: Work pattern as for rows 32 to 53 but work colours of flower heads as follows:

 Row 81: Use F instead of J.
 Row 82: Use F instead of J.
 Row 83: Use T instead of L.
 Row 84: Use J instead of M.
 Row 85: Use U instead of H.

Rows 98 to 117: Work pattern as for rows 54 to 73 but work colours of flowers as follows:

 Row 103: Use F instead of N.
 Row 104: Use F instead of N.
 Row 105: Use L instead of Q.
 Row 106: Use H instead of R.
 Row 107: Use S.

Row 118: 2A (7H, 3A) to last 9 sts, 7H, 2A.

Row 119: make neck as follows: Small and large sizes: K3A (5S, 5A) 3/4 times, then 5S, 2A making 40/50 sts in all. Cast off 11 sts and patt to end. Medium size: K3A (5S, 5A) 4 times, then 2S making 45 sts in all. Cast off 11 sts and patt to end.

Row 120: P in A to centre, join new yarn A to second side of neck, cast off 6 sts and continue in A to end. From now on work across both sides of front at the same time.

Row 121: K in A to neck edge, cast off 6 sts at beginning of second side of neck, K in A to end. Mark each end of row for shoulders.

Row 122: P in A across both fronts. (34/39/44 sts each side).

Rows 123 to 128: From now on work backwards through the rows starting at row 119. The flowers will thus be the right way up on back and front.

Row 129: On this row and every following alternate row increase at each neck edge, in the following manner: 1 st 3 times, 2 sts twice, 5 sts once, making 46/51/56 sts at each side.

Row 130 onwards: Continue working backwards through the rows to row 1. It is easier to follow your own knitting than the pattern at this point. Change to 4½mm (no. 7) needle. Using yarn H, P 3 rows to form turn-over edge, then work 5 rows stocking stitch. Cast off.

Sleeves

Using yarn H and (4½mm (no. 7) needle, cast on 33 sts. Hem as for back.

Change to 6½mm (no. 3) needle.

Row 1 and every following odd numbered row, knit.

Row 2 and every following even numbered row, purl.

Row 1: A.

Row 2: (2F, 2R) to last st, 1F.

Row 3: 1F (2R, 2F) to end.

Row 4: (2F, 2R) to last st, 1F.

Row 5: A.

Row 6: 6A (1B, 9A) twice, 1B, 6A.

Now increase 1 st at each end of the next row, and every following alternate K row until there are 97 sts in all. At the same time place rows of flowers in the following colour sequence. (The increase sts are incorporated into each K row.)

Row 7: (knit) 7A, (1B, 9A) to last 8 sts, 1B, 7A.

Row 8: 6A, (3C, 7A) to last 9 sts, 3C, 6A.

Row 9: 1C, 5A, (1C, 1A, 1C, 1A, 1C, 5A) to last st, 1C.

Row 10: 2C, 3A (2C, 1A, 1C, 1A, 2C, 3A) to last 2 sts, 2C.

Row 11: 1C, 2A, 1C, 1A, (1C, 2A, 3C, 2A, 1C, 1A) to last 4 sts, 1C, 2A, 1C.

Row 12: 1A, 1D, 5A, (1D, 1A, 1D, 1A, 1D, 5A) to last 2 sts, 1D, 1A.

Row 13: 1D, 1A, 2D, 3A (2D, 1A, 1D, 1A, 2D, 3A) to last 4 sts, 2D, 1A, 1D.

Row 14: 2D, 2A, 1D, 1A, (1D, 2A, 3D, 2A, 1D, 1A) to last 5 sts, 1D, 2A, 2D.

Row 15: 1A, 1D, 1A, 1D, 5A, (1D, 1A, 1D, 1A, 1D, 5A) to last 4 sts, 1D, 1A, 1D, 1A.

Row 16: 1A, 1D, 1A, 2D, 3A, (2D, 1A, 1D, 1A, 2D, 3A) to last 5 sts, 2D, 1A, 1D, 1A.

Row 17: 1A, 3D, 2A, 1D, 1A, (1D, 2A, 3D, 2A, 1D, 1A) to last 7 sts, 1D, 2A, 3D, 1A.
Row 18: (1D, 1A, 1D, 1A, 1D, 5A) to last 5 sts, 1D, 1A, 1D, 1A, 1D.
Working the increase stitches into the pattern, continue in the following sequence.
Rows 19 to 35: Work as for rows 81 to 97 (i.e. orange flowers).
Rows 36 to 57: As for rows 54 to 75 (blue flowers).
Rows 58 to 62: As for rows 32 to 36 (stems).
Rows 63 to 65: As for rows 15 to 17 (pink flowers).
Row 66: (3A, 7G) to last 3 sts, 3A.
Row 67: (5A, 5H) to last 5 sts, 5A.
Row 68: A.
Row 69: (2F, 2R) to last stitch, 1F (97 sts in all).
Row 70: 1F (2R, 2F) to end.
Row 71: (2F, 2R) to last st, 1F.
Row 72: A.
Then cast off.

Pockets

RIGHT POCKET

With right side of back of jacket facing you pick up 30 sts up right hand side edge between two pocket markers using Yarn A and 6½mm (no. 3) needle.
Row 1: P to end. Turn. Cast on 4 sts at end of row.
Row 2: K.
Row 3: P2 tog, P to end.
Continue in stocking stitch decreasing 1 st at beginning of every P row until 20 sts remain. Cast off.

LEFT POCKET

Pick up 30 sts as for right pocket.
Row 1: P.
Row 2: K2 tog, K to end. Turn, cast on 4 sts.
Continue decreasing 1 st at beginning of every K row till 20 sts remain, cast off.

POCKET EDGE

With right side of front of jacket facing and using Yarn H and 4½mm (no. 7) needle, pick up 40 sts between pocket markers.
Row 1: K to form turn-over edge.
Row 2: K.
Continue in stocking stitch for 4 more rows. Cast off.
Make left pocket edge to match right one.

Front edges

Using yarn A and 5½mm (no. 5) needle pick up 104 sts down right front edge of jacket.
Row 1: P (2R, 2F) to end.
Row 2: K (2F, 2R) to end and make buttonholes by patt 4, (cast off 2, patt 14 including st on ndl), repeat to last 4 sts, cast off 2, patt 2.
Row 3: Working pattern as for row 1, cast on buttonhole stitches again.
Row 4: K in A.
Row 5: Change to size 4½mm (no. 7) needle, P in H.
Row 6: P in H to form turn-over row.
Row 7: P in H.
Row 8: K in H.
Row 9: Working in H, P2 (cast off 2, P14 including st

already on needle) to last 6 sts, cast off 2, P4.
Row 10: K, casting on buttonholes again.
Work 5 more rows stocking stitch. Cast off loosely.
Knit left front edge as for right, but omit buttonholes.

Finishing

Press.
Backstitch sleeves onto body joining mid-point of sleeves onto shoulder markers. Press seams. Catch down hems of front edges, tucking hem of lower edge under front hems. Catch down pocket edges. Backstitch sleeve and side seams above and below pocket then catch down pockets onto inside fronts. Make sure motifs match at sides. Turn up and hem cuffs and lower edge of jacket. Sew on buttons.

COLLAR

Using Yarn A and 5½mm (no. 5) needle, pick up 78 sts round neck edge.
Row 1: P (2R, 2F) to last 2 sts, 2R.
Row 2: K (2R, 2F) to last 2 sts, 2R.
Row 3: As for row 1.
Row 4: Change to 4½mm (no. 7) needle, K in A.
P 3 rows in H to form turn-over row, then work 6 more rows stocking stitch. Cast off very loosely. Press. Catch down collar hem, stretching it slightly to fit round curve.

Jane Wheeler: Persian Medallion Coat and Daughter's Fair Isle Cardigan

[See colour photograph opposite page 17]

The flame-sharp points from a Navajo blanket, the intricate border patterns of a Persian carpet or the sturdy stitches of English crewel embroidery are all incorporated into Jane Wheeler's knitting.

She lives with her writer husband and daughter Lucy in a picturesque Norfolk cottage, with whipping winds round the door and an undulating bleached landscape outside for inspiration. Yet Jane Wheeler's tiny workroom is crowded with the books she uses for her research – colourful plates of tribal rugs and kelims, of homely woven textiles and exotic Ottoman embroideries.

Jane Wheeler inherits a family interest in textiles from her mother, who teaches the age-old art of spinning at a Norfolk college and whose own weaving is another source of inspiration for Jane's knitwear.

'I was frustrated in my early twenties, because I saw so much that I wanted to copy in knitting. I saw a Flemish tapestry at the Victoria and Albert Museum and nursed the idea of using the design for the next 10 years.'

Her speciality is Fair Isle knitting, in the muted country tones against the pale straw and clear skyscapes she sees around her and in the richer and more exotic colours she sees in her textile books. Most of her knits have been sold to Margaret Howell, but she is increasingly working in her own right, as well as designing a machine-knit collection in cashmere. A full time assistant and a team of 150 hand-knitters enable her to export her craft to the United States, especially San Francisco, as well as selling in England.

Jane likes mixing textures, using blended yarns like linen and silk, cashmere with lambswool, silk and wool, although the warm earthy colours of Shetland wool remain her favourites.

Her studio/stockroom, at the top of the steep wooden cottage stairs, is lined with a rainbow of different yarns and stocked with boxes of buttons that Lucy considers her favourite toys.

Jane works her designs out on paper, often isolating a simple motif, as she did with the coat she designed for this book (see colour photograph), which was from the central medallion of a nineteenth century Quashqa'i rug from the Fars province in Southern Persia. From the first drawings she works out the design in knitting. ('Basically, it means using acres of graph paper,' she explains). Then the pattern is sent off to one of her sample knitters. She seldom has the time to knit herself these days (although she did knit up the bold and insistent patterns on her Navajo sweaters).

Jane Wheeler started her design career studying ceramics at Bath Academy of Arts and from that experience she developed an interest in textiles. Her first experiments in knitting were on a machine. She was taught to knit by her mother ('although she was the kind of knitter who never finished anything.')

Little Lucy seems more interested in her dolls, her kitten and the local farm animals than in picking up stitches. She does have a splendid wardrobe of knits, although her mother is practical enough to realise that machine washable wool is required for her small daughter – and made up the cardigan for this book accordingly. Mother and daughter are in the colour picture.

Sweaters, like the textiles which inspire them, in a sense, can be considered as collectors' items'. 'They are works of art as prints are,' she explains. 'They aren't one-offs. But an original piece of hand-knitting is something special, and I like to think that it will be treasured.'

Persian Medallion Coat

Jane Wheeler designs her knits by researching antique textiles. She isolated the central medallion of a Persian rug for the bold motif on the back of her border-patterned coat that falls to mid-calf. It is worked in wool and mohair, in stocking stitch and moss stitch, using one main colour and four other colours for the magic carpet patterning.

Sizes: One size. Length from nape of neck to hem: 112cm (44in).

Yarn: Harmonieuse Wool/Mohair from Laines Couture, 20 Bedford Street, London WC2.
MY: 9 × 100g balls Cream (Harpe no. 21).
A: 4 × 100g balls Blue (Oliphan no. 47).
B: 3 × 100g balls Old Gold (Violon no. 13).
C: 3 × 100g balls Burnt Orange (Tuba no. 12).
D: 3 × 100g balls Rust (Tenor no. 57).

Needles: 7mm (no. 2); 6mm (no. 4); 5mm (no. 6).

Tension: 12 sts and 16 rows knitted in st.st on 7mm (no. 2) ndls to 10cm (4in) square.

Notions: Five 25mm (1in) diameter natural horn or wood buttons.

Notes: Do not, as a general rule, strand yarns across the back of work. Instead, twist yarns at joins and leave hanging at back of work when not in use. This rule may be broken if there are only one or two st gaps between blocks of the same colour.

The pattern on the charts may not fit exactly into the number of sts on your ndls. Do not worry if you have part of a repeat at one end of the row.

Pocket backs

Cast on 18 sts using MY and size 7mm (no. 2) ndls.
Work 24 rows in st.st and put on holder.

Left front

Cast on 45 sts using yarn A and 6mm (no. 4) ndls.
Work 4 rows in moss st.
Put last 5 sts on holder.
Change to 7mm (no. 2) ndls and work border pattern (see border chart).
Then start main chart, working from st 1 to st 40.
Continue straight following chart until work measures 61cm (24in).
Cast off 18 sts, 6 sts in from under arm edge and replace with pocket back.
When work measures 102cm (40in) cast off 5 sts for neck and then dec 1 st every alt row for neck 5 times.
When work measures 112cm (44in) put on spare ndl.

Right front

As left front, but put *first* 5 sts on holder and work main chart from st 32 to st 72.

Back

Cast on 72 sts using yarn A and 6mm (no. 4) ndls.
Work 4 rows in moss st.
Change to 7mm (no. 2) ndls and work border pattern, then main chart.
When work measures 112cm (44in) keep on ndl.

JOIN SHOULDERS
By casting off back and front sts tog on outside.

Sleeves

Pick up 72 sts from sides, marking 30cm (12in) each side of shoulder seam, 36 sts from each 30cm (12in), using 7mm (no. 2) ndls work border upside down, dec 1 st each side every 4th row.
When border complete, work 4 rows moss st in yarn A on 6mm (no. 4) ndls.
Cast off using 7mm (no. 2) ndls in moss st. Sew underarm seams.

Front bands

Using 5mm (no. 6) ndls and MY, continue the 5 sts of moss st until band measures 91cm (36in) unstretched. Keep on holder.
Sew on, using flat st and leaving 2mm (¾in) gaps for buttonholes, one at top and 4 more down front, 10cm (4in) apart. Sew on buttons.

Neckband

Pick up 63 sts from neck and front bands.
Using 6mm (no. 4) ndls and yarn A work 5 rows in moss st.
Cast off in moss st.

Pocket bands

Pick up 18 sts from pocket tops using MY and 5mm (no. 6) ndls.
Work 4 rows in moss st.
Cast off in moss st.

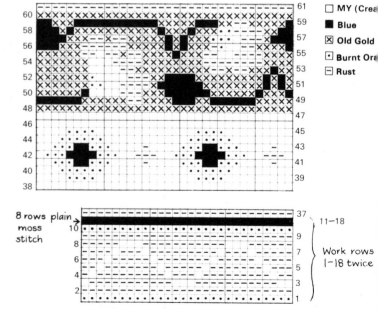

Border pattern

□ MY (Crea
■ Blue
☒ Old Gold
• Burnt Ora
⊟ Rust

8 rows plain moss stitch

Work rows 1–18 twice

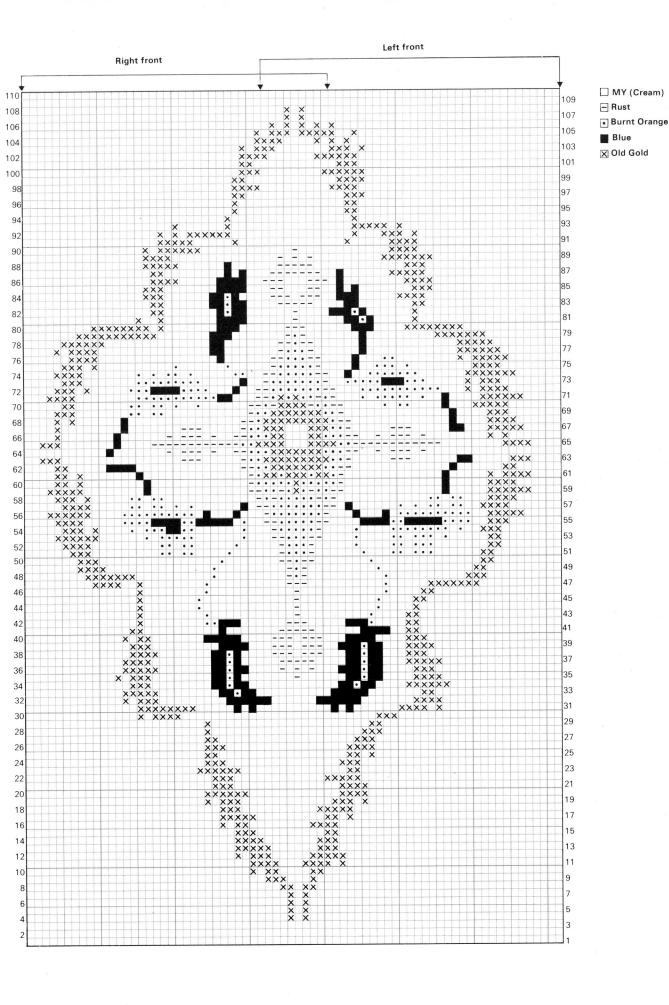

☐ MY (Cream)
⊟ Rust
⊡ Burnt Orange
■ Blue
☒ Old Gold

45

Daughter's Fair Isle Cardigan

Jane Wheeler designed a pretty round-necked Fair Isle cardigan for her daughter Lucy, carrying the pattern symmetrically across the body and raglan sleeves. It is knitted in a main colour with four others in the pattern, using a 4-ply yarn.

Sizes: 1–2 years/2–3 years.

Yarn: Patons Clansman 4-ply.
MY: 3 × 50g balls Cream.
A: 1 × 50g ball Blue.
B: 1 × 50g ball Pink.
C: 1 × 50g ball Maroon.
D: 1 × 50g ball Navy.

Needles: 3¾mm (no. 9); 2¾mm (no. 12); 3¼mm (no. 10).

Tension: 24 sts and 32 rows knitted in st.st on 3¾mm (no. 9) ndls to 10cm (4in) square.

Notions: Six 1.3cm (½in) buttons.

Note: The pattern on the chart may not fit exactly into the number of sts on your ndls. Don't worry if you have part of a rep at one end of the row. Do not carry a yarn across the back of the knitting when it is not needed until the next row, as it spoils the tension.

Fronts

Cast on 40/44 sts and work 4cm (1½in) in K1, P1 rib on 2¾mm (no. 12) ndls.
Change to 3¾mm (no. 9) ndls and Fair Isle (see Chart).
When work measures 18/20cm (7/8in) cast off 4 sts then dec 1 st every alt row on the same side.
When work measures 24/32cm (9½/12½in) cast off 6/10 sts on neck side.
Then dec 1 st each side on every alt row until all sts cast off.
Knit second front as first, reversing all shapings.

Back

Cast on 80/88 sts and work 4cm (1½in) in K1, P1 rib on 2¾mm (no. 12) ndls.
Change to 3¾mm (no. 9) ndls and Fair Isle.
When work measures 18/20cm (7/8in) cast off 4/5 sts each side.
Then dec 1 st each side every alt row until 24/26 sts left.
Put on holder.

Sleeves

(2 alike).
Cast on 40 sts and work 4cm (1½in) on 2¾mm (no. 12) ndls.
On last row inc 1 st every 5th st by working into back and front of st (49 sts).
Increase 1 st each side on every 4th row until 70 sts, working in Fair Isle on 3¾mm (no. 9) ndls.
When sleeve measures 18/20cm (7/8in) cast off 4 sts each side and then dec 1 st every alt row until 10 sts left.
Put on holder.

Finishing

Join side seams, raglan seams and underarm seams with back st as near the edge as possible.
Pick up 80 sts from neckline with 2¾mm (no. 12) ndls and work 6 rows in K1, P1 rib.
Cast off with 3¼mm (no. 10) ndls.

FRONT BANDS
Using 2¾mm (no. 12) ndls and MY cast on 10 sts.
Work bands in K1, P1 rib to fit fronts, making 1 st buttonholes every 5/5.5cm (2/2¼in).
Do not reinforce buttonholes. Sew on buttons.

Fair Isle chart

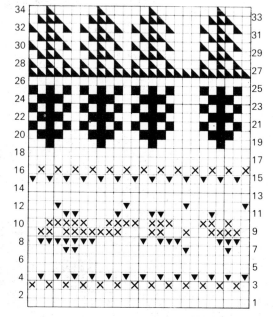

- ☐ MY
- ☒ A
- ▼ B
- ■ C
- ◪ D

Flower Gardens

Susan Duckworth: Flower Market Cardigan and Diamond Lace Summer Sweater

[For cardigan see photograph previous page. For Diamond Sweater see colour photograph opposite page 81]

The flower is a poignant decorative motif, its seeds scattered through the cultures of East and West. The exotically patterned garden carpets of Ancient Persia, delicate blooms of inlaid Indian decoration and the sweet florals printed on English country garden cottons all spring from the same inspiration: to recreate nature in art.

Susan Duckworth was trained as a painter, and she has a painter's eye for colour and pattern, that she absorbs into her knitting from all kinds of artistic stimuli. She is a voracious museum researcher, and Elizabethan blackwork, Victorian samplers and the complex patternings of oriental carpets have all been sources for her designing, with the flowers – graphic, naturalistic or decorative – her favourite motifs.

'There are certain things that work in knitting, but I am constantly frustrated,' she admits. 'The finest Persian carpets can have 1,000 knots to the square inch. Even the most basic rug will have 150. In knitting, you have got just seven stitches to the inch. It is quite difficult to get the same flexibility of pattern into knitting even though I like to work in the finest yarns. I don't really like chunky knitting. I think it always looks too easy.'

The idea of translating woven textiles into knitting is as old as the craft itself. Nordic patterns have been linked directly with the patternings on Berber carpets, brought from their home in North Africa via the Viking trade routes and still seen in Norwegian knitting to this day. The simple rectilinear designs of Nomad rugs are easier to work into garments in small areas to decorate the human body, than are the more rounded shapes that rely for their effect on density of colour and pattern.

Susan is currently trying to create in her knitting one of the most insistent of the Eastern motifs: the Paisley patterns that originated as the teardrop shape of the Persian boteh and came to the Scottish town of Paisley via India in the days of the British Empire.

She relies on the hard core of 100 knitters who have been with her loyally over the last decade, to respond to the challenge of her latest patterns which, she admits 'get progressively more difficult'. Even when her stitchcraft is relatively simple, she will work with 20 different shades of yarn – wool, cotton or even silk. Her graphic sampler sweater and the delicate lace cotton sweater featured here are two different facets of her style.

'I think that colour is one of the most important things that I put into my knitting,' she says. 'The only bit of my business that I absolutely love is the designing. I draw up shapes on graph paper, knit up endless squares and I even dye up my own yarns to get the right kind of linked colours.'

Susan Duckworth started her career as a make-up artist for BBC television and set up in business in a small way in a workshop collective ten years ago. She lives in the gentlest part of rural England, outside Farnham, Surrey, with her husband (who now helps with the business) and two small children. They don't yet have the wardrobe of hand-knits that she once envisaged for them. ('It's always in my mind to knit for them, but somehow I seem to be too busy.')

Like many other designers, Susan finds that all too much time is now spent organizing her business and collating the efforts of her 200 outworkers, rather than in the creative work she really enjoys. She believes that her designs are dependent on absolute mastery of the craft of knitting.

'When I go round museums and see interesting visual ideas, I have to think how to re-interpret them in stitches,' she explains.

'All the time I am trying to invent stitches that can't be put on a machine.'

Flower Market Cardigan

An example of Susan Duckworth's ideas absorbed from museum art and from nature. Her Victorian sampler cardigan has nursery bright flowers knitted in Fair Isle on a neutral ground using a 4-ply wool. The bell frilled cuffs echo the frill at the collar.

Size: Medium.

Yarn:
MY: 5 × 50g balls Natural (Lister Lee Target Motoravia 4-ply, shade 9178).
A: 1 × 50g ball Air Force Blue Aplaca (Pingolaine, from Pinguoin, shade 30).

Other contrast yarns (small quantity of each):
Wine (Pingolaine, shade 12).
Scarlet (Patons Fuzzy Wuzzy Angora, shade 5610).
Forest (Pingolaine, shade 07).
Cerise (Pingolaine, shade 25).
Yellow (Pingolaine, shade 40).
Royal (Sirdar Superwash 4-ply, shade 016).
Sky Blue (Jaeger Langora, shade 247, from Patons).
Rowan (Georges Picaud Lambswool, shade 104).
Saffron (Pingolaine, shade 19).
Yellow Ochre (Patricia Roberts Shetland, shade NC3).
Willow (Pingolaine, shade 29).
Dark Blue (Sirdar Superwash 4-ply, shade 079).
Note: Addresses for Patons, Pinguoin and Sirdar are on page 11, and for Patricia Roberts' Knitting Shops on page 64. If you have difficulty obtaining the specified yarns or shades, similar ones can be substituted.

Needles: 2¾mm (no. 12); 3mm (no. 11); 3¼mm (no. 10).

Tension: 32 sts and 34 rows worked on 3¼mm (no. 10) needles in the Fair Isle pattern to 10cm (4in) square.

Right front

Using 2¾mm (no. 12) needles and MY, cast on 67 sts and work in K1, P1 rib straight for 7.5 cm (3in), knitting into the back of all knit sts throughout to give a firmer rib.
Change to 3¼mm (no. 10) needles and proceed in the Fair Isle patterns in st.st as shown on the chart, starting at row 1 (knit row) and dec 1 st at side on every foll 8th row until there are 62 sts on needles.
Work 100 rows. Work the large Fair Isle motifs individually, having separate balls of yarn for each motif across work. Work only 'whole' motifs at sides and centre front over the two large patterns (i.e. rows 18 to 43 and rows 77 to 100). Try to arrange that the complete motifs are in the centre of work with the same number of plain sts in st.st at each side.

SHAPE ARMHOLE
Next row: Cast off 7 sts at armhole edge, then work in patterns to the end of row.
Dec 1 st at armhole edge on the next and every foll alt row until there are 50 sts left on needle.
Then cont without further shaping until work measures 18cm (7in) from the beg of the armhole shaping, then shape neck.

SHAPE NECK
Keeping to the continuity of the Fair Isle patterns and placing the motifs centrally across shoulders, cast off 8 sts at front edge on the next row. Then cast off 2 sts at front edge on the next and every foll alt row until there are 28 sts left on needle.
Cont without further shaping until the armhole measures 22cm (8½in) from the beg of shaping, then shape shoulder.

SHAPE SHOULDER
Cast off 9 sts at the beg of armhole edge on the next and foll alt 2 rows. Fasten off.
Note: Do not stop half way through a repeat across shoulder. If necessary work the last rows in MY st.st.

Left front

Work to match right front, reversing all shapings, taking care to match patterns at centre front (i.e. having the same Fair Isle pattern positioning on either side of centre front).

Back

Using 2¾mm (no. 12) needles and MY cast on 134 sts and work in K1, P1 rib straight for 7.5cm (3in) to match rib on fronts.
Change to 3¼mm (no. 10) needles and work in Fair Isle patterns from row 1 to row 100 inclusive. Cast off 1 st at each end of every foll 8th row until there are 124 sts on needles.

SHAPE ARMHOLES
Keeping to the continuity of the Fair Isle patterns, cast off 8 sts at the beg of the next 2 rows.
Then dec 1 st at each end of every foll alt row until 100 sts remain.
Cont on these 100 sts straight in Fair Isle patterns until the back measures the same as fronts at the beg of shoulder shaping.

SHAPE SHOULDERS
Cast off 9 sts at the beg of the next 4 rows.
Then cast off 9 sts at the beg of the next 2 rows.
Cast off rem sts.

Sleeves

BELL FRILLING FOR CUFFS
Using 3mm (no. 11) needles and Yarn A, cast on 116 sts.
Row 1: P2 (K7, P7) to last 2 sts, end P2.
Row 2: K2 (K7, P7) to last 2 sts, end P2.
Row 3: P2 (K2 tog tbl, K3, K2 tog, P7) to last 2 sts, end P2.
Row 4: K2 (K7, P5), to last 2 sts, end P2.
Row 5: P2 (K2 tog tbl, K1, K2 tog, P7) to last 2 sts, end P2.
Row 6: K2 (K7, P3) to last 2 sts, end P2.
Row 7: P2 (Sl 1, K2 tog tbl, PSSO, P7) to last 2 sts, end P2.
Row 8: K2 (K7, P1) to last 2 sts, ending P2, (68 sts on needle).
Row 9 (right side row): P2, (K2 tog tbl, P6) to last 2 sts, end P2.

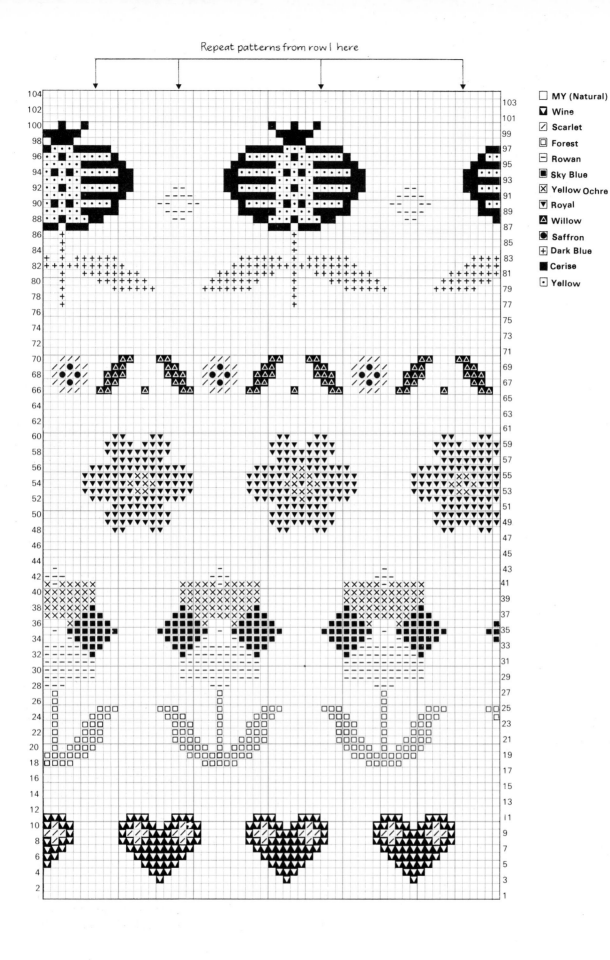

□	MY (Natural)
◹	Wine
☑	Scarlet
⊡	Forest
⊟	Rowan
◼	Sky Blue
☒	Yellow Ochre
▽	Royal
△	Willow
●	Saffron
✛	Dark Blue
■	Cerise
·	Yellow

Row 10: K2, (K6, P1) to last 2 sts, ending P2.
Change to MY and knit one row.
Change to 2¾mm (no. 12) needles (60 sts).
Then still using MY work 12cm (4½in) of K1, P1 rib, knitting into the back of all knit sts.
Now change to 3¼mm (no. 10) needles and inc for the fullness of sleeve as follows:
Next row: K2 (K1, knit into the front and back of the next 3 sts) 13 times, K2 (95 sts).
Now proceed in Fair Isle patterns from row 1 to row 100 inclusive without further shaping.

SHAPE TOP OF SLEEVE
Keeping to the continuity of the Fair Isle pattern, shape top of sleeve by casting off 3 sts at beg of the next 6 rows; then 2 sts at the beg of the next 4 rows.
Then dec 1 st at both ends of every row until 68 sts remain, then every alt row until 58 sts rem; then every 3rd row until 42 sts rem.
Then cast off 6 sts at the beg of the next 4 rows.
Cast off rem sts.
Again, do not work half motifs at sides of sleeve top shapings.

Front band

Using 2¾mm (no. 12) needles and MY, cast on 11 sts and work in K1, P1 rib (knitting into the back of all knit sts).
Make a band to fit right up the front edge, starting at bottom edge and finishing at neck edge.
Then work an identical band but placing buttonholes evenly over the centre 3 sts (i.e. with 4 sts at either side) on every 26th and 27th row up to the neck line.
Place the first buttonhole 13mm (½in) from bottom edge, last buttonhole 13mm (½in) from neckline.

Collar edging and frill

With the right side facing, using 2¾mm (no. 12) needles and MY pick up 90 sts evenly around edge of neck.
Now transfer these 90 sts onto another 2¾mm (no. 12) needle so that the next row will again be worked with the right side facing. Leave these sts.
Now using Yarn A and 3mm (no. 11) needles cast on 186 sts and work in bell sts as for cuffs but working over 186 sts instead of 116.
Continue to decrease down the bell until there are 90 sts left on needle.
Then change to MY and 2¾mm (no. 12) needles and knit both sets of sts tog (i.e. those picked up around neck and those of the frill).
Cont in K1, P1 rib for 7 rows, decreasing 1 st at beg and end of every other row (centre front edge).
Cast off loosely.

Finishing

Using a damp cloth lightly press on the reverse side of work and then join all seams, apart from front band, using a fine backstitch. For front band use a flat seam and sew it on as you go. Sew on buttons.

Diamond Lace Summer Sweater

Susan Duckworth is interested in stitchcraft and likes her patterns to be a challenge. Her creamy square-necked cotton jumper is knitted from the shoulders downwards in a diamond lace stitch, using the diamond motif, large and small, for pattern and colour.

Size: medium.

Yarn:
MY: 7 balls Ivory (Georges Picaud Coton Cannele, shade 1).
Contrast yarns: Small quantity of each of the following:
A: Ash Grey (W.D.C. Dilthey, Beauty, shade 0942).
B: Blue Moon (Georges Picaud Coton Cannele, shade 39).
C: Old Rose (W.D.C. Dilthey, Polo Fil D'Ecosse, shade 0993).
D: Delft Blue (Georges Picaud Coton Cannele, shade 50).
E: Naples Yellow (Georges Picaud Orient Express Silk, shade 5).
F: Dove Grey (Georges Picaud Orient Express Silk, shade 11).
G: Smoke (W.D.C. Dilthey, Polo, shade 0995).
H: Frost Pink (Georges Picaud Orient Express Silk, shade 42).
The address for Georges Picaud is on page 11. W.D.C. Dilthey's address is Eldon House, 92 London Road, Leicester LE2 0PT. If you have difficulty with small quantity orders or with yarns that have been discontinued you can substitute any equivalent 4-ply cotton yarn.

Needles: 3mm (no. 11); 3¼mm (no. 10); 2¾mm (no. 12).

Tension: width across two diamonds should be 13cm (5in). As the tension on knitted cotton can vary greatly, keep as close as possible to this tension check.

Note: This jumper is worked in reverse, i.e. from the shoulders down to the welt, and from the top of the sleeves down towards the cuff.

Diamond pattern

Note: Do not weave the colours from diamond to diamond as the threads will show behind the lace stitch. Work each colour separately, using small balls of coloured yarn (see diagram).
Row 1: * MY, yrn to make a st, SKPO, K13, K2 tog, m1, K1B, in MY m1, SKPO, K13, K2 tog, m1, K1A, rep from * to end.
Row 2 and all foll alt rows: Purl all sts in respective colours.
Row 3: * K1A, in MY m1, SKPO, K11, K2 tog, m1, K3B, in MY m1, SKPO, K11, K2 tog, m1, K2A, rep from * to end.
Row 5: * K2A, in MY m1, SKPO, K9, K2 tog, m1, K5B, in MY m1, SKPO, K9, K2 tog, m1, K3A, rep from * to end.
Row 7: * K3A, in MY m1, SKPO, K7, K2 tog, m1, K7B, in MY m1, SKPO, K7, K2 tog, m1, K4A, rep from * to end.
Row 9: * K4A, in MY m1, SKPO, K5, K2 tog, m1, K9B, in MY m1, SKPO, K5, K2 tog, m1, K5A, rep from * to end.

Row 11: * K5A, in MY m1, SKPO, K3, K2 tog, m1, K11B, in MY m1, SKPO, K3, K2 tog, m1, K6A, rep from * to end.

Row 13: * K6A, in MY m1, SKPO, K1, K2 tog, m1, K13B, in MY m1, SKPO, K1, K2 tog, m1, K7A, rep from * to end.

Row 15: * K7A, in MY m1, Sl 1, K2 tog, PSSO, m1, K15B, in MY m1, Sl 1, K2 tog, PSSO, m1, K8A, rep from * to end.

Row 17: * K6A, in MY K2 tog, m1, K1D, in MY m1, SKPO, K13B, in MY K2 tog, m1, K1C, in MY m1, SKPO, K7A, rep from * to end.

Row 19: * K5A, in MY K2 tog, m1, K3D, in MY m1, SKPO, K11B, in MY K2 tog, m1, K3C, in MY m1, SKPO, K6A, rep from * to end.

Row 21: * K4A, in MY K2 tog, m1, K5D, in MY m1, SKPO, K9B, in MY K2 tog, m1, K5C, in MY m1, SKPO, K5A, rep from * to end.

Row 23: * K3A, in MY K2 tog, m1, K7D, in MY m1, SKPO, K7B, in MY K2 tog, m1, K7C, in MY m1, SKPO, K4A, rep from * to end.

Row 25: * K2A, in MY K2 tog, m1, K9D, in MY m1, SKPO, K5B, in MY K2 tog, m1, K9C, in MY m1, SKPO, K3A, rep from * to end.

Row 27: * K1A, in MY K2 tog, m1, K11D, in MY m1, SKPO, K3B, in MY K2 tog, m1, K11C, in MY m1, SKPO, K2A, rep from * to end.

Row 29: * In MY K2 tog, m1, K13D, in MY m1, Sl 1, K2 tog, PSSO, K2 tog, m1, K13C, in MY m1, Sl 1, K2 tog, PSSO, rep from * to end.

Row 31: * In MY K1, m1, K15D, in MY m1, SKPO, m1, K15C, in MY m1, K1, rep from * to end.

Row 33: In MY yrn to make a st, Sl 2, K1, PSSO, * K13D, in MY K2 tog, m1, K1E, in MY m1, SKPO, K13C, in MY K2 tog, m1, K1, m1, SKPO, rep from * to end, omitting SKPO at end of last repeat.

Row 35: * K1F, in MY m1, SKPO, K11D, in MY K2 tog, m1, K3E, in MY m1, SKPO, K11C, in MY K2 tog, m1, K2F, rep from * to end.

Row 37: * K2F, in MY m1, SKPO, K9D, in MY K2 tog, m1, K5E, in MY m1, SKPO, K9C, in MY K2 tog, m1, K3F, rep from * to end.

Row 39: * K3F, in MY m1. SKPO, K7D, in MY K2 tog,

m1, K7E, in MY m1, SKPO, K7C, in MY K2 tog, m1, 4F, rep from * to end.

Row 41: * K4F, in MY m1, SKPO, K5D, in MY K2 tog, m1, K9E, in MY m1, SKPO, K5C, in MY K2 tog, m1, K5F, rep from * to end.

Row 43: * K5F, in MY m1, SKPO, K3D, in MY K2 tog, m1, K11E, in MY m1, SKPO, K3C, in MY K2 tog, m1, K6F, rep from * to end.

Row 45: * K6F, in MY m1, SKPO, K1D, in MY K2 tog, m1, K13E, in MY m1, SKPO, K1C, in MY K2 tog, m1, K7F, rep from * to end.

Row 47: * K7F, in MY m1, Sl 1, K2 tog, PSSO, m1, K15E, in MY m1, Sl 1, K2 tog, PSSO, m1, K8F, rep from * to end.

Row 48: P all sts in respective colours.

Repeat rows 17 to 32 but substituting the following yarns:
    For yarn A, use F
    For yarn B, use E.
    For yarn C, use G.
    For yarn D, use H.

Repeat rows 33 to 48, but substituting the following yarns:
    For yarn C, use G.
    For yarn D, use H.
    For yarn E, use B.
    For yarn F, use A.

Repeat rows 17 to 26, but substituting the following yarns:
    For yarn A, continue to use A.
    For yarn B, continue to use B.
    For yarn C, use MY.
    For yarn D, use MY.

***Row 91:* * K1A, in MY K2 tog, m1, K5, K1D, in MY K5, m1, SKPO, K3B, in MY K2 tog, m1, K5, K1C, K5, m1, SKPO, K2, rep from * to end.

Row 93: * In MY K2 tog, m1, K5, K3D, in MY K5, m1, Sl 1, K2 tog, PSSO, K2 tog, m1, K5, K3C, in MY K5, m1, Sl 1, K2 tog, PSSO, rep from * to end.

Row 95: * In MY K1, m1, K5, K2D, in MY K1, K2D, in MY K5, m1, Sl 1, K1, PSSO, m1, K5, K2C, in MY K1, K2C, in MY K5, m1, K1, rep from * to end.

Row 97: In MY, yrn to make a st, Sl 2, K1, PSSO, * K5, K3D, in MY K5, K2 tog, m1, K1, m1, SKPO, K5, K3C, in MY K5, K2 tog, m1, K1, m1, SKPO, rep from * to end, omitting SKPO at end of last repeat.

Row 99: * In MY K1, m1, SKPO, K5, K1D, in MY K5, K2 tog, m1, K3, m1, SKPO, K5, K1C, in MY K5, K2 tog, m1, K2, rep from * to end.

Repeat rows 36 to 42, in MY *only.*

Row 107: * In MY K5, m1, SKPO, K3, K2 tog, m1, K5, K1F, in MY K5, m1, SKPO, K3, K2 tog, m1, K5, K1B, rep from * to end.

Row 109: * K1B, in MY K5, m1, SKPO, K1, K2 tog, m1, K5, K3F, in MY K5, m1, SKPO, K1, K2 tog, m1, K5, K2B, rep from * to end.

Row 111: * K2B, in MY K5, m1, Sl 1, K2 tog, PSSO, m1, K5, K2, K1, K2F, in MY K5, m1, Sl 1, K2 tog, PSSO, m1, K5, K2B, in MY K1, rep from * to end.

Row 113: * K1B, in MY K5, K2 tog, m1, K1, m1, SKPO, K5, K3F, in MY K5, K2 tog, m1, K1, m1, SKPO, K5, K2B, rep from * to end.

MY

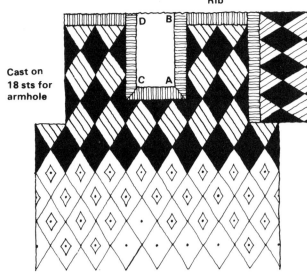

Rib

Cast on 18 sts for armhole

7in rib cuff

Row 115: * In MY, K5, K2 tog, m1, K3, m1, SKPO, K5, K1F, in MY K5, K2 tog, m1, K3, m1, SKPO, K5, K1B, rep from * to end.
Then repeat rows 20 to 26 inclusive (122 rows worked). ***
Repeat from *** (row 91) to *** (row 122).

Sleeves

Start at top of sleeve and work downwards.
Using 3mm (no. 11) needles and MY, cast on 144 sts as loosely as possible.
Then work 8 rows of K1, P1 rib, knitting into the back of every knit st throughout to give a firm rib (work all ribbed areas in this garment in this way).
Change to $3\frac{1}{4}$mm (no. 10) needles and work in pattern starting at row 1 and working straight without shaping until sleeve measures 36cm (14in) or 4 full diamonds lengthwise from the cast on edge. Do not end halfway through a pattern repeat or diamond.
Next row: Using MY only, K2 tog throughout row, so halving the number of sts (72 sts on needles).
Change to 3mm (no. 11) needles and work in K1, P1 rib, decreasing 1 st at each end of the next and every foll 6th row until there are 56 sts on needles.
Then cont without further dec until ribbed cuff measures 18cm (7in) and then cast off firmly in rib.
Work a second sleeve to match.

Back

Start at shoulders and work downwards.
Using 3mm (no. 11) needles and MY cast on 108 sts and work 8 rows of K1, P1 rib.
Change to $3\frac{1}{4}$mm (no. 10) needles and proceed in pattern starting at row 1 and working straight for 2 complete diamonds (up to row 47). Work measures 22cm ($8\frac{1}{2}$in) from the cast on edge.
Then shape bottom of armhole as follows.

SHAPE ARMHOLE
** Cast *on* 18 sts at the beg of the next 2 rows.
Now, keeping to the continuity of the diamond pattern, work straight on these 144 sts until back measures

61–63cm (24–25in) from cast on edge, completing 7 complete diamond patterns.
Then change to 3mm (no. 11) needles and dec for welt as follows.
Next row: K2, * K8, K2 tog, * rep from * to * across row, ending K2.
Work 7.5cm (3in) of K1, P1, rib on these 130 sts.
Then cast off loosely in rib.**

Front

**** Start at shoulders and work down.
Using 3mm (no. 11) needles and MY, cast on 36 sts and work 8 rows of K1, P1 rib.
Change to $3\frac{1}{4}$mm (no. 10) needles and work pattern beginning at row 1 and working straight for 47 rows.****
Leave these 36 sts on a spare needle.
Now repeat instructions from **** to ****.

MAKE SQUARE NECK
Row 48 (wrong side row): Work across one set of 36 sts, then cast on 36 sts, then work across the 36 sts from the other needle (108 sts).
Now cont on these 108 sts until Front measures the same as Back at the point for shaping armholes (i.e. 22cm ($8\frac{1}{2}$in) from cast on edge).
Then work exactly as instructions for back from ** to **

Finishing

Using a flat seam, join the shoulder seams end to end across the rib at shoulder edge.

RIBBED NECK EDGING
Using $2\frac{3}{4}$mm (no. 12) needles and MY, pick up and knit 50 sts up the first side of neck (i.e. between points A and B), the right side of work facing you. Work 5 rows of K1, P1 rib and then cast off firmly in rib, decreasing 1 st at point A on every right side row.
Then pick up 50 sts with the right side of work facing bet points D and C and work 5 rows to match first half, decreasing 1 st on every right side row at point c.
Cast off.
Then pick up, with the right side facing, 32 sts across front of neck bet points C and A, and work 5 rows of rib to match, decreasing 1 st at each end of every right side row.
Sew up the small seams at points A, B, C and D.
Then set in the sleeves squarely and join the underarm seam using a fine backstitch.
Join the side seams.
Press this garment using a damp cloth on reverse side of work.

Sandy Black: Vase of Flowers Angora Coat

[See colour photograph on front of jacket and opposite page 33]

Sandy Black paints pictures in stitches. Her vivid use of colour and pattern, her landscape sweaters that open windows on a rural world, are an interesting fusion of art with craft. 'My inspiration is from nature,' she admits. 'I love looking out of the window, especially in the North of England where I come from. I watch skyscapes and seascapes. I take photographs when I am travelling. And I find that I always respond to stimulating visual information everywhere.'

Across the bare brick wall of her Bermondsey studio/warehouse fly a flock of china ducks, alongside a carefully arranged clutter of antique and interesting objects that she and her partner Kevin Bolger have collected.

The same geese fly against white clouds on the front of one of her most stylish sweaters. It requires a proper understanding of the craft of knitting to be able to translate motifs into pattern form and an aesthetic sense to work out how a picture scales in relation to the human body that it is destined to decorate. The vase of flowers on the fluffy Angora coat featured here was inspired by a real jug in her home. It is used as a vivid simple motif, quite different from the graphic squared cardigan on page 83.

She and Kevin work together on their ideas, planning them on paper, trying them out in stitches but working first from the head rather than with the hands. 'Certain ideas can be developed on paper,' she explains. 'But the most successful patterns tend to come from a mixture of the different processes. We throw around our ideas together, do rough sketches and knit up at the same time. At least, I do the knitting. Kevin doesn't knit at all. He only ever managed one scarf !'

Sandy Black has more than an artist's eye for shape and colour. She started her career as a maths student and she still teaches numeracy on a part-time basis.

'My teaching helps me with writing patterns,' she says. 'I make no assumptions that people understand anything.'

Sandy's first experiment in knitting was a set of three scenic cushions which together make up a striking riviera landscape. The same design theme of lagoon blue shoreline and curving palms appears on some of her most sophisticated sweaters. But the knits that she has done by hand and on the machine over the last ten years show versatility of design. There are some effective animal sweaters with realistic markings and textures. Abstract blocks of colour, jigsaws and zig zags of pattern form a different theme that is especially effective in summer-weight crunchy cottons.

The business is now divided between the sweaters she designs and makes to sell in chic boutiques and her own work as a designer for yarn companies. Sandy has a team of hand-knitters mostly living like herself in the shadow of the Tower of London but her work involves constant experiment with her knitting needles herself, in order to develop new patterns, shapes and textures.

A recent development has been her own range of knitting wools, because she sensed the frustration of hand-knitters who could not find the yarns in interesting enough shades and textures for the work they wanted to do.

She herself is increasingly involved in texture, using fluffy angora or deep pile mohair, often combined with a flatter yarn, to make unusual effects in her geometric patterns or picture designs.

'I am interested in stitches as well as pictures,' she explains. 'I like them to be part of the design, perhaps a cable that grows into a flower. And I like to get curves into my knitting, to follow the lines of the body.'

Sandy Black's artist's eye for shape and colour, and for painting pictures with her stitches, is evident in this featherlight coat in fluffy grey angora, which has a vase of flowers worked in strong dramatic colour spreading from hemline to shoulders. The three-quarter length plain knit coat is curved at the front, wrapped edge-to-edge with a shawl collar.

Size: One size. Bust 97cm (38in). All round width at underarm 120cm (47in). Length (approx) 89cm (35in). Sleeve seam 43cm (17in).

Yarn: Sandy Black 100% Angora.
MY: Charcoal grey, black or white.
Yarn available as a complete kit by mail order from Sandy Black Original Knits, Studio 2, 164 Abbey Street, London SE1. Please write for details enclosing a stamped addressed envelope.
Sandy Black angora also available at Harrods, London; Ritzy Knits, Bond Street, Brighton; C and R Wools, Loughton, Essex; Cloud Nine, Skipton, Yorkshire; Helen Roberts, Cardiff.

Needles: 5½mm (no. 5).

Tension: 18 sts and 22 rows knitted in st.st on 5½mm (no. 5) ndls to 10cm (4in) square.

Notions: 2 shoulder pads

Notes on working from charts: The pieces are knitted in st.st from the charts. One square represents one stitch. Odd rows are knit (read from right to left), even rows are purl (read from left to right). Use separate balls of yarn for each area of colour, and take care to twist yarns when changing from one colour to another to link the yarns and avoid holes. You may find it helpful to wind small bobbins of each colour (made from card) to prevent yarns entangling.
N.B. The colour photograph of the coat has been reversed and therefore shows the pattern the opposite way round to the chart.

Back

With MY, cast on 76 sts and work in st.st, starting with a K row, for 17 rows, increasing 1 st at each side of the 7th row and following 6th row.
Commence working patt from Chart A on next row (18) as follows, joining in new balls of yarn as necessary.
Row 18: P31 MY, 17M, 2F, 30 MY.
Row 19: Inc. in 1st st, K26 MY, 4F, 5M, 11F, 4M, 28 MY, inc in last st.
Cont working from chart, still increasing every 6th row as shown until there are 106 sts. Continue until row 115 is complete.

SHAPE ARMHOLES
Cast off 4 sts at beg of next 2 rows.
Cast off 2 sts at beg of next 4 rows.
Dec 1 st at beg of next 8 rows. (82 sts on needle).
Cont without shaping until row 172 is complete.

SHAPE SHOULDERS
Cast off 6 sts at beg of next 6 rows, and 7 sts at beg of next 2 rows. Cast off remaining 32 sts.

Right front

Cast on 20 sts in MY and work in st.st, starting with a knit row, shaping as follows: Inc 1 st at side edge of every 6th row throughout and *at the same time, shape front edge only* as follows.
Cast on 4 sts at beg of 3rd and 5th rows. Inc 1 st on following 7 rows (37 sts). Inc 1 st on following 8 alt rows. Inc 1 st on every following 3rd row, 4 times. (53 sts on needle.)
Work straight at front edge, but continue increasing at side edge until there are 62 sts. Work straight until front matches back to armhole, ending with a knit row.

SHAPE ARMHOLE AND NECK EDGE
Cast off 4 sts at beg, and dec 1 st at end of next row. Dec 1 st at neck edge on every following alt row and *at the same time* cast off on alt rows at armhole edge, 2 sts twice, and 1 st 4 times to 43 sts, ending on a wrong side row.
Work straight at armhole edge, but continue to dec at neck edge every alt row.
Commence pattern from Chart B at row 1 and work until row 45 is complete.

SHAPE SHOULDER
Cast off 6 sts at beg of next row and following 2 alt rows, cast off remaining sts.

Left front

Work as right front, but reverse shapings by starting with a purl row, and finishing with a purl row before armhole shaping, then work pattern from Chart C.

Sleeves

LEFT SLEEVE
With MY, cast on 46 sts and work in st.st for 5cm (2in). Inc 1 st at each end of every following 4th row until there are 82 sts. Continue straight until sleeve measures 46cm (18in).
Shape top and commence pattern: Cast off 4 sts at beg of next 2 rows and 3 sts at beg of following 2 rows. * Join in appropriate colours and start working pattern from Chart D at row 5, noting that one flower shape is omitted at left edge. (Work these sts in MY instead.)
Dec 1 st at each end of every alt row until row 31 is complete, then dec 1 st each end of next 7 rows (26 sts). Cast off 5 sts at beg of next 2 rows. Cast off remaining sts.

RIGHT SLEEVE
Work as left to *.
Commence pattern, joining in correct colours and noting one flower is left out at right edge.

Edging and collar

(Worked in one piece.)
With MY, cast on 29 sts, and knit 1 row.
Work in slip st pattern as follows:
Row 1 (right side): P1, (Sl 3, P1), rep to end.
Row 2 (wrong side): Knit.
Row 3: Purl.
Row 4: K2, (K next st tog with strand of yarn on P side, K3), rep to end, ending last rep K2.

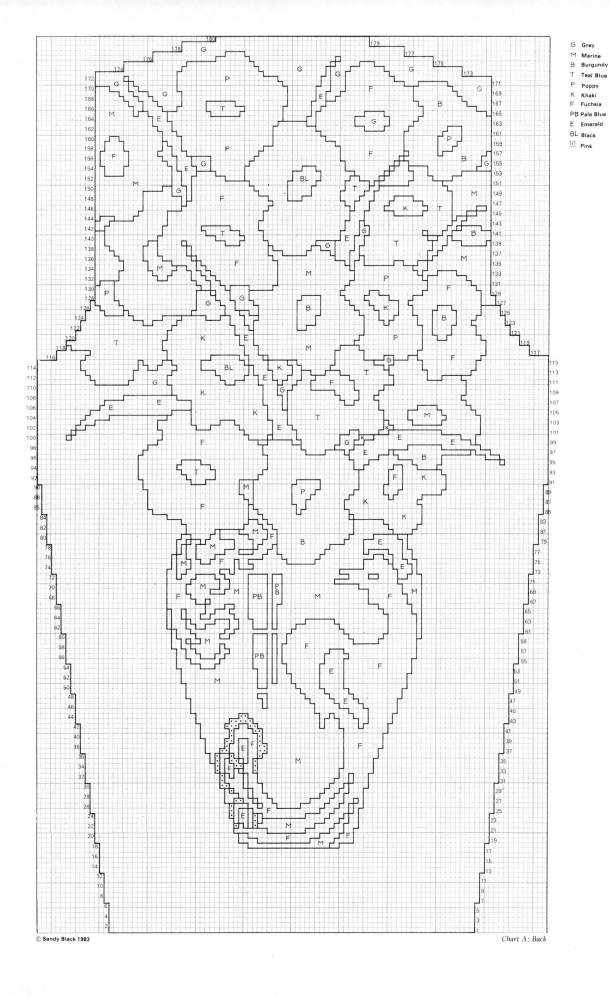

G Grey
M Marine
B Burgundy
T Teal Blue
P Poppy
K Khaki
F Fuchsia
PB Pale Blue
E Emerald
BL Black
⊡ Pink

© Sandy Black 1983

Chart A: Back

56

Row 5: P3, (Sl 3, P1) rep to last 2 sts, P2.
Row 6: Knit.
Row 7: Purl.
Row 8: K4, (K next st tog with strand on P side, K3), rep to end, ending last rep K4.
These 8 rows form pattern.
Continue in pattern until work measures 76cm (30in).

SHAPE COLLAR
Keeping continuity of pattern, inc 1 st at each end of the next and every following 6th row until there are 57 sts.
Work straight until edging measures 134.5cm (53in) from beg. Dec 1 st at each end of next and every following 6th row until 29 sts remain.
Continue straight for a further 127cm (50in). Cast off.

Finishing
Do not press.
Darn in loose ends carefully on inside of work, closing any gaps.
Join shoulder, side and sleeve seams. Set in sleeves.
Turn up 2.5cm (1in) at cuff to inside and slip st in place.
With right sides together, place centre of collar to centre back, and pin edging all round front and lower edges, easing around front curves, until the two ends meet at a side seam. Backstitch edging in position, join edging seam, turn to inside and slip st neatly in place. Insert shoulder pads.

© *Sandy Black 1983.*

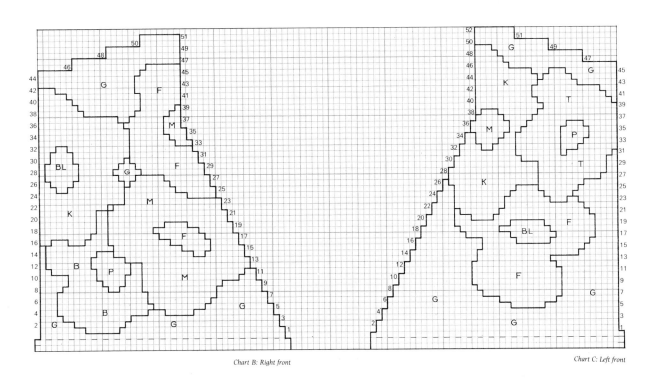

Chart B: Right front

Chart C: Left front

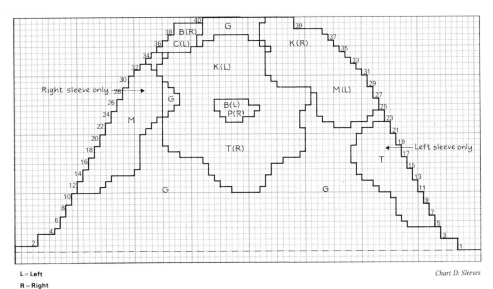

L = Left
R = Right

Chart D: Sleeves

Jean Muir: Cashmere Sweater

Jean Muir is a purist and a perfectionist. Not for her the quick effect put together with more dash than detail, nor the sweet-toothed and romantic frills so beloved by British designers.

Jean Muir's designs are classics, but ones that she herself conceived: the fluid and feminine dress; the suedes cut, tucked and printed like cloth; the artists' smock in draped jersey. Her approach is architectural rather than artistic, for she assembles her collections with meticulous attention from the first directional sketch, to a toile, altered and adjusted on a dummy (and on her own size ten figure), before ever a seam is cut or stitched.

She designs, of course, for herself. But like all really creative designers, her clothes can be and are worn by many women who do not have her own neat figure, unadorned style and preference for dark, plain colours. She is seen mainly in navy blue, always in neutral colours, yet her design palette sizzles with cobalt blue, tomato red and fuchsia pink.

Knitwear is a relatively new addition to her range, but her experience of working in wool is as old as her fashion career. As a designer for Jaeger in 1956, she was in sole charge of their influential knitwear range for her final year with them.

'Then, in the fifties, knitwear was really dire,' she admits. 'It was a question of starting all over again to get the body shapes right and to make the knits, as they should be, a part of fashion.'

Knitwear has sporadically been made since she set up in business in 1966 with her husband Harry Leuckert, but she cannot now remember why she decided to work seriously three years ago with a knitwear company in Hawick the cashmere centre of Scotland.

The Jean Muir knitwear consists of neat hand-framed sweaters, wrapped carefully to the body, with puffed sleeves or raglan shoulders, all in the finest cashmere and with that deceptive simplicity which comes from absolute attention to the detail of cut and decoration. Miss Muir works as closely with her knitwear specialist as she does with her senior pattern cutter. In many cases, including the gentle dolman sleeved hand-knit sweater she designed especially for this book, she cuts a toile first to fit the body shape, and then works out the design and tension in knitting.

For her knits, she favours nature's law for sheep and goats. She chooses natural beige, black, cloud grey or creamy white, although her collection sometimes includes splashes of strong colour. The sweaters, she says, are essentially accessories to her own separates, although she believes that every garment she makes must be acceptable in its own right.

Perfect proportion is the hallmark of the Jean Muir style, and the sweaters that go with her godet skirts in fine angora or plain pleated linen are relatively high waisted, small and neat in the bodice, but sometimes with a puffed shoulder line.

She believes passionately in the craft of fashion, and her lectures to fashion students and would-be stars emphasise the need for technical skill and dedicated craftmanship, rather than just a strong creative urge.

Jean Muir also believes that the expertise and the raw materials for fashion creations can be found in Britain.

'I suppose I started working with cashmere because it is the finest and because I believed that they could do what I wanted,' says Jean Muir, who has spent several seasons teaching and explaining her demands to the factory. 'You can get anything you want out of Britain if you are prepared to work at it.'

Jean Muir, photographed here by Shirley Beljon, is Britain's leading designer with an international reputation. She has won many design awards in Britain and in the United States and is a member of the Royal Society of Arts and a Fellow of the Society of Industrial Artists and Designers.

Jean Muir's knits are as classic, fluid and understated as her famous jersey dresses. Her silversand cashmere jumper (photograph page 58) is worked from a long waist ribbing in stocking stitch with a lacy pattern. The sleeves are set into a very deep armhole to give a dolman effect but a neat shoulder line. A long ribbed cuff and ribbed cowl neck give symmetry to the sweater.

Size: One size. Bust 80–85cm (32–34in).

Yarn: 10 × 25g balls Woollybear Cashmere by Patricia Roberts.
Yarn available from Patricia Roberts Knitting Shops at 31 James Street, London WC2; 16 Kensington Church Walk, London W8; 60 Kinnerton Street, London SW1. Mail order is available from the last two shops. Please write enclosing a stamped addressed envelope for price list.

Needles: 2¾mm (no. 12) and 3¼mm (no. 10).

Tension: 28 sts and 36 rows knitted in st.st on 3¼mm (no. 10) ndls to 10cm (4in) square.

Back

Using 2¾mm (no. 12) ndls cast on 117 sts and work 13cm (5in) in K1, P1 rib. * Change to 3¼mm (no. 10) ndls and work in st.st for 18 rows.

SHAPE ARMHOLES
Right side facing, cast off 16 sts at beg of next 2 rows, 85 sts remain. Continue until armhole measures 31cm (12in).

SHAPE NECK
Right side facing, work 23 sts, turn.
P one row.
Dec 1 st at neck edge on next 9 rows.
Cast off remaining 14 sts.
Put centre 39 sts onto spare needle for polo neckband.
Rejoin yarn at neck edge to remaining 23 sts.
Work 2nd side to match, reversing shapings.

Front

Work as Back to *.
Change to 3¼mm (no. 10) ndls and work in st.st for 4 rows. Now work in lace pattern throughout, setting first row as follows:
K20, (pattern panel 23 sts, K4) twice, pattern panel 23 sts, K20. (117 sts). (Start armhole shaping at Row 15.)

LACE PATTERN PANEL
Row 1: K11, YFD, K2 tog, K10.
Row 2 and every alternate row: P.
Row 3: K10, (YFD, K2 tog) twice, K9.
Row 5: K8, K2 tog tbl, YFD, K3, YFD, K2 tog, K8.
Row 7: K7, K2 tog tbl, YFD, K5, YFD, K2 tog, K7.
Row 9: K6, K2 tog tbl, YFD, K3, YFD, K2 tog, K2, YFD, K2 tog, K6.
Row 11: K5, K2 tog tbl, YFD, K3, (YFD, K2 tog) twice, K2 YFD, K2 tog, K5.
Row 13: K4, K2 tog tbl, YFD, K2, K2 tog tbl, YFD, K3, YFD, K2 tog, K2, YFD, K2 tog, K4.

Row 15: K3, K2 tog tbl, YFD, K2, K2 tog tbl, YFD, K5, YFD, K2 tog, K2, YFD, K2 tog, K3.
Row 17: K2, K2 tog tbl, YFD, K2, K2 tog tbl, YFD, K7, YFD, K2 tog, K2, YFD, K2 tog, K2.
Row 19: K1, K2 tog tbl, YFD, K2, K2 tog tbl, YFD, K9, YFD, K2 tog, K2, YFD, K2 tog, K1.
Row 21: K2 tog tbl, YFD, K2, K2 tog tbl, YFD, K11, YFD, K2 tog, K2, YFD, K2 tog.
Row 23: K3, K2 tog tbl, YFD, K13, YFD, K2 tog, K3.
Row 25: K2, K2 tog tbl, YFD, K15, YFD, K2 tog, K2.
Row 27: K1 (K2 tog tbl, YFD) twice, K13, (YFD, K2 tog) twice, K1.
Row 29: K2 tog tbl, YFD, K1, K2 tog tbl, YFD, K13, YFD, K2 tog, K1, YFD, K2 tog.
Rows 31, 33, 35: K3, K2 tog tbl, YFD, K13, YFD, K2 tog, K3.
Row 37: K3, K2 tog tbl, YFD, K6, YFD, K2 tog, K5, YFD, K2 tog, K3.
Row 39: K3, K2 tog tbl, YFD, K5, (YFD, K2 tog) twice, K4, YFD, K2 tog, K3.
Row 41: K4, K2 tog tbl, YFD, K2, K2 tog tbl, YFD, K3, YFD, K2 tog, K2, YFD, K2 tog, K4.
Row 43: K5, (K2 tog tbl, YFD) twice, K5, (YFD, K2 tog) twice, K5.
Row 45: K6, K2 tog tbl, YFD, K7, YFD, K2 tog, K6.
Row 47: As row 43.
Row 49: As row 41.
Row 51: K4, K2 tog tbl, YFD, K3, K2 tog tbl, YFD, (K2, YFD, K2 tog) twice, K4.
Row 53: K4, K2 tog tbl, YFD, K4, K2 tog tbl, YFD, K5, YFD, K2 tog, K4.
Row 54: P.
These 54 rows form the lace pattern panel.

SHAPE ARMHOLES
As for Back, starting at row 15 of lace pattern panel.
Continue lace panels as follows:
K4, (pattern panel 23 sts, K4) twice, pattern panel 23 sts, K4. (85 sts).
After completing 54 rows lace panels, work 4 rows st.st then work 2nd set of lace panels followed by 4 rows of st.st.

SHAPE NECK
Next row: Right side facing, work across 26 sts, turn.
P one row.
Dec 1 st at neck edge on next 12 rows.
Work straight until Front measures the same as Back.
Cast off remaining 14 sts.
Put centre 33 sts onto spare ndl for polo neckband.
Rejoin yarn at neck edge to remaining 26 sts.
Work 2nd side to match, reversing shapings.

Sleeves

Using 2¾mm (no. 12) ndls cast on 55 sts and work 12cm (4¾in) in K1, P1 rib.
Change to 3¼mm (no. 10) ndls and work 4 rows st.st.
Now work the 54 rows of lace pattern, setting first row as follows:
K16, pattern panel 23 sts, K16.
At the same time, inc 1 st at each end of every other row to 191 sts.

Place markers at this point.
Work straight for 5cm (2in).
Cast off loosely.

Polo neck

Join right shoulder seam.
Right side facing and using 2¾mm (no. 12) ndls pick up
and K21 sts down left front neck, K across 33 sts along
centre front, pick up and K21 sts up right front neck,
pick up and K16 sts down right back neck, K across
39 sts along centre back, pick up and K15 sts up left
back. (145 sts).
Work 20cm (8in) in K1, P1 rib.
Cast off loosely.

Finishing

Join left shoulder seam and polo neckband seam.
Sew in sleeves to armhole edges.
Sew sleeves above markers to cast off edges on front and
back.
Sew sleeve and side seams.

Patricia Roberts: Patchwork Jacket and Grapes and Cherries Child's Cardigan

[*See colour photograph opposite page 32*]

Patricia Roberts is a magician with stitches. She will give an additional dimension to her knitted landscapes with bobbles of wool that make snowflakes, rosebuds or clusters of berries. Delicate, intricate and lacy stitches turn a basic cotton sweater into an airy mesh. 'I do think that my technical ability is my strength,' she says. 'I have spent ten years learning my technical skills. I could never give someone a drawing and ask them to turn it into a hand-knit. I write all my own patterns. For me it is part and parcel of knitting, like mixing the oils on a palette if you are a painter.'

Patricia Roberts studied fashion at Leicester Polytechnic, taking hand-knitting as a subsidiary subject. By the time she worked for IPC magazines in the early 1970s, she had realised that nobody was making interesting hand-knits, and spotting that gap in the market gave her the courage to set up as a freelance knitwear designer. Her earliest work sold to the influential London Fashion shop Browns and to important stores in the United States, and from that auspicious beginning, she has built up a thriving export business, which is particularly strong in the fashion capitals of Italy and France.

The first Patricia Roberts knitting book, filled with unusual patterns, imaginatively photographed, launched a small London shop in 1976. That has now been followed by two more London shops where colourful yarns are stacked against the walls like an old-fashioned sweet shop. New editions of her pattern books come out each year.

As soon as she had her own retail outlet, Patricia and her brother and partner Keith Roberts, spotted yet another dropped stitch in the knitwear business. Because the only yarns they could find in good colours and textures had to be imported, Pat decided to colour and market her own yarns, which have become an important part of her business.

Now she divides her time between her West London design studio and her all-white High Tech home where her small daugher Amy's toys add the only bright splash of colour to the stark walls and angular furnishings. Mother and dauther are photographed in the High Tech kitchen (opposite page 32). Unlike many knitwear designers who find their inspiration from traditional textiles and ancient oriental rugs and surround themselves with these visual stimuli, Patricia Roberts is stimulated by working with stitches. She starts a collection by drawing, knitting up sample pieces, and then drawing again. 'For me, the stitches and the body shapes go together,' she says. 'Quite often I can't even adapt a design for a different size because it is just too complicated. I am sometimes inspired by things around me. I do need more input than working with my needles or on graph paper. The patchwork design I am wearing was actually inspired by some quilted china plates I have. It can be something you live with for years that suddenly triggers off an idea.'

Her most seminal patterns themselves become classics, like the bunches of grapes and cherries that she first produced in 1978. 'Although I am not just a fashion designer, I do respond to fashion' she admits. 'I have always done different things for each season, but often on more than one theme at once. For example, when picture knits were very important, I did at the same time plain Arans, but with complicated stitches.' 'Now,' says Patricia, she hardly ever knits up a garment, not even for Amy. 'I feel that if I am knitting, I ought to be making stitch blocks'.

Her patterns tend to fall into two different groups: simple shapes in natural fibres (like the luxurious cashmere she introduced into her own range) worked in complex stitches. Or there is plainer knitting made up in graphic combinations of colour to give lozenge or geometric patternings. Texture, from fancy and tweedy yarns or from stitches that give surface interest, is yet another facet of her knitting style.

'The thing with my patterns, is that I do like to give them a slight technical challenge, so that they don't become boring to knit', she explains. 'Even my own knitters don't always know quite what they are knitting up.'

Patchwork Jacket

Patricia Roberts believes that her stitchcraft is her strength. Her patchwork cardigan with striped shawl collar is made in fluffy angora with lambswool, silk or fine cotton as you choose. The pattern is worked basically in stocking stitch, in squares of contrasting colour, pattern and texture.

Materials
Either: 10 × 20 gram balls of 'Woollybear Angora' by Patricia Roberts in main colour, 6 balls in third contrast and 4 balls in each of the 3 other contrasts, or 11 × 25 gram balls of 'Woollybear Lambswool' in main colour, 7 balls in third contrast and 5 balls in each of the 3 other contrasts; a pair each of size 2¼mm (No 13) and size 2¾mm (No 12) Aero knitting needles; 4 buttons.

Stockists
Woollybear yarns are available from Patricia Roberts Knitting Shops at 31 James Street, Covent Garden, London, WC2; 60 Kinnerton Street, London, SW1; and 1b Kensington Church Walk, London, W8. Mail order is available from the last 2 shops. Please write enclosing a stamped self-addressed envelope for price list.

Tension
The pattern is based on a stocking stitch tension of 16 stitches and 20 rows to 5 centimetres (2 inches) using size 2¾mm (No. 12) needles. If you cannot obtain this tension using the size needles suggested, use larger or smaller needles accordingly.

Abbreviations
k., knit; p., purl; st., stitch; tog., together; dec., decrease (by working 2 sts. tog.); inc., increase (by working twice into same st.); single rib is k.1 and p.1 alternately; s.s., stocking stitch is k. on the right side and p. on the wrong side; up 1, pick up the loop, which lies between the needles, slip it onto the left hand needle; then k. into back of it; sl., slip; p.s.s.o., pass sl.st. over; y.r.n., yarn round needle; s.s.k., sl.1, k.1, p.s.s.o.; m., main colour; a., first contrast colour; b., second contrast colour; c., third contrast colour; d., fourth contrast colour; 3 from 1, k.1, y.r.n., k.1 all into next st.; 24 from 16 is (k.1, inc. in next st.) 8 times; m.b., make bobble thus, k.1, y.r.n., k.1 all into next st., turn, p.3, turn, sl.1, k.2tog., p.s.s.o.; m.b. p.wise, make bobble purlwise as m.b but reading p. for k. and k. for p.; 5 from 1, k.1, y.r.n, k.1, y.r.n., k.1 all into one st.; 4 over 1, pass 2nd, 3rd, 4th and 5th sts. on left hand needle over first st., then with m. k. this st.

Measurements
The measurements are given in centimetres followed by inches in brackets.

Underarms   92.5 (37).
Side seam   37.5 (15).
Length   57.5 (23).
Sleeve seam 42.5 (17).
NOTE: Instructions in brackets are worked the number of times stated after the brackets.

The Back
With size 2¼ mm. (No. 13) needles and m. cast on 116 sts, and work 35 rows in single rib.
Now divide the sts. for easier working: Next row: Rib 58, and leave these sts. on a spare needle until required for left half back, work to end and continue on these 58 sts. for the right half back.
The right half back: Change to size 2¾ mm. (No. 12) needles and, beginning with a k. row s.s. 2 rows. Now work in pattern as follows, using separate short lengths of m. for each vertical stripe and separate balls of contrast colours for each square. On wrong side rows take care to wrap m. firmly round contrast colours at the edges of the squares.
Row 1: With m. k.2, with a. 24 from 16, turn, with a. p.24, turn, with a. k.24, with m. k.3, with b. 24 from 16, turn, with b. p.24, turn, with b. k.3, (with a. k.2, with b. k.2) 5 times, with b. k.1 more, with m. k.3, with c. 24 from 16, turn, with c. p.24, turn, with c. k.24, with m. k.2.
Row 2: With m. p.2, with c. p.24, with m. p.3, with b. p.3, (with a. p.2, with b. p.2) 5 times, with b. p.1 more, with m. p.3, with a. p.24, with m. p.2.
Row 3: With m. k.2, with a. k.24, turn, with a. p.24, turn, with a. k.24, *with m. k.3, with b. k.1, (with a. k.2, with b. k.2) 5 times, with a. k.2, with b. k.1, turn, with b. p.1, (with a. p.2, with b. p.2) 5 times, with a. p.2, with b. p.1, **turn, with b. k.3, (with a. k.2, with b. k.2) 5 times, with b. k.1 more*, with m. k.3, with c. k.24, turn, with c. p.24, turn, with c. k.24, with m. k.2.
Rows 4 to 9: Repeat 2nd and 3rd rows 3 times.
Row 10: As row 2.
Row 11: Work as given for 3rd row until ** is reached, turn, with b. k.24, with m. k.3, with c. k.24, turn, with c. p.24, turn, with c. k.24, with m. k.2.
Row 12: With m. p.2, with c. p.24, with m. p.3, with b. p.24, with m. p.3, with a. p.24, with m. p.2.
Row 13: With m. k.2, *(k.2 tog., k.1) 8 times, k.3, repeat from * ending last repeat k.2.
Rows 14 to 16: With m. in s.s.
Row 17: With m. k.2, with d. 24 from 16, turn, with d. p. 24, turn, with m. k.2tog., k.1, 3 from 1, k.2, (sl.1, k.2tog., p.s.s.o., k.2, 3 from 1, k.2) twice, s.s.k., k.3, still with m. 24 from 16, turn, with m. p.24, turn, with m. k.24, then k.3, with a. 24 from 16, turn, with a. p.24, turn, with a. k.2, (with c. m.b., with a. k.3) 5 times, with c. m.b., with a. k.1, with m. k.2.
Row 18: With m. p.2, with a. p.24, with m. p.30, still with m. k.24, p.2.
Row 19: With m. k.2, with d. k.2tog., k.1, 3 from 1, k.2, (sl.1, k.2tog., p.s.s.o., k.2, 3 from 1, k.2) twice, s.s.k., turn, with d. p.24, turn, with d. k.24, with m. k.3, then k.24, turn, with m. p.24, turn, with m. k.24, then k.3, with a. k.24, *turn, with a. p.24, turn, with a. k.24, with m. k.2.
Row 20: With m. p.2, (with a. p.3, with c. m.b. p.wise) 5 times, with a. p.4, with m. p.30, with d. p.24, with m. p.2.
Row 21: With m. k.2, still with m. *k.2tog., k.1, 3 from 1, k.2, (sl.1, k.2tog., p.s.s.o., k.2, 3 from 1, k.2) twice, s.s.k.*, turn, with m. k.24, turn, with d. repeat from * to *, with m. k.3, then k.24, turn p.24, turn, k.24, then

Artwork's paisley patterned mohair sweater decorated with beads (page 107)

k.3, with a. k.24, turn, p.24, **turn, k.24, with m. k.2.
Row 22: With m. p.2, with a. p.24, with m. p.30, with d. p.24, with m. p.2.
Row 23: With m. k.2, with d. k.24, turn, p.24, turn, with m. work from * to * on row 21, then with m. k.3, then k.24, turn, p.24, turn, k.24, then k.3, with a. k.2, (with c. m.b., with a. k.3) 5 times, with c. m.b., with a. k.1, turn, with a. p.24, turn, with a. k.24, with m. k.2.
Row 24: As row 18.
Row 25: Work as for row 19 until * is reached, turn, (with a. p.3, with c. m.b p.wise) 5 times, with a. p.4, turn, with a. k.24, with m. k.2.
Row 26: As row 22.
Row 27: Work as for row 21 until ** is reached, turn, with a. k.2, (with c. m.b., with a. k.3) 5 times, with c. m.b., with a. k.1, with m. k.2.
Row 28: As row 22.
Rows 29 to 32: As rows 13 to 16.
Row 33: With m. k.2, with b. 24 from 16, turn, p.24, turn, k.24, with m. k.3, with c. 24 from 16, turn, with c. p.24, turn, with d. k.24, with m. k.3, with d. 24 from 16, turn, with d. p.24, turn, with d. k.24, with m. k.2.
Row 34: With m. p.2, with d. p.24, with m. p.3, with d. k.24, with m. p.3, with b. p.24, with m. p.2.
Row 35: With m. k.2, with b. k.24, turn, p.24, turn, k.24, with m. k.3, with c. k.24, turn, p.24, turn, k.24, with m. k.3, with d. k.24, turn, p.24, turn, k.24, with m. k.2.
Row 36: With m. p.2, with d. p.24, with m. p.3, with c. p.24, with m. p.3, with b. p.24, with m. p.2.
Row 37: With m. k.2, with b. k.24, turn, p.24, turn, k.24, with m. k.3, with d. k.24, turn, with d. k.24, turn, with c. k.24, with m. k.3, with d. k.24, turn, p.24, turn, k.24, with m. k.2.
Row 38: As row 36.
Row 39: With m. k.2, with b. k.24, turn, p.24, turn, k.24, with m. k.3, with c. k.24, turn, p.24, turn, with d. k.24, with m. k3, with d. k.24, turn, p.24, turn, k.24, with m. k.2.
Rows 40 to 44: As rows 34 to 38.
Rows 45 to 48: As rows 13 to 16.
Row 49: With m. k.2, with m. 24 from 16, turn, with m. p.24, turn, with m. k.3, (with b. 5 from 1, with m. k.7) twice, with b. 5 from 1, with m. k.4, then k.3 more, with a. 24 from 16, turn, with a. p.24, turn, with a. k.24, with m. k.3, with b. 24 from 16, turn, with b. p.24, turn, with b. k.3, (with a. k.2, with b. k.2) 5 times, with b. k.1 more, with m. k.2.
Row 50: With m. p.2, with b. p.3, (with a. p.2, with b. p.2) 5 times, with b. p.1 more, with m. p.3, with a. p.24*, (with m. p.7, with b. p.5 winding yarn round needle twice for each st.) 3 times, with m. p.5.
Row 51: With m. k.5, (slip 5 dropping extra loops, with m. k.7) twice, slip 5 dropping extra loops, with m. k.4, turn, with m. p.4, (sl.5, p.7) twice, sl.5, p.3, turn, with m. k.3, (4 over 1, k.7) 3 times, with a. k.24, turn, p.24, turn, k.24**, work as for row 3 from * to *, with m. k.2.
Row 52: Work as given for row 50 until * is reached, with m. p. to end.
Row 53: With m. k.2, then still with m. k.24, turn, p.24, turn, (with m. k.7, with b. 5 from 1) twice, with m. k.11, with a. k.24, turn, p.24, turn, k.24, work as

given for row 3 from * to *, with m. k.2.
Row 54: Work as given for row 50 until * is reached, with m. p.11, (with b. p.5 winding yarn round needle twice for each st., with m. p.7) twice, with m. p.2.
Row 55: With m. k.2, then (with m. k.7, sl.5 dropping extra loops) twice, with m. k.8, turn, with m. p.8, (sl.5, p.7) twice, turn, (with m. k.7, 4 over 1) twice, with m. k.11, with a. k.24, turn, p.24, turn, k.24, work as given for 3rd row from * to *, with m. k.2.
Row 56: As row 52.
Row 57: With m. k.26, turn, p.24, turn, with m. k.3, (with b. 5 from 1, with m. k.7) 3 times, with a. k.24, turn, p.24, turn, k.24, work as given for row 3 from * to *, with m. k.2.
Row 58: As row 50.
Row 59: Work as for row 51 until ** is reached, then as given for row 3 from * to **, turn and with b. k.24, with m. k.2.
Row 60: With m. p.2, with b. p.24, with m. p.3, with a. p.24, with m. p.29.
Rows 61 to 64: As rows 13 to 16.
Row 65: With m. k.2, with c. 24 from 16, turn, with c. p.24, turn, with c. k.24, with m. k.3, with d. 24 from 16, turn, p.24, turn, with m. k.2tog., k.1, 3 from 1, k.2, (sl.1, k.2tog., p.s.s.o., k.2, 3 from 1, k.2) twice, s.s.k., still with m. k.3, then 24 from 16, turn, with m. p.24, turn, with m. k. to end.
Row 66: With m. p.29, still with m. k.24, then p.3, with c. p.24, with m. p.2.
Row 67: With m. k.2, with c. k.24, turn, p.24, turn, k.24, with m. k.3, with d. k.2tog., k.1, 3 from 1, k.2, (sl.1, k.2tog., p.s.s.o., k.2, 3 from 1, k.2) twice, s.s.k., turn, with d. p.24, turn, k.24, with m. k.27, turn, p.24, turn, k.26.
Row 68: With m. p.29, with d. p.24, with m. p.3, with c. p.24, with m. p.2.
Row 69: With m. k.2, with c. k.24, turn, p.24, turn, k.24, with m. k.3, then still with m. *k.2tog., k.1, 3 from 1, k.2, (sl.1, k.2tog., p.s.s.o., k.2, 3 from 1, k.2) twice, s.s.k.*, turn, with m. k.24, turn, with d. repeat from * to *, with m. k.27, turn, p.24, turn, k.26.
Row 70: As row 68.
Row 71: With m. k.2, with c. k.24, turn, p.24, turn, k.24, with m. k.3, with d. k.24, turn, with d. p.24, turn, with m. work from * to * on row 69, still with m. k.27, turn, p.24, turn, k.26.
Rows 72 to 76: As rows 66 to 70.
Rows 77 to 80: As rows 13 to 16.
Row 81: With m. k.2, with a. 24 from 16, turn, with a. p.24, turn, with a. k.2, (with c. m.b, with a. k.3) 5 times, with c. m.b, with a. k.1, with m. k.3, with b. 24 from 16, turn, with b. p.24, turn, with b. k.24, with m. k.3, with c. 24 from 16, turn, with c. p.24, turn, with d. k.24, with m. k.2.
Row 82: With m. p.2, with d. k.24, with m. p.3, with b. p.24, with m. p.3, with a. p.24, with m. p.2.
Rows 83 to 94: The last 2 rows set the position of the pattern squares, thus work one square in a. with bobbles in c. as on rows 17 to 30, one in b. alone and the other in c. with garter st. stripes as on rows 33 to 46.

To shape the armhole:

Row 95: With m. cast off 8, k. to end. – 50 sts.

Row 96: With m. all p.

Row 97: With m. k.2, with d. (k.1, inc. in next st.) 4 times, turn, with d. p.12, turn, k.12, with m. k3., then still with m. 24 from 16, turn, p.24, turn, with m. k.3, (with b. 5 from 1, with m. k.7) 3 times, **with a. 24 from 16, turn, with a. p.24, turn, k.24, then with m. k.2.

Row 98: With m. p.2, with a. p.24, (with m. p.7, with b. p.5 winding yarn round needle twice for each st.) 3 times, with m. p.6, with d. p.12, with m. p.2.

Rows 99 to 108: The last 2 rows set the colours and pattern of the squares, thus work one in d. alone, one in m. with dots in b. as on rows 51 to 60 and one in a. alone.

Row 109: With m. k.2, (k.2tog., k.1) 4 times, k.3, (k.2tog., k.1) 8 times, k.3, (k.2tog., k.1) 8 times, k.2.

Rows 110 to 112: With m. in s.s.

Row 113: With m. k.2, with b. (k.1, inc. in next st.) 4 times, turn, with b. p.12, turn, with b. k.3, with a. k.2, with b. k.2, with a. k.2, with b. k.3, with m. k.3, with c. 24 from 16, turn, with c. p.24, turn, with c. k.24, with m. k.3, ** with d. 24 from 16, turn, with d. p.24, turn, with m. k.2tog., k.1, 3 from 1, k.2 (sl.1, k.2tog., p.s.s.o., k.2, 3 from 1, k.2) twice, s.s.k., with m. k.2.

Rows 114 to 124: The last row sets the position of the patterns and colours, thus work one square in b. with checks in a. as on rows 2 to 12, and in c. alone and one in d. with zig-zags as on rows 18 to 28.

Rows 125 to 128: As rows 109 to 112.

Row 129: With m. k.2, still with m. (k.1, inc. in next st.) 4 times, turn, with m. p.12, turn, k.12, then k.3, with a. 24 from 16, turn, p.24, turn, with a. k.2, (with c. m.b., with a. k.3) 5 times, with c. m.b, with a. k.1, with m. k.3**, with b. 24 from 16, turn, with b. p.24, turn, k.24, with m. k.2.

Rows 130 to 140: Work in pattern as set, one square in m., one in a. with bobbles in c. and one in b. alone.

Rows 141 to 144: As rows 109 to 112.

Row 145: With m. k.2, with c. (k.1, inc. in next st.) 4 times, turn, p.12, turn, with d. k.12, with m. k.3, with d. 24 from 16, turn, p.24, turn, k.24, with m. k.3, then still with m. 24 from 16, turn, p.24, turn, with m. k.3, (with b. 5 from 1, with m. k.7) twice, with b. 5 from 1, with m. k.6.

Rows 146 to 156: Work in pattern as set, one square in c. with garter st. stripes in d., one in d. alone and one in m. with dots in b.

Rows 157 and 158: As rows 109 and 110.

To slope the shoulder: With m. cast off 29 sts. loosely, using a size larger needle.

On 21 sts. work 1 row, then cast off very loosely, using a size larger needle.

The left half back: With right side of work facing rejoin m. to inner edge of the 58 sts. left on spare needle. With size 2¾ mm. (No. 12) needles and m. beginning with a k. row s.s. 2 rows.

Now using separate short lengths of m. for the vertical stripes and taking care to wrap m. firmly round contrast colours at the edges of the squares, work in pattern as follows:

Work the pattern rows 17 to 94 given for right half back.

Rows 79 and 80: With m. in s.s.

Row 81: With m. k.2, with d. 24 from 16, turn, with d. p.24, turn, k.24, with m. k.3, then still with m. 24 from 16, turn, with m. p.24, turn, with m. k.3, (with b. 5 from 1, with m. k.7) 3 times, with a. 24 from 16, turn, p.24, turn, k.24, with m. k.2.

Rows 82 to 95: Work in pattern as set working one square in d. only, one in m. with dots in b. as before and one in a. only.

To shape the armhole: *Row 96:* With m. cast off 8 sts., p. to end. – 50 sts.

Row 97: With m. k.2, with b. 24 from 16, turn, with b. p.24, turn, with b. k.3 (with a. k.2, with b. k.2) 5 times, with b. k.1 more, **with m. k.3, with c. 24 from 16, turn, with c. p.24, turn, with c. k.24, with m. k.3, with d. (k.1, inc. in next st.) 4 times, turn, with d. p.12, turn, with m. k.2tog., k.1, 3 from 1, k.2, sl.1, k.2tog., p.s.s.o., k.2, inc. in next st., with m. k.2.

Rows 98 to 108: In pattern as set, working one square in b. with checks in a., one in c. and one in d. with zig-zags in m.

Row 109: With m. k.2, (k.2tog., k.1) 8 times, k.3, (k.2tog., k.1) 8 times, k.3, (k.2tog., k.1) 4 times, k.2 more.

Rows 110 to 112: With m. in s.s.

Row 113: With m. k.2, still with m. 24 from 16, turn, p.24, turn, k.27, with a. 24 from 16, turn, with a. p.24, turn, with a. k.2, (with c. m.b., with a. k.3) 5 times, with c. m.b., with a k.1, with m. k.3, with b. (k.1, inc. in next st.) 4 times, turn, p.12, turn, k.12, with m. k.2.

Rows 114 to 128: In pattern as set, working one square in m., one in a. with bobbles in c. and one in b. as set.

Row 129: With m. k.2, with c. 24 from 16, turn, with c. p.24, turn, with d. k.24, with m. k.3, with d. 24 from 16, turn, with d. p.24, turn, k.24, with m. k.3, then still with m. (k.1, inc. in next st.) 4 times, turn, p.12, turn, k.3, with b. 5 from 1, with m. k.7, with b. 5 from 1, with m. k.2.

Rows 130 to 144: In pattern as set, working one square in c. with stripes in d., one in d. alone and one in m. with dots in b. as set.

Row 145: With m. k.2, with a. 24 from 16, turn, p.24, turn, k.24, with m. k.3, with b. k.24, turn, p.24, turn, with b.k.3, (with a. k.2, with b. k.2) 5 times, with b. k.1 more, with m. k.3, with c. (k.1, inc. in next st.) 4 times, turn, p.12, turn, k.12, with m. k.2.

Rows 146 to 157: In pattern as set, working one square in a., one in b. with checks in a. and one in c.

To slope the shoulder: With m. cast off 29 sts. loosely using a larger needle.

On 21 sts. work 1 row, then cast off very loosely, using a larger needle.

The sleeves (both alike)

With size 2¼ mm. (No. 13) needles and m. cast on 64 sts. and work 35 rows in single rib.

Increase row: Rib 2, *up 1, rib 5; repeat from * ending rib 2. – 77 sts.

Change to size 2¾ mm. (No. 12) needles and beginning with a k. row s.s. 2 rows.

Now work in pattern as follows, using separate lengths of m. for the vertical stripes and taking great care to wrap m. firmly round contrast colours at the edges of squares on wrong side rows.

Row 1: With m. k.2, with b. 24 from 16, turn, p.24, turn, with b. k.3, (with a. k.2, with b. k.2) 5 times, with b. k.1 more, with m. k.3, with c. 24 from 16, turn, with c. p.24, turn, k.24, with m. k.3, with d. 24 from 16, turn, with d. p.24, turn, with m. k.2tog., k.1, 3 from 1, k.2, (sl.1, k.2tog., p.s.s.o., k.2, 3 from 1, k.2) twice, s.s.k., then with m. k.3, still with m. 24 from 16, turn, p.24, turn, k.26.

The last row sets the position of the pattern, this is the same as the centre of the back.

Now work the rows 2 to 112 as set, increasing 1 st. at the end of the last row. – 78 sts. Break off m., join in b. and a. and work in check pattern as follows; taking great care, not to pull colours tightly across the back of the work.

Row 1: With b. k.2, *with a. k.2, with b. k.2; repeat from * to end.

Row 2: With b. p.2, *with a. p.2, with b. p.2; repeat from * to end.

Row 3: With a. k.2, *with b. k.2, with a k.2; repeat from * to end.

Row 4: With a. p.2, * with b. p.2, with a. p.2; repeat from * to end.

Continuing in pattern as set, work 8 rows straight, marking each end of the last row with coloured threads.

Dec. 1 st. at each end of the next row and the 18 following alternate rows.

On 40 sts. work 1 row.

Cast off 3 sts. at the beginning of the next 6 rows, then 4 sts. on the 4 following rows.

Cast off the remaining 6 sts.

The left front

With size 2¼ mm. (No. 13) needles and m. cast on 58 sts. and work 36 rows in single rib.

Change to size 2¾ mm. (No. 12) needles and beginning with a k. row s.s. 2 rows.

Work pattern rows 1 to 81 given for right half back.

To slope the front edge: Decrease row: With m. p.2, with appropriate colour p.2tog., work to end as set.

Pattern 1 row as set.

Repeat the last 2 rows 4 times, then work the dec. row again, thus ending with the 92nd pattern row.

Row 93: With m., k.2, (k.2tog., k.1) 8 times, k.3, (k.2tog., k.1) 8 times, k.3, (k.2tog., k.1) 6 times, k.2. – 54 sts.

Row 94: With m. all p.

To shape the armhole: *Row 95:* With m. cast off 8, k. to end. – 46 sts.

Row 96: With m. all p.

Row 97: As given for row 97 on right half back until ** is reached, with a. (k.1, inc. in next st.) 6 times, turn, with a. p.18, turn k.18, then with m. k.2.

Dec. 1 st. as before on the next row and the 5 following alternate rows.

Row 109: With m. k.2, (k.2tog., k.1) 4 times, k.3, (k.2tog., k.1) 8 times, k.3, (k.2tog., k.1) 4 times, k.2.

Rows 110 to 112: With m. in s.s.

Row 113: As given for row 113 on right back until ** is reached, with d. (k.1, inc. in next st.) 4 times, turn, with d. p.12, turn, with m. k.2tog., k.1, 3 from 1, k.2, sl.1, k.2tog., p.s.s.o., k.2, inc. in next st., with m. k.2.

Rows 114 to 124: In pattern as set, but decreasing 1 st. as before for front edge on each wrong side row.

Row 125: With m. k.2, (k.2tog., k.1) 4 times, k.3, (k.2tog., k.1) 8 times, k.3, (k.2tog., k.1) twice, k.2.

Rows 126 to 128: With m. in s.s.

Row 129: Work as for row 129 on right half back until ** is reached, with b. (k.1, inc. in next st.) twice, turn, with b. p.6, turn, k.6, with m. k.2.

Rows 130 to 140: In pattern as set, but decreasing as before for front edge on each wrong side row.

Row 141: With m. k.2, (k.2tog., k.1) 4 times, k.3, (k.2tog., k.1) 8 times, k.1, k.2tog., k.2.

Rows 142 to 158: In pattern as set, but decreasing by working the 3rd and 4th sts. from front edge tog. as before on 143rd and 145th rows.

To slope the shoulder: Cast off the remaining 31 sts. loosely using a size larger needle.

The right front

With size 2¼ mm. (No. 13) needles and m. cast on 58 sts. and work 36 rows in single rib.

Change to size 2¾ mm. (No. 12) needles and beginning with a k. row s.s. 2 rows.

Work the pattern rows 1 to 81 given for left half back.

To slope the front edge: Decrease row: Pattern as set until 4 remain, with appropriate colour p.2tog., with m. p.2.

Pattern 1 row as set.

Repeat the last 2 rows 4 times more, then work the decrease row again, ending with pattern row 92.

Row 93: With m. k.2, (k.2tog., k.1) 6 times, k.3, (k.2tog., k.1) 8 times, k.3, (k.2tog., k.1) 8 times, k.2.

Rows 94 and 95: With m. in s.s.

To shape the armhole: *Row 96:* With m. cast off 8 sts., p. to end. – 46 sts.

Row 97: With m. k.2, with b. (k.1, inc. in next st.) 6 times, turn, p.18, turn, with b. k.1, (with a k.2, with b. k.2) 4 times, with b. k.1 more, work as for row 97 on left half back from ** to end.

Work rows 98 to 159 as set, but decreasing at front edge, by working the 3rd and 4th sts. from front edge tog. on row 98 and the 5 following alternate rows, then on row 114 and the 5 following alternate rows, then on row 130 and 5 following alternate rows and finally on row 141 and 2 following alternate rows.

To slope the shoulder: Cast off the remaining 31 sts. loosely with a size larger needle.

The buttonband

With right side of work facing rejoin m. to left front edge at the pattern row 80 and using size 2¾ mm. (No. 12) needles pick up and k. 104 sts. from row end edge up to cast on edge.

Work 11 rows in single rib, then cast off loosely in rib, using a size larger needle.

The buttonhole band

With right side of work facing rejoin m. at cast on edge of right front and using size $2\frac{3}{4}$ mm. (No. 12) needles pick up and k. 104 sts. from row end edge, up to pattern row 80.

Work 5 rows in single rib.

1st Buttonhole row: Rib 6, *cast off 6, rib next 23 sts; repeat from * ending last repeat rib 1.

2nd Buttonhole row: Rib 2, *turn, cast on 6, turn, rib 24; repeat from * ending last repeat rib 6.

Rib 4 rows, then cast off in rib very loosely.

The half collar (2 pieces alike)

With size $2\frac{3}{4}$ mm. (No. 12) needles and c. cast on 64 sts. and work in pattern as follows:

Row 1: With c. all k.
Row 2: With c. all p.
Rows 3 and 4: With d. all k.
Rows 5 and 6: As rows 1 and 2.

The last 6 rows form the pattern; repeat them 11 times more, then work the first 2 rows again.

Continuing in pattern as set, dec. 1 st. at each end of the next row and the 23 following alternate rows. On 16 sts. work 1 row, then cast off.

The pocket backs (2 alike)

With size $2\frac{3}{4}$ mm. (No. 12) needles and m. cast on 48 sts. and work 60 rows in s.s., then cast off.

To make up the cardigan

Do not press. Neatly join centre back seams; do not do this too firmly. Join shoulder seams. Set in sleeves, so that the 12 check pattern rows below the marking threads on sleeve top are sewn to the cast off groups at underarms. Neatly sew one row end edge of each pocket back to the row ends of the first 3 squares on each side of back. Join sleeve seams. Join side seams, neatly slip-stitching pockets in place at back of fronts. Join cast on edges of half collar pieces. Fold in half lengthways. Neatly sew row end edges of collar in place at neck edge, neatly sewing cast off edges of collar to row ends of button and buttonhole bands.

Grapes and Cherries Child's Cardigan

Patricia Roberts made her daughter Amy a fluffy cardigan decorated with bobbles of grapes and cherries in relief. It can also be knitted in Shetland wool or fine cotton. The cardigan is worked in stocking stitch in five colours in the front and separate bands for buttons and buttonholes.

Materials
Either 6(7)(8) 20 gram balls of 'Woollybear Angora' by Patricia Roberts in main colour and 2 balls in each of 5 contrast colours or 5(6)(7) 28 gram (ounce) hanks of 'Woollybear Real Shetland' in main colour and 2 hanks in each of 5 contrast colours or for summer 6(7)(8) 25 gram balls of 'Woollybear Fine Cotton' in main colour and 2 balls in each of 5 contrast colours; a pair each of size $2\frac{1}{4}$mm. (No. 13) and size $2\frac{3}{4}$mm. (No. 12) Aero knitting needles; 6 buttons.

Stockists
Woollybear Yarns are available from Patricia Roberts Knitting Shops at 31 James Street, Covent Garden, London WC2, 60 Kinnerton Street, London SW1 and 1b Kensington Church Walk, London W8. Mail order is available from the last 2 shops. Please write enclosing a stamped self-addressed envelope for price list.

Tension
16 stitches and 20 rows to 5 centimetres (2 inches) over the stocking stitch using size $2\frac{3}{4}$mm. (No. 12) needles. If you cannot obtain the correct tension using the size needles suggested, use larger or smaller needles accordingly.

Abbreviations
k., knit; p., purl; st., stitch; tog., together; dec., decrease (by working 2 sts. tog.); inc., increase (by working twice into same st.); single rib is k.1 and p.1 alternately; y.r.n., yarn round needle; s.s., stocking stitch is k. on the right side and p. on the wrong side; sl., slip; p.s.s.o., pass sl.st. over; up1, pick up the loop, which lies between the needles, slip it onto left hand needle, then k. into back of it; 5 from 1, k.1, y.r.n., k.1, y.r.n., k.1 all into next st.; m.b., make bobble, thus, with appropriate contrast colour, k.1, y.r.n., k.1 all into next st., turn, p.3, turn, k.3, turn, p.3, turn, sl.1, k.2tog., p.s.s.o.; m., main colour; a., first contrast; b., second contrast; c., third contrast; d., fourth contrast; e., fifth contrast.

Note
The instructions are given for the first size. Where they vary, work the instructions in the first brackets for the second size or the instructions in the second brackets for the third size.

Measurements
The measurements are given in centimetres followed by inches in brackets.

Underarms	55	(22)	60.5	$(24\frac{1}{4})$	66	$(26\frac{1}{2})$
Side seam	22.5	(9)	25	(10)	27.5	(11)
Length	35.5	$(14\frac{1}{4})$	39	$(15\frac{3}{4})$	43	$(17\frac{1}{4})$
Sleeve seam	24	$(9\frac{1}{2})$	26	$(10\frac{1}{2})$	29	$(11\frac{1}{2})$

The pocket backs

(2 alike)

With size 2¾mm. (No. 12) needles and m. cast on 20 sts. and beginning with a k. row s.s. 28 rows, then leave these sts. on a stitch-holder until required.

The main part

With size 2¼mm. (No. 13) needles and m. cast on 154(170)(186) sts. and work 29 rows in single rib.
Increase row: Rib 5, *up 1, rib 8; repeat from * ending last repeat rib 5. – 173(191)(209) sts.
Change to size 2¾mm. (No. 12) needles and work in pattern as follows: Use short lengths or small balls of contrast colour for each individual motif.
Row 1: With m. all k.
Row 2: With m. all p.
Row 3: With m. k.3, *with a. 5 from 1, with m. k.17; repeat from * ending last repeat with m. k.7.
Row 4: With m. p.7, *with a. p.5, with m. p.17; repeat from * ending last repeat with m. p. 3.
Row 5: With m. k.3, *with a. k.5, with m. k.17; repeat from * ending last repeat with m. k.7.
Row 6: As row 4.
Row 7: With m. k.3, *with a. sl.1, k.1, p.s.s.o., k.1, k.2tog., with m. k.3, with a. 5 from 1, with m. k.13; repeat from * ending last repeat with m. k.3.
Row 8: With m. p.3, *with a. p.5, with m. p.3, with a. p.3tog., with m. p.13; repeat from * ending last repeat with m. p.3.
Row 9: With m. k.3, *with b. k.1, with m. k.3, with a., k.5, with m. k.13; repeat from * ending last repeat with m. k.3.
Row 10: With m. p.3, *with a. p.5, with m. p.3, with b. p.1, with m. p.13; repeat from * ending last repeat with m. p.3.
Row 11: With m. k.3, *with m. up1, with b. k.1, with m. k.2tog., k.1, with a. sl.1, k.1, p.s.s.o., k.1, k.2tog., with m. k.13; repeat from * ending last repeat with m. k.3.
Row 12: With m. p.3, *with a. p.3tog., with m. p.2, with b. p.1, with m. p.14; repeat from * ending last repeat with m. p.4.
Row 13: With m. k.4, *with m. up1, with b. k.1, with m. k.2tog., with b. k.1, with m. k.14; repeat from * ending last repeat with m. k.3.
Row 14: With m. p.3, *with b. p.1, with m. p.1, with b. p. 1, with m. p. 15; repeat from * ending last repeat p.5.
Row 15: With m. k.5, *with m. up1, with b. sl.1, k.1, p.s.s.o., k.1, with m. k.15; repeat from * ending last repeat with m. k.3.
Row 16: With m. p.3, *with b. p.2, with m. p.16; repeat from * ending last repeat p.6.
Row 17: With m. k.6, *with m. up1, with b. sl.1, k.1, p.s.s.o., with m. k.16; repeat from * ending last repeat with m. k.3.
Row 18: With m. all p.
Row 19: With m. all k.
Row 20: With m. all p.
Row 21: With m. k.16, *with c. m.b., with m. k.17; repeat from * ending last repeat with m. k.12.
Row 22: With m. p.11, *with c. p.3, with m. p.15; repeat from * ending last repeat p.15.
Row 23: With m. k.15, *with c. m.b., k.1, m.b., with m. k.15; repeat from * ending last repeat with m. k.11.
Row 24: With m. p.10, *with c. p.5, with m. p.13; repeat from * ending last repeat with m. p.14.
Row 25: With m. k.14, *with c. m.b., k.1, m.b., k.1, m.b., with m. k.13; repeat from * ending last repeat with m. k.10.
Row 26: With m. p.9, *with c. p.7, with m. p.11; repeat from * ending last repeat with m. p.13.
Row 27: With m. k.13, *with c. m.b., k.1, m.b., k.1, m.b., k.1, m.b., with m. k.11; repeat from * ending last repeat with m. k.9.
Rows 28 and 29: As rows 24 and 25.
Row 30: With m. p.11, *with b. p.3, with m. p.15; repeat from * ending last repeat with m. p.15.
Row 31: With m. k.14, *with b. k.5, with m. k.13; repeat from * ending last repeat with m. k.10.
Row 32: With m. p.12, *with b. p.1, with m. p.17; repeat from * ending last repeat with m. p.16.
Row 33: With m. k.16, *with b. k.1, with m. k.17; repeat from * ending last repeat with m. k.12.
Row 34: As row 32.
The last 34 rows form the pattern. Continuing in pattern as set, but using d. instead of a. and e. instead of c. on every alternate pattern repeat, work as follows.
Pocket row: With m. k.12, *sl. next 20 sts. onto a stitch-holder and leave at front of work, in their place k. across the 20 sts. of one pocket back*, k.109(127)(145) sts.; then repeat from * to *, k.12.
Pattern 30(40)(50) rows.
Now divide the sts. for the armholes: Next row: Pattern 41(45)(49) and leave these sts. on a spare needle until required for left half front, cast off 4(5)(6), work across next 82(90)(98) sts. and leave these 83(91)(99) sts. on a spare needle, until required for back, cast off 4(5)(6) sts., pattern to end and continue on these 41(45)(49) sts. for the right half front.
The right half front: To shape the armhole: Maintaining the continuity of the pattern as set, dec. 1 st. at the armhole edge on each of the next 7(8)(9) rows.
On 34(37)(40) sts. pattern 21(24)(25) rows.
To shape the neck: Cast off 6(7)(7) sts. at the beginning of the next row, then dec. 1 st. at the neck edge on each of the next 8(8)(9) rows.
On 20(22)(24) sts. work 10(12)(13) rows.
To slope the shoulder: Cast off 10(11)(12) sts. at the beginning of the next row. On 10(11)(12) sts. work 1 row, then cast off.
The back: With right side of work facing rejoin yarn to the 83(91)(99) sts. left on spare needle and work as follows.
To shape the armholes: Continuing in pattern as set, dec. 1 st. at each end of the next 7(8)(9) rows.
On 69(75)(81) sts. pattern 41(46)(49) rows.
To slope the shoulders: Cast off 10(11)(12) sts. at the beginning of the next 4 rows, then leave the remaining 29(31)(33) sts. on a spare needle until required for neckband.
The left half front: With right side of work facing rejoin yarn to inner edge of sts. left on spare needle and work to end of row, then work as given for right half front to end.

The sleeves

(both alike)

With size 2¼mm. (No. 13) needles and m. cast on
47(51)(55) sts. and work 18 rows in single rib.
Change to size 2¾mm. (No. 12) needles and beginning
with a k. row s.s. 2 rows.
Now work in pattern as follows:
Row 21: With m. k.5(7)(9), *with e. m.b., with m. k.17;
repeat from * ending last repeat k.5(7)(9).
The last row sets the position of the pattern given for
the back. Pattern 7 rows more.
Continuing in pattern as set and working the extra sts.
into the pattern as they occur, inc. 1 st. at each end of
the next row and the 8 following 8th(8th)(10th) rows.
On 65(69)(73) sts. pattern 7(17)(11) rows.
To shape the sleeve top: Cast off 2(3)(3) sts. at the
beginning of the next 2 rows, then dec. 1 st. at each
end of the next row and the 5(6)(8) alternate rows.
On 49 sts. work 1 row.
Dec. 1 st. at each end of the next 16 rows.
Cast off 3 sts. at the beginning of the next 4 rows. Cast
off the remaining 5 sts.

The pocket tops

(2 alike)

With right side of work facing rejoin m. to the 20 sts.
left on stitch-holder and using size 2¼mm. (No. 13)
needles work 6 rows in single rib, then cast off in rib.

The neckband

First join shoulder seams. With right side of work facing
rejoin m. at right front neck edge and using size 2¼mm.
(No. 13) needles pick up and k. 28(30)(31) sts. from
right front neck edge, k. across the 29(31)(33) sts. left
on spare needle at back neck edge, then pick up and k.
28(30)(31) sts. from left front neck edge.
On 85(91)(95) sts. work 5 rows in single rib, then cast
off in rib.

The buttonband

With size 2¼mm. (No. 13) needles and m. cast on 6 sts.
and work 132(148)(160) rows in single rib, then cast
off in rib.

The buttonhole band

With size 2¼mm. (No. 13) needles and m. cast on 6 sts.
and work 6(8)(10) rows in single rib.
1st Buttonhole row: Rib 2, cast off 2, rib to end.
2nd Buttonhole row: Rib 2, turn, cast on 2, turn, rib to
end.
Rib 22(24)(26) rows.
Repeat the last 24(26)(28) rows 4 times more, then
work the 2 buttonhole rows again.
Rib 4(6)(6) rows, then cast off.

To make up the cardigan

Pin out to size and press all parts except the ribbing
lightly on the wrong side with a warm iron over a
damp cloth. Join sleeve seams. Set in sleeves. Sew
button and buttonhole bands in place. Sew pocket backs
and row ends of pocket tops in position. Sew on
buttons.

Suzanne Russell for Rococo: Crunchy Cardigan

A pair of knickers for her teddy bear, knitted when she was four years old, started Suzanne Russell on her fashion career. She comes from a family of knitters and her earliest memories are of her grandmother knitting socks and giving her needles and a ball of wool to play with.

If you handed her that yarn today, Suzanne would produce the most delicate and refined of knits, very carefully made and with the emphasis on stitchcraft, like the white lacy stitch cardigan she wears in the picture on page 73. To underline the personal and rustic nature of knitting, each Rococo sweater has a swing label saying 'Knitted by the fireside of . . .' and the name of the hand-knitter, one of a thousand who now work for the company.

Suzanne started her career in fashion as an assistant to Mary Quant. Then her fascination with fabrics encouraged her to do her own collection of textile designs which she took to New York and Los Angeles. 'Then, by 1975, I was trying to work in textiles with texture,' she explains. 'I was fed up with them being flat. And that was when I started off with picture knitting.'

One of her earliest successes should have been knitted up by the kitchen sink, rather than the fireside. Suzanne Russell found a yarn that was used to make old-fashioned dishcloths ('it actually smelt and had bits in it') and she turned it into a casual sweater that chimed absolutely with the mood for natural fibres, for workwear-inspired fashion and for the growing trend for summer knits.

The texture is still an important part of the Rococo collections, with crunchy yarns and open-weave stitches adding a new dimension to a simple cardigan or sweater. Suzanne likes natural shades or fresh white cotton, although she also uses colour. 'But it must always be in the right balance with the proportions of what you are making'.

She admits that she designs for herself. 'I start with what I would like to wear,' she explains. 'I like very plain, well-made clothes. Hand-knits are expensive and I would not want to spend £100 to look ugly. I want to look attractive'.

The changing shapes of fashion are important to her and all her knits are fitted on a dummy 'because they are clothes, not just hand-knitted garments'. Her attention to detail has been rewarded by a strong export business, in America, Japan and Europe, and she is especially proud that Rococo's best customer is Italy, the one-time home of hand-knitting.

Detail is important to Suzanne, whether it is the narrow half-moon buttons that close the delicate open-weave cardigan or the subtle embroidery on the front of a wool sweater. She says that all knitwear design is to do with balance. Sometimes she starts by working out a pattern on a sheet of graph paper, another time she sits down with needles and yarn and develops her design theme from there. 'But I don't sit down and design a sweater with bobbles on it. That comes from thinking about texture and surface interest and the idea just grows,' she explains.

The Rococo designs are detailed and delicate, but Suzanne also liked to think that they are timeless, rather than fashion garments that happen to be on a wave of popularity at present. 'I think,' she says, 'that knitting should be in its own way creating a modern classic.'

Suzanne Russell likes delicate knits with surface interest and texture. The crisp white cotton cardigan she wears here is worked in cable, rib and a lacy openwork pattern formed by knitting through the back of the loops.

Sizes: To fit bust 81–86/89–94cm (32–34/35–37in). Length 51.5/54.5cm (20$\frac{1}{4}$/21$\frac{1}{2}$in). Sleeve seam 41/43cm (16/17in).

Yarn: 11/12 × 50g balls of Mercerised Cotton available only by Mail Order from: Rococo, 27 Harcourt Street, London, W1H 1DT (shade card available on receipt of a stamped, addressed envelope).

Needles: 3$\frac{1}{4}$mm (no. 10) and 2$\frac{3}{4}$mm (no. 12); 3mm (no. 11) circular knitting needle; cable needle.

Notions: 7 buttons.

Tension: 12 sts and 16 rows knitted over basic sts of Bell pattern to 5cm (2in) square.

Special abbreviations: C2f = slip next 2 sts onto cable needle and hold at front, K2, then K2 from cable needle.

Note: Where a number of sts is given, this refers to the basic number and does not include those made in the pattern.

Back

With 2$\frac{3}{4}$mm (no. 12) needles and using the thumb method cast on 103/113 sts.
Row 1: K2, * P1, K1, rep from * to the last st, K1.
Row 2: *K1, P1, rep from * to the last st, K1.
Rep these 2 rows 8 times more, and then row 1 once.
Next row: Rib to end, increasing 7 sts evenly spaced (110/120 sts).
Change to 3$\frac{1}{4}$mm (no. 10) needles and pattern as follows:

PATTERN
Row 1: (P2, K1 tbl) 3 times, *P2, K6, P2, (K1 tbl, P4) 6/7 times K1 tbl, rep from * once more, P2, K6, P2, (K1 tbl, P2) 3 times.
Row 2: (K2, P1 tbl) 3 times, *K2, P6, K2, (P1 tbl, K4) 6/7 times. P1 tbl, rep from * once more, K2, P6, K2, (P1 tbl, K2) 3 times.
Row 3: (P2, K1 tbl) 3 times, * P2, K6, P2, (K1 tbl, P2, turn, cast on 8 sts, P2) 6/7 times, K1 tbl, rep from * once more, P2, K6, P2, (K1 tbl, P2) 3 times.
Row 4: (K2, P1 tbl) 3 times, K2, P6, K2, (P1 tbl, K2, P8, K2) 6/7 times, P1 tbl, rep from * once more, K2, P6, K2, (P1 tbl, K2) 3 times.
Row 5: (P2, K1 tbl) 3 times, * P2, C3b, P2, (K1 tbl, P2, K8, P2) 6/7 times, K1 tbl, rep from * once more, P2, C3b, P2, (K1 tbl, P2) 3 times.
Row 6: As row 4.
Row 7: (P2, K1 tbl) 3 times, * P2, K6, P2, (K1 tbl, P2, K2 tog tbl, K4, K2 tog, P2) 6/7 times, K1 tbl, rep from * once more, P2, K6, P2 (K1 tbl, P2) 3 times.
Row 8: (K2, P1 tbl) 3 times, * K2, P6, K2, (P1 tbl, K2, P2 tog, P2, P2 tog tbl, K2) 6/7 times, P1 tbl, rep from * once more, K2, P6, K2, (P1 tbl, K2) 3 times.
Row 9: (P2, K1 tbl) 3 times, * P2, K6, P2, (K1 tbl, P2, K2 tog tbl, K2 tog, P2) 6/7 times, K1 tbl, rep from * once more, P2, K6, P2, (K1 tbl, P2) 3 times.
Row 10: (K2, P1 tbl) 3 times, * K2, P6, K2, (P1 tbl, K1, K2 tog tbl, K2 tog, K1) 6/7 times, P1 tbl, rep from * once more, K2, P6, K2, (P1 tbl, K2) 3 times.
These 10 rows form patt.
Work until the 10th row of the 8th/9th patt from commencement has been completed.

SHAPE ARMHOLES
Cast off 4 sts at beg of next 2 rows.
Now dec 1 st at each end of next 5 rows (92/102 sts).
Work until the 10th row of the 14th/15th patt from commencement has been completed.
Continue in patt as rows 1 and 2 only.

SHAPE SHOULDERS
Cast off 10/11 sts at beg of next 4 rows, and 11/12 sts at beg of 2 following rows.
Cast off remaining sts.

Left front

With 2$\frac{3}{4}$mm (no. 12) needles and using the thumb method, cast on 59/63 sts, and work 19 rows in rib as back.
Next row: Rib 10, inc in next st, * rib 8/7, inc in next st, rep from * to the last 3/4 sts, rib to end. (65/70 sts).
Change to 3$\frac{1}{4}$mm (no. 10) needles and patt.
Row 1: (P2, K1 tbl) 3 times, P2, K6, P2, (K1 tbl, P4) 5/6 times, K1 tbl, P2, K6, P2, turn leaving remaining sts on a st holder for border.
Continue in patt as set.
Work until the 10th row of the 8th/9th patt from commencement has been completed.

SHAPE ARMHOLE
Cast off 4 sts at beg of next row.
Work 1 row.
Now dec 1 st at armhole edge of the next 5 rows (46/51 sts).
Work until the 1st row of the 13th/14th patt from commencement has been completed.

SHAPE NECK
Next row: Cast off 8/9 sts, patt to end.
Next row: Patt to last 7 sts, K1 tbl, P4, K1 tbl, P1.
Now dec 1 st at neck edge on next 7/8 rows.
Work until the 10th row of the 14th/15th patt from commencement has been completed, but working 3/4 bells instead of 4/5 bells in last patt. Continue in patt as rows 1 and 2.

SHAPE SHOULDER
Cast off 10/11 sts at beg of next 2 rows.
Work 1 row.
Cast off 11/12 remaining sts.

BUTTON BORDER
Rejoin yarn at inside edge of 10 sts on st holder.
Work 112/124 rows in rib.
Cast off firmly in rib.

Right front

With 2¾mm (no. 12) needles and using the thumb method, cast on 59/63 sts and work 6 rows in rib.
Make buttonhole: rib 4, cast off 3, rib to end.
Next row: rib to end, casting on 3 sts over those cast off.
Work 11 more rows in rib.
Next row: rib 3/4, inc in next st, * rib 8/7, inc in next st, rep from * to the last 10 sts, rib to end.
Next row: rib 10 sts and slip on st holder, change to 3¼mm (no. 10) needles; P2, K6, P2, (K1 tbl, P4) 5/6 times, K1 tbl, P2, K6, P2, (K1 tbl, P3) 3 times.
Continue in patt as set until the 1st row of the 9th/10th patt from commencement has been completed.
Shape armhole as left front.
Work until the 2nd row of the 13th/14th patt from commencement has been completed.
Shape neck and complete to match left front.

BUTTONHOLE BORDER
Rejoin yarn at inside edge of 10 sts on st holder.
Work 5/7 rows in rib.
Make buttonhole in next 2 rows as before.
Make 5 more buttonholes with 18/20 rows between each.
Work 4 rows after last buttonhole has been completed.
Cast off firmly in rib.

Sleeves

With 2¾mm (no. 12) needles and using the thumb method, cast on 52/56 sts.
Work 19 rows in K1, P1 rib.
Next row: rib 5/3, inc in next st, * rib 5/6, inc in next st, rep from * to the last 4/3 sts, rib to end. (60/64 sts).
Change to 3¼mm (no. 10) needles and patt.
Row 1 (smaller size only): P1, K1 tbl, (P2, K1 tbl) 5 times, P2, K6, P2, K1 tbl, P4, K1 tbl, P2, K6, P2, (K1 tbl, P2) 5 times, K1 tbl, P1.
Row 1 (larger size only): K1 tbl, (P2, K1 tbl) 6 times, P2, K6, P2, K1 tbl, P4, K1 tbl, P2, K6, P2, (K1 tbl, P2) 6 times, K1 tbl.
Continue with 2 cable panels, 1 bell panel, and the remainder in K1 tbl, P2 rib.
Work 9 more rows.
Inc 1 st at each end of next row, and then every 6th row until 14 inc have been made at each side (88/92 sts).
Work until the 6th row of the 11th/12th patt from commencement has been completed.

SHAPE TOP
Cast off 4 sts at beg of next 2 rows.
Work 4 rows.
Dec 1 st at each end of next row, and then every 3rd row 9 times more (60/64 sts).
Work 1 row.
Now dec 1 st at each end of next row, and then every alt row 4 times more. (The 15th/16th bell from commencement should now be completed).
Cast off 50/54 remaining sts.

Collar

With the 3mm (no. 11) circular needle and using the thumb method, cast on 350/383 sts.
Work backwards and forwards.
Row 1: P.
Row 2: K.
Rows 3 to 5: Rep rows 1 and 2 once more, and then row 1 once.
Row 6: K3, (K2 tog) 8 times, K to last 19 sts, (K2 tog) 8 times, K3.
Row 7: (P2 tog) 4 times, now P3 tog to last 8 sts, (P2 tog) 4 times (114/125 sts).
Break yarn and sew in ends.
Row 8: Sl first 7 sts and keep at end of needle to be worked into pattern as instructed. Join in yarn and pick up loop from between needles and P it, * K1 tbl, P3, K4, P3, rep from * 8/9 times more, K1 tbl, pick up loop from between needles and P it. Turn leaving 7 sts unworked.
Row 9: Sl 1, * P1 tbl, K3, P4, K3, rep from * 8/9 times more, P1 tbl, K2, pick up loop from between needles and K it. Turn.
Row 10: Sl 1, P2, * K1 tbl, P3, K4, P3, rep from * 8/9 times more, K1 tbl, P2, pick up loop from between needles and P it. Turn.
Row 11: Sl 1, K2, * P1 tbl, K3, P4, K3, rep from * 8/9 times more, P1 tbl, K4, Sl 1 with yarn at front of st, turn.
Row 12: P5, * K1 tbl, P3, C2f, P3, rep from * 8/9 times more, K1 tbl, P4, Sl 1 with yarn at back of st, turn.
Row 13: K5, * P1 tbl, K3, P4, K3, rep from * 8/9 times more, P1 tbl, K4, K2 tog, turn.
Row 14: P5, * K1 tbl, P3, K4, P3, rep from * 8/9 times more, K1 tbl, P4, P2 tog, turn.
Row 15: As row 13.
Row 16: As row 14.
Row 17: As row 13.
Row 18: P5, * K1 tbl, P3, C2f, P3, rep from * 8/9 times more, K1 tbl, P4, P2 tog, turn.
Row 19: As row 13.
Row 20: As row 14.
Change to 2¾mm (no. 12) needles.
Row 21: K5, * P1 tbl, K3, P4, K3, rep from * 8/9 times more, P1 tbl, K5.
Continuing in pattern cast off 14 sts at beg of next 2 rows, and 14/16 sts at beg of 2 following rows.
Cast off remaining sts.

Finishing

Sew borders to fronts.
Join shoulders, side and sleeve seams.
Sew sleeves into armholes, making pleats on sleeve top at side edges of cable panels.
Sew cast off edge of collar to neck edge.
Press seams. Sew on buttons.

The New Graphics

Lumière: Greek Key Pattern

[See photograph previous page]

When knitting developed beyond the idea of a warm covering, it became, like any other garment, a part of fashion. The ebb and flow of interest in knitwear this century has depended almost entirely on fashion, with the growth of sportswear for both sexes favouring knitted styles, and any return to formal or sophisticated clothes slightly discouraging it. This has been particularly true of hand-knits, which were challenged by machine knits, especially from Italy during the fifties, and only recovered their fashion force with the revolt against modern technology and the enthusiasm for craft, ethnic cultures and back-to-nature dressing.

Now fashion has moved on again, and the role of knitwear designers is to find a thread to link hand-knits with new styles.

The problem is mainly one of proportions. Even the classic hand-knits need subtle changes of body shape and shoulder line to dovetail with the current line in clothes.

The Lumière label is synonymous with knits that change quite radically according to fashion, but always have a strong and individual look. The company makes hand and machine knits as part of a high fashion collection and behind it are two women: tall, fair Barbara Kennington and her partner Megumi Ohki who is small dark and Japanese.

These two designers met when they were both studying for their MA degrees in fashion design at the Royal College of Art, and they have stayed together for five years because they both think and work in the same way. 'Because we both look so different, and because our collections have various different strands, people tend to think that Meg and I both contribute quite different ideas,' says Barbara.

'In fact,' says Megumi, 'we've worked so long together that we discuss things first and then work out the whole collection.'

The first thing that they do is to go out and look for cloth. Then they 'face up to a blank sheet of paper'. But they are always thinking of a development from the previous season and when they buy the cloth, it is with that sense of continuity in mind.

The resulting knits are very much part of a total fashion style, which currently means shapes and textures inspired by Japan (co-incidentally Megumi's cultural background). Previous collections have been inspired by Renaissance tapestries or even worked out on an African theme.

The cable front oversweater with asymmetric hemline and geometric Fair Isle patterning shown here is an example of the cross-fertilisation of their fashion ideas. Their frilled cotton sweater (page 116) is in a different mood but has a similar panelled body shape.

They both have a good technical understanding of the possibilities of knitting. Megumi's grandmother back home in Osaka, Japan, taught her to knit while her mother made clothes and inspired an interest in sewing. Barbara was brought up in Durban, South Africa, and learned hand-knitting from her mother. Both of them have now discovered the limitations, as well as the strengths of working by hand. 'Hand-knitting can be very restricting,' says Barbara. 'Not so much personally, but when you are trying to run a business, the production is very difficult and the price prohibitive.'

They have around 100 knitters, mostly in Scotland, but since Lumière became part of the Jeffrey Rogers knitwear group in 1981, they have been able to work at the creative machine knitting they were taught at College and make that too an important part of fashion.

Lumière use a high fashion mix of different styles and skills. Their graphic over-sweater in black double knitting with silver lurex geometric patternings is shaped asymmetrically with the back longer than the front. The main panels are worked in cable, with side and underarm panels knitted in Fair Isle using the two yarns. All the panels are joined with an over-stitch to represent thonging.

Size: One size.

Yarn: MY: 15 × 50g balls Patons Clansman DK. A: 2 × 50g balls Patons Clansman DK. 1 × 20g ball Pinguoin Place de Vendome lurex (one strand of each worked together).

Needles: 4mm (no. 8) and 3¼mm (no. 10); 1 cable needle.

Tension: 22 sts and 28 rows knitted in st.st on 4mm (no. 8) needles to 10cm (4in) square.

Special abbreviations:
MK = make knot as follows: (K1, P1, K1, P1, K1, P1, K1) in one st, making 7 sts from 1 st. Then with point of left-hand needle pass 2nd, 3rd, 4th, 5th, 6th and 7th sts on right-hand needle separately over last st made, completing knot.

Side panels
(2 the same)
Using 3¼mm (no. 10) ndls and MY cast on 44 sts and work 4 rows in K1, P1 rib.
Change to 4mm (no. 8) ndls and work next 2 rows in st.st.
Now work Fair Isle pattern and shaping as chart.

Underarm panels
(2 the same)
Using 4mm (no. 8) ndls and MY cast on 12 sts.
Now work Fair Isle pattern and shaping as chart.

Front cable panel
Using 4mm (no. 8) ndls and MY cast on 116 sts.
Row 1: K1, P1, K1, (P2, K2) to last 5 sts, P2, K1, P1, K1.
Row 2: K1, P1, K1, (K2, P2) to last 5 sts, K2, K1, P1, K1.
Repeat these 2 rows until 5cm (2in) have been worked.
Now work cable panel as chart, until piece measures 56cm (22in), including rib, ending with a wrong side row.

NECKLINE
Next row: work 44 sts in pattern. Cast off 28 sts. Work 44 sts in pattern. (Work on these 44 sts for right shoulder.)

RIGHT SHOULDER
Work 1 row.
Next row: cast off 15 sts at neck edge. Work in pattern to end.
Work 1 row.
Next row: cast off 5 sts at neck edge. Work in pattern to end.
Work 1 row.
Next row: cast off remaining 24 sts.
Now work left shoulder to correspond.

Back cable panel
Work as for front cable panel, until piece measures 63cm (25in), including rib.
Work neckline as for front.

Sleeve cable panel
(2 the same)
Using 4mm (no. 8) ndls and MY, cast on 68 sts and work 2 rows in st.st.
Now work panel as chart, until piece measures 56cm (22in) from cast on.
Cast off.

Collar
Using 4mm (no. 8) ndls and MY cast on 118 sts, and work 2 rows in K1, P1 rib.
Row 3: (with right side facing, in st.st Fair Isle): 5MY, (8A, 2MY), end 3MY.
Row 4: 5MY, (1A, 6MY, 1A, 2MY), 3MY.
Row 5: 5MY, (1A, 1MY, 4A, 1MY, 1A, 2MY) 3MY.
Row 6: 5MY, (1A, 1MY, 1A, 2MY, 1A, 1MY, 1A, 2MY) 3MY.
Row 7: as row 6.

Row 8: 5MY, (1A, 1MY, 2A, 1MY, 1A, 1MY, 1A, 2MY) 3MY.

Row 9: 5MY, (1A, 1MY, 1A, 4MY, 1A, 2MY) 3MY.

Row 10: 5MY, (6A, 1MY, 1A, 2MY) 3MY.

Row 11: 5MY, (1A, 9MY) 3MY.

Row 12: 5MY, (8A, 2MY) 3MY.

Work next 12 rows in st.st using MY only.

Work next 2 rows in K1, P1 rib.

Cast off in rib pattern, not too tightly.

Cuffs

Using 3¼mm (no. 10) ndls and MY pick up 60 sts evenly around wrist edge.

Row 1: (K2, P2) to end.

Row 2: (K2, P2) to end.

Repeat these 2 rows until 6.5cm (2½in) have been worked.

Cast off in rib pattern.

Finishing

Finish all yarn ends securely and neatly.

Press all pieces lightly on wrong side using warm iron and damp cloth.

Join shoulder seams using neat back st.

Lightly press collar in half, join seam, then back st onto neck edge.

Using A join side panels to front and back panels with large overstitches (giving thonged effect). In same manner join top-sleeve panel to underarm panel.

Using MY back st. join underarm seam.

Sleeve cable panel (2 the same)

STITCH GUIDE

Hollow oak cable (worked over 15 sts)

Row 1: P5, K5, P5.

Rows 2, 4, 6, 8: K5, P5, K5.

Row 3: P5, K2, MK, K2, P5.

Row 5: P5, MK, K3, MK, P5.

Row 7: Repeat row 3.

Row 9: P4, BC, P1, FC, P4.

Row 10: K4, P2, K1, P1, K1, P2, K4.

Row 11: P3, BC, K1, P1, K1, FC, P3.

Row 12: K3, P3, K1, P1, K1, P3, K3.

Row 13: P2, BC, (P1, K1) twice, P1, FC, P2.

Row 14: K2, P2, (K1, P1) 3 times, K1, P2, K2.

Row 15: P2, K3, (P1, K1) twice, P1, K3, P2.

Rows 16, 18, 20: Repeat rows 14, 12, 10.

Row 17: P2, FC, (P1, K1) twice, P1, BC, P2.

Row 19: P3, FC, K1, P1, K1, BC, P3.

Row 21: P4, FC, P1, BC, P4.

Repeat rows 2–21.

Bobble stitch (worked over 5 sts)

Row 1: P2, make bobble by (P1, K1) twice into next st, then take 2nd, 3rd, 4th sts over first st, P2.

Row 2: K2, P1, K2.

Row 3: P5.

Row 4: as row 2.

Fancy cable (worked over 8 sts)

Rows 1 and 5: K8.

Row 2 and all even-numbered rows: P8.

Row 3: Sl 2 sts onto a cable needle and leave at front of work, K2, then K2 from cable needle, Sl 2 sts onto a cable needle and leave at back of work, K2, then K2 from cable needle.

Row 7: Sl 2 sts onto a cable needle and leave at back of work, K2, then K2 from cable needle, Sl 2 sts onto a cable needle and leave at front of work, K2, then K2 from cable needle.

Row 8: P8.

Corn stitch (worked over 9 sts)

Row 1: K9.

Row 2: P9.

Row 3: Sl 3 sts onto a cable needle and leave at back of work, K1, then K3 from cable needle, K1, Sl 1 st onto a cable needle and leave at front of work, K3, then K1 from cable needle.

Row 4: P9.

Moss stitch (worked over 3 sts)

Row 1: K1, P1, K1.

Row 2: K1, P1, K1.

Front and back cable panels

Underarm panel (2 the same)

Side panels (2 the same)

Single rib

Moss stitch

☒ A

Sarah Dallas: Chessboard Checks

[*See photograph page 81*]

Sarah Dallas teaches the craft of knitting – especially by machine – to groups of textile and fashion students.

She herself studied weaving and knitting at Middlesex Polytechnic, went on to do a textile course at the Royal College of Art and now has a designer knitting business in Skipton, Yorkshire.

When Sarah sets a project for her Brighton students, she tries to think of a theme that they can exploit by using it with other fashion fabrics. She has currently been fired with enthusiasm for Japanese knits and made the graphic wool sweater featured here in that mood. Sarah is also interested in Japanese experiments with distressed and surface-worn fabrics. 'In a way, that is against everything I believe in, because it is anti-fashion,' she says. 'But I think it is very important for students to be inspired to experiment, to do knitting that is absolutely free instead of always being bound by shaping and design.'

She sees a divide between textile students (as she herself was) and fashion students. 'A fashion student will think of knitwear as part of a total outfit and will not be much concerned with the technical side. The textile student will experiment more with texture, dyeing yarns and working with them to get surface effects.'

In her own collections, which are primarily machine knits, she tries to work in the two separate strands. She commissions specially woven fabrics for the garments that co-ordinate with her knits (which make up two-thirds of her business) as she finds it difficult to search Interstoff or the other large fabric fairs for suitable materials.

Sarah Dallas says that she never designs for herself, although she always tries on each of her designs to check its shaping on the body. 'A sweater has got to be part of fashion,' she explains. 'You can tell when people haven't tried on their creations. That's why I still knit all my own samples and for several seasons I tried on every single thing we made.' With nearly 100 knitters working for her, that kind of stock control has now become an impossible task.

The pretty sweater, often in white and decorated with ribbons or beading was once the hallmark of a Sarah Dallas sweater (see page 120). However, she finds increasingly that her collections are schizophrenic: the pretty, delicate cotton open weave jumpers on the one side; on the other, and usually in wool, more graphic much darker designs, using grey, black and indigo.

In her teaching, she encourages her students to work with positive groups of colour to make a design statement. 'Some people just pick colours from the sky, but colour is so important,' she says, 'I do loads of little swatches to get things right.'

She enjoys hand-knitting, but she is also interested in teaching her students to be creative on a machine. 'In the end, it comes down to the same thing,' she says. 'It's a question of making the machine or the knitting do what you want it to do.'

Zandra Rhodes in her exotic bedroom wearing her 'Bubble' dress
(page 127)

Sarah Dallas is experimenting with graphic knits, using geometric patterns to give interest to flat weaves. This asymmetric checked sweater is knitted in stocking stitch relying for its effect entirely on the bi-colour blocks of black, white and grey and on the varied width of the stripes.

Sizes: To fit an 80/85/90cm (32/34/36in) bust loosely. Back length: 51/53/55cm (20½/21¼/22in). Length of sleeve: 42/43/44cm (16¾/17¼/17¾in).

Yarn: Real Shetland 2-ply Jumper Yarn from T. M. Hunter Ltd, Sutherland Wool Mills, Brora, Sutherland, Scotland (Tel: 040-82366/7).
MY: approx. 6 × 1oz hanks Black.
A: approx. 2 × 1oz hanks Grey.
B: approx. 2 × 1oz hanks White.

Needles: 3¼mm (no. 10); 3¾mm (no. 9); 1 st holder.

Tension: 24 sts and 28 rows on 3¾mm (no. 9) needles in st.st to 10cm (4in) square.

Susan Duckworth's sweet pea summer sweater with diamond lace motifs (page 51)

Back

With $3\frac{1}{4}$mm (no. 10) needles cast on 128/134/140 sts using MY and work 10 rows in K1, P1 rib.

Change to $3\frac{3}{4}$mm (no. 9) needles and starting with a K row (right side) work in st.st for 12 rows.

* Next row: (right side) Knit 64/67/70 sts using A, then K rem 64/67/70 sts using MY. Continue in st.st for a further 11 rows working sts in colours as set remembering to twist yarns when changing yarns to avoid a hole forming. **

Next row: (right side) K all sts in MY.

Continue in st.st for a further 11 rows using MY only.

Now rep from * to ** once more.

*** Next row: (right side) K 64/67/70 sts in MY then K rem 64/67/70 sts in B. Continue in st.st for a further 5 rows in colours as set. Then work 6 rows in st.st using MY only on all sts. ****

Rep from *** to **** 3 times (36 rows).

SHAPE ARMHOLES

Work one more rep from *** to **** *but at same time* cast off 6/7/8 sts at beg of next 2 rows. (116/120/124 sts).

Then K4 rows in colours as set, then 6 rows MY only.

Next row: (right side) K 58/60/62 sts using A then K rem 58/60/62 sts in MY.

Next row: P all sts in colours as set by previous row.

Next row: K all sts using MY only.

Next row: P all sts using MY only.

These 4 rows are repeated for the remainder of back.

SHAPE SHOULDERS

When work measures 49/52/54cm ($19\frac{1}{4}$/$20\frac{1}{2}$/$21\frac{1}{4}$in) shape shoulders as follows (ending with a wrong side row): Continuing with stripe sequence, cast off 9 sts at beg of next 6 rows then cast off 11/12/13 sts at beg of foll 2 rows. Place remaining 40/42/44 sts for back neck on a spare needle.

Front

Follow exactly as for back but reversing stripe pattern till 41/43/45cm ($16\frac{1}{2}$/$17\frac{1}{4}$/18in) have been worked from beg ending with a wrong side row.

SHAPE NECK

Maintaining stripe sequence correctly, place centre 20 sts onto a st holder and work on left side of neck shaping (48/50/52 sts).

Knit 45/47/49 sts, K2 tog, K1, *turn.*

Next row: P.

Continue decreasing at neck edge on every alt row as set 10/11/12 times in all. *At the same time* when work measures same as back to shoulder, *shape shoulder* to match back left shoulder. Return to remaining 48/50/52 sts for right side of neck. With right side of work facing you, K1, Sl 1, K1 PSSO, Knit to end.

Next row: P.

Repeat last 2 rows 10/11/12 times in all. When work measures same as back to shoulder, shape right shoulder to match.

Left sleeve

With $3\frac{1}{4}$mm (no. 10) needles cast on 64/66/68 sts using MY and work 10 rows in K1, P1 rib. Change to $3\frac{3}{4}$mm (no. 9) needles and starting with a K row work 2 rows in st.st in MY, then work 2 rows in st.st with B. Repeat these 4 rows 11 times in all then complete sleeve in st.st using MY only. *But at same time* shape sleeve as follows:

Inc 1 st each end of 4th and every following 4th row till 120/124/126 sts. When sleeve measures 44/45/46cm (17/18/$18\frac{1}{2}$in) from beg cast off loosely.

Right sleeve

Follow exactly as for left sleeve but work in MY only till sleeve measures 14cm ($5\frac{1}{2}$in) from beg. Now work stripes as follows (still increasing as required): Work 6 rows st.st in A then work 6 rows st.st in MY. Repeat these 12 rows twice more, then do another 6 rows st.st in A, then complete sleeve using MY to match left sleeve.

Neckband

Using backstitch neatly join right shoulders. With right side of work facing you using $3\frac{1}{4}$mm (no. 10) needles K across the 40/42/44 sts from back neck, neatly pick up and K18/20/22 sts from left neck edge, K across the centre 20 sts, pick up and K18/20/22 sts from right neck edge (96/102/108 sts). Work 10 rows in K1, P1 rib. Cast off evenly.

Finishing

Join left shoulder. Pin sleeves in position and sew. Pin side and sleeve seams and neatly sew. Press according to yarn instructions.

Sandy Black: Grid Cardigan

The geometric grid of Sandy Black's silky cardigan is a reflection of her background. For ex-maths student Sandy (see page 54) works out all her patterns with meticulous and logical care on graph paper.

The new graphic designs can seem flat and two-dimensional after the richness of pattern and colour of the last decade or in contrast with the vivid picture knits that Sandy Black herself makes so realistically (see colour plate opposite page 33). An extra dimension is given to the flat squares of the maths textbook design shown here in two different ways: by the texture of the yarns (fine silk, embroidered in fluffy angora) and by the knitting itself.

Sandy Black learned crochet from her grandmother even before her mother taught her to knit. Her earliest experiments with the needles were a combination of hand-knitting with crochet, and she used her crochet hook to work the grid on the jacket – although it can equally well be done with a tapestry needle.

'Because I have a background in numeracy, I bring a logical mind to my knitting,' says Sandy. She was also logical enough to see the potential of knitwear for all seasons and occasions. This cardigan is in a fine summer weight, but is also ritzy enough to wear out at night.

The body of the cream cardigan jacket is worked in silk, used double. The horizontal lines of the graph paper grid are knitted in fuchsia pink and electric blue angora. To give an optical illusion of depth and added textural interest, the vertical lines are embroidered on top of the knitting in chain stitch.

Sizes: Bust 86–91/97cm (34–36/38in). Length 60cm (23½in).

Yarn:
MY: Sandy Black 100% silk (ecru).
Yarn A: Sandy Black 100% angora (marine blue).
Yarn B: Sandy Black 100% angora (fuchsia).
Yarn is available as a complete kit by mail order from Sandy Black Original Knits, Studio 2, 164 Abbey Street, London SE1. Please write for details, enclosing a stamped, addressed envelope.

Needles: 4mm (no. 8) and 5mm (no. 6); medium crochet hook.

Tension: 18 sts and 22 rows knitted in st.st on 5mm (no. 6) ndls to 10cm (4in) square, using main yarn.

Notions: 8 buttons.

Notes: The silk yarn is used double throughout. Cut each yarn when changing colour in stripe sequence.

Back

With 4mm (no. 8) ndls and MY (used double), cast on 84/90 sts and work in K1, P1 rib for 2.5cm (1in).
Change to 5mm (no. 6) ndls and st.st and work in stripes as follows, starting with a K row:
* 12 rows in MY, 1 row A, 3 rows MY, 1 row B. *
These 17 rows form the stripe sequence. Rep from * to * 3 times more. Work 4 rows in MY. (Work measures 35.5cm (14in) from beg.)
Keeping continuity of stripe sequence:

SHAPE ARMHOLES
Cast off 4 sts at the beg of next 2 rows, then 3 sts, then 2 sts. Dec 1 st at each end of following 2/3 alt rows. (62/66 sts.)
Cont straight in stripe sequence until work measures 57cm (22½in) from beg.

SHAPE SHOULDERS
Cast off 6 sts at beg of next 6/4 rows.
Second size only: Cast off 7 sts at beg of next 2 rows.
Cast off remaining 26/28 sts.

Right front

With 4mm (no. 8) ndls and MY, cast on 42/45 sts and work in K1, P1 rib for 2.5cm (1in). Change to 5mm (no. 6) ndls and work in stripe sequence as back until work matches back to armhole, ending with a K row.

SHAPE ARMHOLE
Cast off 4 sts at beg of next row.
Cast off 3 sts at beg of following alt row, then 2 sts on following alt row.
Dec 1 st at armhole edge on following 2/3 alt rows. (31/33 sts.)
Continue in stripes until front measures 53.5cm (21in) ending with a purl row.

SHAPE NECK
Cast off 6/7 sts at beg of next row. Dec 1 st on neck edge of following 7 rows. (18/19 sts.)
Continue straight until work matches back, ending with a knit row.

SHAPE SHOULDER
Cast off 6 sts at beg of next and following alt row.
Work 1 row.
Cast off remaining sts.

Left front

Work as right front, but reversing all shapings thus: finish on a purl row for armhole shaping, a knit row for neck shaping and a purl row for shoulder shaping.

Sleeves
(2 alike)
With 4mm (no. 8) needles and MY, cast on 40/42 sts and work in K1, P1 rib for 2.5cm (1in).
Change to 5mm (no. 6) ndls and st.st. Knit 1 row in B, then start stripes sequence working from * to * of back. *At the same time* inc 1 st at each end of every alt row until there are 64/68 sts. Continue in stripes without shaping until sleeve measures 43cm (17in) from beg.

SHAPE TOP
Cast off 3 sts at beg of next 2 rows. Continue straight until sleeve measures 56cm (22in) from beg.
Dec 1 st at each end of every row until 42/46 sts remain.
Cast off.

Front bands
(2 alike)
With 4mm (no. 8) ndls and MY, cast on 8 sts and work in garter st until band fits up front edge when slightly stretched. Cast off.

Collar

With 4mm (no. 8) ndls and A, cast on 21 sts and knit 2 rows.
Change to MY and work in garter st in stripes as follows:
26 rows MY * 2 rows B, 8 rows MY, 2 rows A, 26 rows MY * Rep from * to * 4 times more.
Knit 2 rows in B and cast off.

Embroidery
Using either a crochet hook or a large needle, and starting from just above the rib, work lines of chain st in angora as follows:

BACK
Counting from right side edge, work a fuchsia line up the 8th/7th st and every following 12th/13th st across. Work a blue line up the 3rd st to the right of every fuchsia line.

LEFT FRONT
Work blue lines up the 8th/8th, 20th/21st and 32nd/34th sts from side edge. Work a fuchsia line up the 3rd st to the right of every blue line, and up the 2nd st from centre front.

RIGHT FRONT

Counting from the centre front, work a blue line up the 2nd/2nd, 14th/15th, 26th/28th and 38th/41st sts. Work a fuchsia line up the 3rd st to the right of every blue line.

SLEEVES

Counting from the right side edge, work a blue line up the 10th st and every following 12th st. Work a fuchsia line on the 3rd st to the right of every blue line.

Finishing

Using backstitch seams, join shoulders, side seams and sleeve seam, taking care to match stripes. Set in sleeves, making 2 pleats in the sleeve head either side of shoulder seam. Join front bands to front edge, taking care to follow coloured line. Oversew collar to neck edge. Sew on buttons, positioning one at the top and bottom and the rest where horizontal lines meet the front band. With crochet hook, make chain st loops at edge of right front band to correspond to buttons, taking care to match pattern. If desired, make twisted cord in silk and thread through neckline.

Geometrics from Four Student Designers

[See double page photograph overleaf]

Art college students are developing hand-knitting along new lines. Rectilinear and geometric designs and the flat square shapes of Japanese knits inspire student knitters today rather than the concentrations of pattern and texture that the previous wave of creative designers has favoured.

The new graphic approach was particularly striking among the designs submitted for the student competition, sponsored jointly by the International Wool Secretariat, the yarn company Lister-Lee and *Woman* magazine. I selected four sweaters for this book.

Dorinda Binns, a fashion student at Hastings College of Art and Technology, is interested in geometrically based patterns using only two or three colours (another contrast with the previous trend for multi-colour and pattern). 'My designs include a lot of straight edges and stark shapes in contrast to the fluidity of the human body,' she explains. 'I like to think that my designs have a mannish elegance that can be adapted to men and women alike'. Dorinda is now working on a collection of patterned knits inspired by the London Underground and she hopes to go on to take a further fashion degree course at a London art college. Her checkerboard sweater is in the bottom left of the picture on page 88.

Jan Miller of Leicester Polytechnic thinks that her work has developed further since she designed her graphically stepped sweater for the student competition (see bottom right, page 89). She still tends to design strong colour combinations and bold flat patterns with texture adding a further dimension of interest. 'My most recent work includes materials other than yarn,' she says. 'I am using lengths of fabric and braid to give interesting effects.' Her Honours degree covers fashion, textile design and knitting by hand and machine. But hand-knitting is her major interest and she plans to set up her own hand-knitting business in the Oxford area where she had already sold her knitwear through specialist shops.

Helen Richards of Ravensbourne was taught to knit as a child by her mother, and it was her mother's skill which helped her make the hand-knit square-cut sweater with a chain mail effect which she submitted for the student competition (see top right page 89.) Helen is interested in hand-knitting, but since she has been at college she has also become involved with machine knitting and she hopes that in the future she will be able to make her knitting part of an integrated fashion collection.

Sharon Peake is also at Ravensbourne, studying fashion with knitting as a subsidiary subject. 'During this final year we are encouraged to integrate our subsidiary subject with our fashion studies, but not always in its usual form' she explains. 'For example, we may not actually knit; but instead we may try macramé, knotting and threading. On the other hand, we may find ourselves knitting with plastics or lace.' The sweater Sharon submitted (see top left, page 88) was ispired by Gothic architecture, using the shapes and colours of the stonework. She worked out the shape first in a toile form and then knitted it up 'with help from good old mum!'

Sharon's thesis for her degree is on the wool industry in the Faroe Islands, which she visited in order to talk to knitters and spinners and study their intricate traditional designs. When she leaves college she hopes to work, perhaps as an assistant, with someone already established in the knitwear business. 'I feel that however much we are taught at college, there is no substitute for actual experience in the process of learning. But eventually I would like to organise my own business through which I can express what I want to say about fashion.'

Dorinda Binns

See photograph overleaf, bottom left.

Dorinda Binns likes geometric patterns contrasting straight angles against the curve of the body. Her graphic checkerboard sweater in an Aran yarn is worked in stocking stitch in just two colours, using stripes and zig-zag patterns within the squares for effect. The flapped neckband is knitted in squares to form a castellated collar.

Size: 86cm (34in).

Yarn: Lister-Lee Pure Wool Aran.
MY: 6 × 50g balls Peat.
A: 5 × 50g balls Light Stone.

Needles: 6mm (no. 4) and 4mm (no. 8).

Tension: 21 rows and 19 sts to 10cm (4in) square.

Back

* With 4mm (no. 8) needles and MY cast on 86 sts.
Work 16 rows K1, P1 rib.
Change to 6mm (no. 4) needles. Work 2 rows st.st in MY, then work the pattern st.st according to the chart, starting with stitches 4 to 46, then 1 to 46, and then 1 to 43. Continue until 60 pattern rows have been completed.

ARMHOLE SHAPING
Cast off 3 sts at beg of next 2 rows. Dec 1 st at each end of the next and every following 2nd row 5 times until 70 sts remain.**
Continue straight patterning until a total of 36 pattern rows have been completed from beg of armhole shaping.

SHOULDER SHAPING
Cast off 7 sts at beg of next 4 rows.
Cast off 8 sts at beg of next 2 rows.
Cast off remaining 26 sts.

Front

Work as back from * to ** (but when patterning starts begin 3rd row, MY 2 sts then cross pattern).
Continue straight patterning until 26 pattern rows are completed.

NECK SHAPING
Next row, patt 32 sts. Cast off 6 sts, pattern to end of row.
Working right hand side only, leave remaining left hand side sts on needle.
K2 tog at neck edge of next 10 rows.
Continue patterning, keeping neck edge straight.
Shape the shoulder.
Cast off 7 sts at beg of next 2 rows at armhole edge.
Knit 1 row and cast off remaining 8 sts.
Work left hand side the same but reverse neck and shoulder shaping.

Sleeves

With 4mm (no. 8) needles and MY cast on 42 sts. Work 16 rows K1, P1 rib.
Change to 6mm (no. 4) needles.
Work 2 rows st.st in MY inc 1 st at each end of first and every following 6th row. Continue st.st following sequence of pattern from the chart, starting with st 2 and ending with st 45, and then working increase sts into the pattern as set. Work until 72 rows have been completed since the ribbing.

SLEEVE TOP SHAPING
Keeping pattern correct, cast off 3 sts at beg next 2 rows.
Then K2 tog beg of next 16 rows. K2 tog at each end of following 13 rows.
Cast off remaining 18 sts.

Neckband

Join right shoulder seams, with right side facing using 4mm (no. 8) needles and MY pick up 40 sts around front neck and 32 sts evenly around back neck.
Rib 16 rows.
Cast off in rib.

Finishing

Press. Join left shoulder and neckband seam, turn neckband under and sew down.
Join side and sleeve seams.

FLAPS AROUND NECKBAND
Using 4mm (no. 8) needles and MY, starting at shoulder seam, pick up 18 sts evenly around base of front neckband. Work st.st MY1, A1, repeat for stripes.
Work 16 rows, cast off.
Repeat this three more times at front and three times at back.

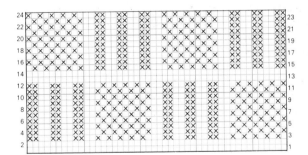

Jan Miller

See photograph page 89, bottom right

Jan Miller uses bold, flat textured patterns in strong colour combinations. Her geometrically stepped sweater in double knitting uses just three colours worked in dramatic zig-zags of pattern. A mixture of plain knitting and basket weave adds interest to the texture.

Size: 86cm (34in). Actual measurement: 101cm (40in). Length: 63cm (25in). Sleeve seam: 49cm (19in).

Yarn: Lister-Lee Motoravia D.K. (used double throughout).
MY: 13 × 50g balls Ginger.
A: 5 × 50g balls Devon Cream.
B: 3 × 50g balls Light Navy.

Needles: $4\frac{1}{2}$mm (no. 7) and $5\frac{1}{2}$mm (no. 5).

Tension: 16 sts and 24 rows knitted over st.st on $5\frac{1}{2}$mm (no. 5) needles to 10cm (4in) square.

Special abbreviation: pw = purlwise.

Back

With $4\frac{1}{2}$mm (no. 7) needles and MY cast on 80 sts and work in K1, P1 rib for 18 rows.
Change to $5\frac{1}{2}$mm (no. 5) needles and continue in pattern as follows:
Row 1 and every following odd numbered row, knit.
Row 2 and every following even numbered row, purl.
Row 1: 34B, 4A, 2B, 13A, with MY k2 (YFD, Sl 3, pw, YBK, K5) 3 times, K1.
Row 2: With MY P1 (P5, YBK, Sl 3, pw, YFD) 3 times, P2, 13A, 2B, 4A, 34B.
Row 3: As Row 1.
Row 4: 27MY, 13A, 2B, 4A, 34B.
Row 5: 34B, 4A, 2B, 13A, with MY K1, (K5, YFD, Sl 3, pw, YBK) 3 times, K2.
Row 6: With MY P2, (YBK, Sl 3, pw, YFD, K5) 3 times P1, 13A, 2B, 4A, 34B.
Row 7: 34MY, 4A, 9B, 6A, with MY K1 (K5, YFD, Sl 3, pw, YBK) 3 times, K2.
Row 8: 27MY, 6A, 9B, 4A, 34B.
Row 9: 34B, 4A, 9B, 6A, with MY K2, (YFD, Sl 3, pw, YBK, K5) 3 times, K1.
Row 10: With MY P1, (P5, YBK, Sl 1, pw, YFD) 3 times, P2, 6A, 2B, 11A, 34B.
Row 11: 34B, 11A, 2B, 6A, with MY K2, (YFD, Sl 3, pw, YBK, K5) 3 times, K1.
Row 12: 27MY, 6A, 2B, 11A, 34MY.
Row 13: 41B, 4A, 2B, 6A, with MY K1, (K5, YFD, Sl 3, pw, YBK) 3 times, K2.
Row 14: With MY P2, (YBK, Sl 3, pw, YFD, P5) 3 times, P1, 6A, 2B, 4A, 41B.
Row 15: As Row 13.
Row 16: 27MY, 6A, 2B, 4A, 41B.
Row 17: 41B, 4A, 2B, 13A, with MY K3, (YFD, Sl 3, pw, YBK, K5) twice, K1.
Row 18: With MY P1, (P5, YBK Sl 3, pw, YFD) twice, P3, 13A, 2B, 4A, 41B.
Row 19: As Row 17.
Row 20: 20MY, 13A, 2B, 4A, 41B.
Row 21: 41B, 4A, 2B, 13A, with MY K2, (K5, YFD, Sl 3, pw, YBK) twice, K2.
Row 22: With MY P2, (YBK, Sl 3, pw, YFD, P5) twice, P2, 13A, 2B, 4A, 41B.
Row 23: 41B, 4A, 9B, 6A, with MY K2, (K5, YFD, pw, YBK) twice, K2.
Row 24: 20MY, 6A, 9B, 4A, 41B.
Row 25: 41B, 4A, 9B, 6A, with MY K3, (YFD, Sl 3, pw, YBK) twice, K1.
Row 26: With MY P1, (P5, YBK, Sl 3, pw, YFD) twice, P3, 6A, 2B, 11A, 41B.
Row 27: 41B, 11A, 2B, 6A, with MY, K3, (YFD, Sl 3, pw, YBK, K5) twice, K1.
Row 28: 20MY, 6A, 2B, 11A, 41B.
Row 29: 48B, 4A, 2B, 6A, with MY K2, (K5, YFD, Sl 3, pw, YBK) twice, K2.
Row 30: With MY P2 (YBK, Sl 3, pw, YFD, P5) twice, P2, 6A, 2B, 4A, 48B.
Row 31: As Row 29.
Row 32: 20MY, 6A, 2B, 4A, 48B.
Row 33: 48B, 4A, 2B, 13A, with MY K4, YFD, Sl 3, pw, YBK, K6.
Row 34: With MY P6, YBK, Sl 3, pw, YFD, p4, 13A, 2B, 4A, 48B.
Row 35: 5A, 43B, 4A, 2B, 13A, with MY K4, YFD, Sl 3, pw, YBK, K6.
Row 36: 13B, 13A, 2B, 4A, 43B, 5A.
Row 37: 5A, 43B, 4A, 2B, 13A, with MY K8, YFD, Sl 3, pw, YBK, K2.
Row 38: With MY P2, YBK, Sl 3, pw, YFD, P8, 13A, 2B, 4A, 43B, 5A.
Row 39: 5A, 43B, 4A, 9B, 6A, with MY K8, YFD, Sl 3, pw, YBK, K2.
Row 40: 13MY, 6A, 9B, 4A, 43B, 5A.
Row 41: 5A, 43B, 4A, 9B, 6A, with MY K4, YFD, Sl 3, pw, YBK, K6.
Row 42: With MY P6, YBK, Sl 3, pw, YFD, P4, 6A, 2B, 11A, 43B, 5A.
Row 43: 5A, 43B, 11A, 2B, 6A, with MY K4, YFD, Sl 3, pw, YBK, K6.
Row 44: 13MY, 6A, 2B, 11A, 43B, 5A.
Row 45: 5A, 50B, 4A, 2B, 6A, with MY K8, YFD, Sl 3, pw, YBK, K2.
Row 46: With MY P2, YBK, Sl 3, pw, YFD, P8, 6A, 2B, 4A, 50B, 5A.
Row 47: As Row 45.
Row 48: 13MY, 6A, 2B, 4A, 50B, 5A.
Row 49: 5A, 50B, 4A, 2B, 13A, 6MY.
Row 50: 6MY, 13A, 2B, 4A, 50B, 5A.
Row 51: 12A, 43B, 4A, 2B, 13A, 6MY.
Row 52: 6MY, 13A, 2B, 4A, 43B, 12A.
Row 53: 12A, 43B, 4A, 2B, 13A, with MY K1, YFD, Sl 3, pw, YBK, K2.
Row 54: With MY P2, YBK, Sl 3, pw, YFD, P1, 13A, 2B, 4A, 43B, 12A.
Row 55: 12A, 43B, 4A, 9B, 6A, with MY K1, YFD, Sl 3, pw, YBK, K2.

Row 56: 6MY, 6A, 9B, 4A, 43B, 12A.
Row 57: 6B, 6A, 43B, 4A, 9B, 6A, 6MY.
Row 58: 6MY, 6A, 2B, 11A, 43B, 6A, 6B.
Row 59: 6B, 6A, 43B, 11A, 2B, 6A, 6MY.
Row 60: 6MY, 6A, 2B, 11A, 43B, 6A, 2B, 4A.
Row 61: 4A, 2B, 6A, 50B, 4A, 2B, 6A, with MY K1, YFD, Sl 3, pw, YBK, K2.
Row 62: With MY P2, YBK, Sl 3, pw, YFD, P1, 6A, 2B, 4A, 50B, 6A, 2B, 4A.
Row 63: As Row 61.
Row 64: 6MY, 6A, 2B, 4A, 50B, 6A, 2B, 4A.
Row 65: 4A, 2B, 6A, 50B, 4A, 2B, 12A.
Row 66: 12A, 2B, 4A, 50B, 6A, 2B, 4A.
Row 67: 4A, 2B, 13A, 43B, 4A, 2B, 12A.
Row 68: 12A, 2B, 4A, 43B, 13A, 2B, 4A.
Row 69: As Row 67.
Row 70: As Row 68.
Row 71: 4A, 2B, 13A, 43B, 4A, 9B, 5A.
Row 72: 5A, 9B, 4A, 43B, 13A, 2B, 4A.
Row 73: 4A, 9B, 6A, 43B, 4A, 9B, 5A.
Row 74: 5A, 2B, 11A, 43B, 6A, 9B, 4A.
Row 75: 4A, 9B, 6A, 43B, 11A, 2B, 5A.
Row 76: 5A, 2B, 11A, 43B, 6A, 2B, 11A.
Row 77: 11A, 2B, 6A, 50B, 4A, 2B, 5A.
Row 78: 5A, 2B, 4A, 50B, 6A, 2B, 11A.

ARMHOLE SHAPING
Row 79: With MY cast off 4 sts, 2MY, 4A, 2B, 6A, 50B, 4A, 2B, 5A.
Row 80: With A cast off 4 sts, 2B, 4A, 50B, 6A, 2B, 4A, 3MY.
Row 81: With MY K2 tog, 1MY, 4A, 2B, 6A, 50B, 4A, 2B, 1A.
Row 82: With B P2 tog, 1B, 4A, 50B, 6A, 2B, 4A, 2MY.
Row 83: With MY K2 tog, 4A, 2B, 13A, 43B, 4A, 2B.
Row 84: With B P2 tog, 4A, 43B, 13A, 2B, 5A.
Row 85: With A K2 tog, 3A, 2B, 13A, 43B, 4A, 1B.
Row 86: With A, P2 tog, 3A, 43B, 13A, 2B, 4A.
Row 87: With A K2 tog, 2A, 2B, 13A, 43B, 4A.
Row 88: With A, P2 tog, 2A, 43B, 13A, 2B, 3A.
Row 89: With A, K2 tog, 1A, 9B, 6A, 43B, 3A.
Row 90: 3A, 9B, 6A, 43MY, 2A.
Row 91: 2A, 9B, 6A, 43MY, 3A.
Row 92: 2A, 43MY, 6A, 9A.
Row 93: 9A, 2B, 6A, with MY K4, (YFD, Sl 3, pw, YBK, K5) 5 times, K1.
Row 94: With MY P1, (P5, YBK, sl 3, pw, YFD) 5 times, P4, 6A, 2B, 9A.
Row 95: 5MY, 4A, 2B, 6A, with MY K4 * YFD, Sl 3 pw, YBK, K5, rep from * 5 times, K1.
Row 96: 45MY, 6A, 2B, 4A, 5MY.
Row 97: With MY K1, YFD, Sl 3, pw, YBK, K1, 4A, 2B, 6A, with MY K3, (K5, YFD, Sl 3, pw) 5 times, K2.
Row 98: With MY P2, (YBK, Sl 3, pw, YFD, P5) 5 times, P3, 6A, 2B, 4A, with MY P1, YBK, Sl 3, pw, YFD, P1.
Row 99: With MY K1, YFD, Sl 3, pw, YBK, K1, 4A, 2B, 13A, with MY K1, (YFD, Sl 3, pw, YBK, K5) 5 times, ending last repeat K2.
Row 100: 38MY, 13A, 2B, 4A, 5MY.
Row 101: 5MY, 4A, 2B, 13A, with MY K5, (YFD, Sl 3, pw, YBK, K5) 4 times, K1.
Row 102: With MY P1, (P5, YBK, Sl 3, pw, YFD) 4 times, P5, 13A, 2B, 4A, 5MY.
Row 103: As Row 101.
Row 104: 38MY, 13A, 2B, 4A, 5MY.
Row 105: With MY, K1, YFD, Sl 3, pw, YBK, K1, 4A, 9B, 4A, with MY K1, (YFD, Sl 3, pw, YBK, K5) 5 times, ending last repeat K2.
Row 106: With MY P2, YBK, Sl 3, pw, YFD, (P5, YBK, Sl 3, pw, YFD) 4 times, P1, 6A, 9B, 4A, with MY P1, YBK, Sl 3, pw, YFD, P1.
Row 107: As Row 105.
Row 108: 38MY, 6A, 2B, 11A, 5MY.
Row 109: 5MY, 11A, 2B, 6A, with MY (K5, YFD, Sl 3, pw, YBK) 4 times, K6.
Row 110: With MY P6 (YBK, Sl 3, pw, YFD, P5) 4 times, 6A, 2B, 11A, 5MY.
Row 111: 12MY, 4A, 2B, 6A, with MY (K5, YFD, Sl 3, pw, YBK) 4 times, K6.
Row 112: 38MY, 6A, 2B, 4A, 12MY.
Row 113: With MY K1, YFD, Sl 3, pw, YBK, K8, 4A, 2B, 6A with MY K4, (K5, YFD, Sl 3, pw, YBK) 4 times, K2.
Row 114: With MY P2 (YBK, Sl 3, pw, YFD, p5) 4 times, P4, 6A, 2B, 4A, with MY P8, YBK, Sl 3, pw, YFD, P1.
Row 115: With MY K1, YFD, Sl 3, pw, YBK, K8, 4A, 2B, 13A, with MY K2 (YFD, Sl 3, pw, YBK, K5) 4 times, ending last repeat K2.
Row 116: 31MY, 13A, 2B, 4A, 12MY.
Row 117: With MY, K5, YFD, Sl 3, pw, YBK, K4, 4A, 2B, 13A, with MY K1, (K5, YFD, Sl 3, pw, YBK) 3 times, K6.
Row 118: With MY P6 (YBK, Sl 3, pw, YFD, P5) 3 times, P1, 13A, 2B, 4A with MY P4, YBK, Sl 3, pw, YFD, P5.
Row 119: As Row 117.
Row 120: 31MY, 13A, 2B, 4A, 12MY.
Row 121: With MY K1, YFD, Sl 3, pw, YBK, K8, 4A, 9B, 6A, with MY K2, (YFD, Sl 3, pw, YBK, K5) 4 times, ending last repeat K2.
Row 122: With MY P2, YBK, Sl 3, pw, YFD, (P5, YBK, Sl 3, pw, YFD) 3 times, P2, 6A, 9B, 4A, with MY P8, YBK, Sl 3, pw, YFD, P1.
Row 123: As Row 121.
Row 124: 31MY, 6A, 2B, 11A, 12MY.
Row 125: With MY K5, YFD, Sl 3, pw, YBK, K4, 11A, 2B, 6A, with MY K6, (YFD, Sl 3, pw, YBK, K5) 3 times, K1.
Row 126: With MY P1, (P5, YBK, Sl 3, pw, YFD) 3 times, P6, 6A, 2B, 11A, with MY P4, YBK, Sl 3, pw, YFD, P5.
Row 127: With MY K5, YFD, Sl 3, pw, YBK, K11, 4A, 2B, 6A, with MY K6 (YFD, Sl 3, pw, YBK, K5) 3 times, K1.
Row 128: 31MY, 6A, 2B, 4A, 19MY.
Row 129: With MY cast off 4 sts, 14MY, 4A, 2B, 6A, 31MY.
Row 130: With MY cast off 4 sts, 26MY, 6A, 2B, 4A, 15MY.
Row 131: With MY cast off 5 sts, 9MY, 4A, 2B, 6A, 27MY.
Row 132: With MY cast off 5 sts, 21MY, 6A, 2B, 4A, 10MY.

Row 133: 44MY.

Leave these stitches on a thread for neckband.

Front

Work as for back until Row 111 has been completed

DIVIDE FOR NECK

P20 MY leave these sts on a spare needle for right front. Leave next 22 sts on thread for Neckband. Continue on remaining 20 sts as follows:

Row 112 (Purl): 2A, 2B, 4A, 12MY.

Row 113: With MY K1, YFD, Sl 3, pw, YBK, K8, 4A, 2B, K2 tog A.

Row 114: P2 tog B, 1B, 4A, with MY P8, YBK, Sl 3, pw, YFD, P1.

Row 115: With MY K1, YFD, Sl 3, pw, YBK, K8, 4A, K2 tog 5B.

Row 116: P2 tog A, 3A, 12MY.

Row 117: With MY K5, YFD, Sl 3, pw, YBK, K4, 2A, K2 tog A.

Row 118: P2 tog A, 1A, with MY P4, YBK, Sl 3, pw, YFD, P5.

Row 119: With MY, K5, YFD, Sl 3, pw, YBK, K4, K2 tog A. Break off A and B and continue in MY only.

Row 120: P2 tog, P11.

Row 121: K1, YFD, Sl 3, pw, K6, K2 tog.

Row 122: P7, YBK, Sl 3, pw, YFD, P1.

Row 123: K1, YFD, Sl 3, pw, YBK, K5, K2 tog.

Row 124: P10.

Row 125: K5, YFD, Sl 3, pw, YBK, K2 tog.

Row 126: P1, YBK, Sl 3, pw, YFD, P5.

Row 127: K5, YFD, Sl 3, pw, YBK, K1.

Row 128: P9.

Row 129: Cast off 4 sts, K to end.

Row 130: P5.

Cast off remaining 5 sts.

RIGHT FRONT

Rejoin yarn to remaining 20 sts at neck edge using MY throughout.

Row 113: K2 tog, (K5, YFD, Sl 3, pw, YBK) twice, K2.

Row 114: P2, (YBK, Sl 3, pw, YFD, P5) twice, ending last repeat P4, P2 tog.

Row 115: K2 tog, K3 (YFD, Sl 3, pw, YBK, K5) twice, ending last repeat K2.

Row 116: P15, P2 tog.

Row 117: K2 tog, K5, YFD, Sl 3, pw, YBK, K6.

Row 118: P6, YBK, Sl 3, pw, YFD, P4, P2 tog.

Row 119: K2 tog, K3, YFD, Sl 3, pw, YBK, K6.

Row 120: P11, P2 tog.

Row 121: K2 tog, K5, YFD, Sl 3, pw, YBK, K2.

Row 122: P2, YBK, Sl 3, pw, YFD, P6.

Row 123: K2 tog, K4, YFD, Sl 3, pw, YBK, K2.

Row 124: P10.

Row 125: K2 tog, K8.

Row 126: P9.

Row 127: K9.

Row 128: Cast off 4 sts, P to end.

Row 129: K5.

Row 130: Cast off remaining 5 sts.

Sleeves

Using 4½mm (no. 7) needles and MY cast on 42 sts and work 16 rows in K1, P1 rib increasing 15 sts evenly across last row (57 sts).

Change to 5½mm (no. 5) needles and continue in pattern as follows (sleeves are worked in MY throughout):

Row 1: (K5, YFD, Sl 3, pw, YBK) 7 times, K1.

Row 2: P1 (YBK, Sl 3, pw, YFD, P5) 7 times.

Row 3: As Row 1.

Row 4: Purl.

Row 5: K1, (YFD, Sl 3, pw, YBK, K5) 7 times.

Row 6: (P5, YBK, Sl 3, pw, YFD) 7 times, P1.

Row 7: As Row 5.

Row 8: Purl.

Repeat these 8 rows until 132 rows have been completed.

SHAPE HEAD

Keeping pattern correct, continue as follows:

Cast off 4 sts at beg of next 2 rows.

Work 2 rows straight.

Cast off 1 st at beg of next 2 rows.

Repeat the last 4 rows 4 times (39 sts).

Cast off 1 st at beg of every row to 24 sts.

Cast off loosely.

Neckband

Join right shoulder seam. Using 4½mm (no. 7) needles and MY pick up and knit 22 sts down Left Front, K across 22 sts at Centre Front, pick up and knit 22 sts up Right Front and knit across 44 sts at Centre Back (110 sts).

Work 9 rows K1, P1, rib.

Cast off ribwise.

Finishing

Follow pressing instructions on ball band. Join left shoulder seam and neckband seam. Join side and sleeve seams.

Helen Richards

See photograph page 89, top right

Helen Richards' square cut and chain mail effect show twin preoccupations with shape and surface interest. The flat Aran sweater in garter stitch and purl knitting is worked square, with no hip band ribbing, the garter stitch used in one colour for the sleeves and long polo collar.

Size: 86cm (34in).

Yarn: Lister-Lee Aran.
MY: 13 × 50g balls Peat.
A: 5 × 50g balls Miss Scarlet.

Needles: 7½mm (no. 1) and 6¾mm (no. 3).

Tension: 30 sts and 16 rows knitted in st.st on 7½mm (no. 1) ndls to 10cm (4in) square.

Back

Cast on 142 sts in MY with 7½mm (no. 1) ndls.
Row 1: P2 MY, P2 A, rep to end.

PATTERN
Row 2: 2 MY * slip the A sts onto a cable needle, leave at back, K next 2 sts with MY then K the sts on cable needle with A, rep from * to end of row.
Row 3: Purl all sts.
Row 4: * Slip the first 2 sts onto cable needle, leave at front, K2 MY then knit sts on cable needle in A. Repeat from * to last 2 sts, K2.
Row 5: Purl all sts.
These 4 rows form pattern.
Cont in pattern to row 55.
Cast off 4 sts at beg of next 2 rows.
Cont in pattern to row 92.

SHOULDER SHAPING
Row 93: Cast off 10 sts on shoulder edge on this and any following alt row to row 101. At same time shape neckline.

NECKLINE
Row 93: Knit 58 sts, hold remaining 67 sts on spare needle.
Row 94: Cast off 3 sts at neck edge.
Row 95: Purl.
Row 96: Knit. Cast off 10 sts at neck edge.
Row 97: Purl.
Row 98: As row 96.
Row 99: Purl.
Row 100: Cast off 6 sts at neck edge.
Row 101: Purl.
Cast off.
Reverse shaping on sts on spare needle.

Front

As Back to row 85.

NECKLINE
Hold 67 sts on spare needle.
Row 86: On neck edge cast off 6 sts on this and every foll alt row to row 93 (see back for shoulder shaping).
Row 94: Cast off 2 sts at neck edge.
Row 95: Purl.
Repeat last 2 rows to row 101. Cast off.
Reverse shaping on sts on spare needle.

Sleeves

(two alike)
Using MY, cast on 42 sts with 7½mm (no. 1) needles. Knit in garter st. On 8th and every foll 8th row increase by 1 st both ends to row 124. Cast off.

Collar

Using MY, cast on 42 sts with 7½mm (no. 1) needles. In garter st knit straight to row 120. Cast off.

Cuffs

(two alike)
Using MY, cast on 12 sts with 6½mm (no. 3) needles. In garter st knit straight to row 50, cast off.

Binding

Using yarn A, cast on 8 sts with 6½mm (no. 3) needles. In st.st knit three lengths to stretch slightly around arm holes and bottom of jumper.

Finishing

Stitch shoulder and side seams together. Sew ends of collar together. Attach collar by oversewing. Oversew cuffs to sleeves, stretching the cuffs to fit. Sew seams. Attach sleeves, sew binding and sleeves to bodice, with seam on outside. Bring binding over seam, stitch onto bodice.
Stitch binding to bottom.

Sharon Peake

See photograph page 88, top left

Sharon Peake was inspired by Gothic church windows and the quiet grey colours of mediaeval stonework to make a two-colour sweater with a window pattern across the body. Pattern and texture from the double rib welt complement the angular effect of the square-cut sleeves.

Size: 86cm (34in).

Yarn: Lister-Lee Aran.
MY: 16 × 50g balls Peat.
A: 4 × 50g balls Irish Cream.

Needles: 4½mm (no. 7) and 4mm (no. 8).

Tension: 20 sts and 28 rows to 10cm (4in) square.

Special Abbreviations: wwrt = winding wool round twice. Cross sts = knit the 4th, 5th and 6th sts, then the 1st, 2nd and 3rd sts, dropping the 4th, 5th and 6th from the left hand ndl as the 1st, 2nd and 3rd are knitted.

Front

With 4mm (no. 8) needles and MY cast on 114 sts.
Work 15 rows K2, P2.
Change to 4½mm (no. 7) needles.
Row 16: P3 in MY * Sl 1, P6 in A, wwrt, Sl 2, P6 in A, wwrt, Sl 2, P6 in A, wwrt, Sl 2, P6 in A, wwrt, Sl 1 *, P6 in MY, rep from * to *, P6 in MY, rep from * to *, P3 in MY.
Row 17: K3 in MY * Sl 1, Sl next 6 sts onto right needle, dropping the extra loops, then pass the 6 sts back onto left needle and cross sts all in A, Sl 2, cross sts, Sl 2, cross sts, Sl 2, cross sts, Sl 1 * K6 in MY, rep from * to *, K 6 in MY, rep from * to *, K3, in MY.
Row 18: P3 in MY * Sl 1, P6 A, Sl 1 * P6 in MY, rep from * to *, P6 in MY, rep from * to *, P3 in MY.

Row 19: K3 in MY * Sl 1, K6 A, Sl 2, K6 A, Sl 2, K6 A, Sl 2, K6 A, Sl 1 * K6 MY, rep from * to *, K6 MY, rep from * to *, K3 MY.
Row 20: P row: with MY P the slip st of previous rows, inserting needle through the st and under the threads drawn across the back of work.
Row 21: P row MY.
Row 22: P3 MY, * P3, Sl 2., P6 A, wwrt, Sl 2, P6 A, wwrt, Sl 2, P6 A, wwrt, Sl 2, P3 A, * P6 MY, rep from * to *, P6 MY, rep from * to * P3 MY.
Row 23: K3 MY. * K3 A, Sl 2, cross sts, Sl 2, cross sts, Sl 2, cross sts, Sl 2, K3 A * K6 MY rep from * to *, K6 MY, rep from * to * K3 MY.
Row 24: P3 MY * P3 A, Sl 2, P6 A, Sl 2, P6 A, Sl 2, P6 A, Sl 2, P3 A, * P6 MY, rep from * to * P6 MY, rep from * to *, P3 MY.
Row 25: K3 MY, * K3 A, Sl 2, K6 A, Sl 2, K6 A, Sl 2, K6 A, Sl 2, K3 A * K6 MY, rep from * to *, K6 MY, rep from * to *, K3 MY.
Row 26: P row MY: P the slip stitch of previous rows inserting needle through the st and under the threads drawn across the back of work.
Row 27: P row MY.
Repeat rows 16 to 27 over and over (ending with a row 21) until row 81.
Row 82: P6 MY, * Sl 2, P6 A, wwrt, Sl 2, P6 A, wwrt, Sl 2, P6 A, wwrt, Sl 2 * P12 MY, rep from * to *, P12 MY, rep from * to *, P6 MY.
Rows 83 to 87: complete pattern as laid down in row 82.
Row 88: P10 MY * Sl 2, P6 A, wwrt, Sl 2, P6 A, wwrt, Sl 2 * P20 MY, rep from * to *, P20 MY, rep from * to *, P10 MY.
Rows 89 to 93: Complete pattern as laid down in row 88.
Row 94: P14 MY, * Sl 2, P6 A, wwrt, Sl 2 * P28 MY, rep from * to *, P28 MY, rep from * to *, P14 MY.
Rows 95 to 99: Complete pattern as laid down in row 94.
Row 100: Purl in MY.
Row 101: Knit in MY.
Row 102: Purl in MY.
Row 103: Knit in MY.

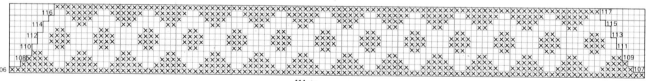

114 sts

Chart 1: Front

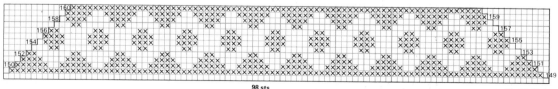

98 sts

Chart 2: Sleeve

⊠ **MY**
☐ **A**

Row 104: Purl in MY.
Row 105: Purl in MY.
Working in stocking stitch (1st row purl), work pattern as shown in chart 1. Decrease at ends of rows as shown.
Continue in MY only.
Rows 118 to 120: Purl.
Row 121: K.
Row 122: P.
Row 123: K.
Repeat the last 4 rows to Row 134.
Cast off centre 20 sts.
Cont in st.st (1st row knit) working one side at a time and decreasing 1 st at neck edge on every 4th row to row 170.

SHAPE SHOULDER
Cast off 10 sts at armhole edge on next 2 rows.
Cast off remaining sts.

Back

Work as for Front to row 134, then continue in st.st to row 168. Cast off centre 20 sts, working one side at a time cast off 1 st at the neck edge on the next 5 rows. When 2 of these rows have been completed cast off 10 sts at armhole edge on next 2 rows.
Cast off remaining sts.
Rejoin yarn to second side and complete to match.

Sleeves

Using 4mm (no. 8) needles and MY cast on 54 sts.
Work 15 rows K2, P2 rib.
Change to 4½mm (no. 7) needles.
Row 1: P.
Row 2: K.
Row 3: P.
Row 4: K.
Row 5: P.
Row 6: P. Increase one st at each end of this row.
Repeat these 6 rows until there are 98 sts on ndl. Then work straight to row 148.
Continue in st.st (1st row knit) from chart 2 decreasing 1 st at each end of every row.
Continue decreasing 1 st at each end of every row.
Row 161: P.
Row 162: P.
Row 163: K.
Row 164: P.
Row 165: K.
Row 166: P.
Row 167: P.
Row 168: P.
Row 169: K.
Row 170: P.
Cast off loosely.

Collar

Using 4mm (no. 8) needles and MY cast on 120 sts.
Work 20 rows K2, P2 rib.
Cast off in rib.

Finishing

Join raglan seams. Join side and sleeve seams. Sew on collar as illustrated. Press as instructions on ball band.

Warm and Wonderful: Bee Sweater

Jokey pictures, witty motifs and trompe l'oeil effects are all inventions of fashion. Such sophisticated ideas had no place in the work baskets of women who knitted to keep their families warm.

The first witty knits were conceived in France's capital of high fashion. Elsa Schiaparelli was the Italian-born designer who stunned Paris in the thirties with her use of dazzling colour and her sense of fun. The inventor of 'shocking' pink (and a perfume of the same name) was an implacable enemy of Chanel and her refined simplicity. 'Schiap' was a close friend of Dali and the surrealists, and both Dali and Picasso drew decorative designs for her collections. In her search for originality, she picked out surreal motifs in sequins on her sweaters and even worked Impressionist painting in hand-knitting.

Her most famous surreal sweater was a skeleton design – the bones standing out across the front in white on a black ground. She was also the first to use trompe l'oeil effects in knitting, like her much copied cravat sweater with a floppy Chanel-style bow worked as a pattern at the neck.

Such rarified and exquisite handwork is a far cry from today's witty picture sweaters run off for mass production on a computerized machine, or even the T-shirt with a message, that is a direct descendant of the witty knits. But the famous 'Schiap' might be pleased to know that the original, witty and one-off sweaters that she invented are still being made fifty years on.

Joanna Osborne and Sally Muir started by counting sheep – especially a black one who regularly turned up amid a fleecy textured flock grazing across the body of their simple sweaters.

Sally Muir's mother had given her a knitting machine for Christmas and Joanna was working for Granada Television when they decided to team their two home knitting machines and start a business in Battersea, South London. With a nice sense of tongue in chic, they called their company 'Warm and Wonderful'.

Both girls had a feeling for the fun of wearing a woolly and from sheep they exploited a whole range of domestic animals: pigs, chickens, calves, geese. Their Christmas inspiration was a sweater scattered with strutting poultry with a turkey served up on a plate in the middle.

The buzzing 'Z' motif in the pattern for this book is in black on waspish golden yellow, with four fat-bodied knitted bees planted strategically on the shoulder and body.

The first stitches of Warm and Wonderful were knitted in Joanna's bedroom five years ago. Now forty knitters work for them and they have a small shop filled with their colourful creations. Both partners learned to knit as children – Sally at school, Jo at her mother's knee – and they find hand-knitting more creative than working rows of rams on the machine that dominates the shop.

Perhaps because they have had no art school training, they start work on a collection by thinking of a theme and choosing their yarns. They consider texture and colour to be important in hand-knitting and their newest thoughts are for a pot pourri of yarns and stitches. 'We've done so many sheep in rows,' says Sally, 'that we have a sudden urge to do something irregular and mad.'

Warm and Wonderful knit wit into their stitches. Their chunky yellow and black buzzing bee jumper, with four fat bees perched on shoulder and body, is knitted in stocking stitch, with the Z motif every ten rows. The bees are knitted in garter stitch stripes, stuffed, trimmed with wings and sewn on near the rouleau neck.

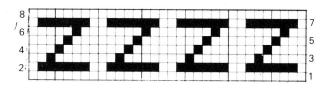

Sizes: To fit bust 85/90/95cm (34/36/38in). Actual chest measurement: 91/97/102cm (36/38/40in). Length from top of shoulder 57/59/60cm (22½/23/23½in). Sleeve seam 43cm (17in) for all sizes.

Yarn: St John's Chunky pure wool.
MY: 7 × 100g hanks Yellow.
A: 2 × 100g hanks Black.
Yarn available by mail order from St. John's Knitting Wool Company Ltd, P.O. Box 55, 39 Well Street, Bradford, West Yorkshire DD1 5NG.

Needles: 6mm (no. 4); 5mm (no. 6) and 4½mm (no. 7).

Tension: 15 sts and 19 rows knitted in st.st on 6mm (no. 4) ndls to 10cm (4in) square.

Special abbreviations: follow chart for 'z' throughout jumper, repeating every 10 rows.

Back

Using 5mm (no. 6) ndls and yellow cast on 70/74/78 sts and work 10 rows in K1, P1 rib. Change to 6mm (no. 4) ndls and work 2 rows st.st. Start the 'z' pattern following the chart weaving the yarn across the back. Repeat the 'z' pattern every 10 rows and continue in st.st until the back measures 34/35/36cm (13/13½/14in) ending with a P row.

RAGLAN SHAPING
Cast off 4 sts at beg of next 2 rows.
Then dec 1 st at both ends of this and every foll alt row until 22/24/26 sts remain. Cast off.

Front

Work as for back until 34/36/38 sts rem in armhole shaping, ending with a P row.

SHAPE NECK
K2 tog, K9, turn and leave rem sts on spare ndl. Now dec 1 st at each end of every alt row until 3/3/4 sts rem. Cont dec at raglan edge only as before until 2 sts rem ending with a P row. K2 tog and fasten off. Go back to other sts, slip centre 12/14/16 sts onto a st holder, then with right side facing, rejoin yarn to rem sts and work to match other side.

Sleeves

Using 5mm (no. 6) ndls and yellow cast on 30/32/34 sts and work 10 rows of K1, P1 rib. Change to 6mm (no. 4) ndls and work 2 rows in st.st. Start the 'z' pattern, and repeat as for back and front. Inc 1 st at both ends of the 5th (after the ribbing) and every foll alt 6th row until there are 52/54/56 sts. Work straight until sleeve measures 43cm (17in) ending with a P row.

SHAPE TOP
Cast off 4 sts at beg of next two rows then dec 1 st at both ends of this and every foll alt row until 6 sts remain, ending after a P row. Cast off.

Neckband

Join raglan seams leaving left back seam open. Now with right side facing, using 6mm (no. 4) ndls and yellow pick up sts across back and around the front neck and sleeve tops.
St.st for 14 rows and cast off loosely.

Finishing

Press st.st parts with a warm iron using a damp cloth. Join rem raglan seam and neckband. Join side and sleeve seams.

TO KNIT THE BEES
(4 alike)
Using 4½mm (no. 7) ndls cast on 3 sts in black.
Continue in garter st.
Row 1: inc 1 st at both ends of this row (5 sts).
Row 2: K5 in yellow.
Row 3: K5 in yellow.
Row 4: inc 1 st at both ends of this row in black (7 sts).
Row 5: K7 in black.
Row 6: K7 in yellow.
Row 7: K7 in yellow.
Row 8: in black inc 1 st at both ends of this row (9 sts).
Row 9: K9 in black.
Row 10: K9 in yellow.
Row 11: K9 in yellow.
Row 12: in black dec 1 st at both ends (7 sts).
Row 13: K7 in black.
Row 14: in black dec 1 st at both ends (5 sts).
Row 15: K5 in black.
Row 16: K5 in black.
Cast off.
Using one of the black ends, sew up, stuffing the bee with the spare ends. Wind the wool around the black end to form the head. Sew on two wings. Sew the bees onto the jumper leaving the head free.

Jenny Kee: The Royal Connection

When the Princess of Wales appeared in a jolly koala bear jumper, it was greeted as a fashion innovation. The idea of a Princess (and a pregnant one at that) wearing a sloppy sweater appeared to some as lèse-majesté, as though the humble peasant craft of knitting was not suitable for the royal family.

Yet the history of hand-knitting has been closely bound up with royalty. The flourishing knitted hose industry in the sixteenth century is credited to Queen Elizabeth I, who was inspired by a pair of hand-knitted silk stockings brought back from France and given to her as a present by the Earl of Oxford. 'Let me have a shirt more than ordinary,' said King Charles I, to his servant on the morning of his execution, 'by reason the season is so sharp as probably may make me shake, which some will imagine proceeds from fear. I would have no such imputation; I fear not death. Death is not terrible to me. I bless my God I am prepared.' He chose knitted silk as his additional shirt, to keep him warm and as suitable covering for a King on his way to the scaffold.

To Queen Victoria we owe the fact that many Scottish knitwear patterns were saved from extinction. The royal interest in British arts and crafts at the Great Exhibition of 1851, revived an enthusiasm for hand-knitting and helped to preserve and disseminate examples of Fair Isle and Shetland knitting.

Hand-knitting has been worn by most modern monarchs, and even by the late Duke of Windsor (then Prince of Wales) whose portrait by John St. Helier Lander painted in 1925 shows him wearing an autumnal coloured V-necked Fair Isle jumper and tweed knickerbockers – a fashion he helped to popularise in the twenties.

Our own Queen, as Princess Elizabeth, was often seen in the neat, nannified twin sets so much a part of pre-war childhood, and portraits of her and her sister Margaret Rose show them in kilts and sweaters. Even now, the Queen is often photographed at Balmoral in her woollies, including a traditional Aran sweater.

The shock of Diana's pullover was that it was a joke, with its bright koala bear on the front. It is actually Prince Charles' sweater (her own version is a kangaroo that was too small to fit over the baby bulge) and the pair of jumpers were a royal wedding gift from Kim Wran, daughter of the Premier of New South Wales.

Their creator Jenny Kee who produced a simpler version of the royal sweater for this book, sees her designs not as witty knits on an Australian theme, but as a patriotic attempt to boost interest in Australian fashion.

'I started off with the idea of creating an Australian fashion image,' explains Jenny, who worked as a designer in London in the sixties and now has her own small shop called Flamingo Park in Sydney. 'Wool and sheep are as typical of Australia as kangaroos and koalas, so I took our pure new wool and created the hand-knitted sweaters with the Australian motifs.'

Jenny Kee worked in the Chelsea Antique Market when she lived in London, and she dates from that time her interest in beautifully made couture clothes. She feels that good hand-knits have the same quality of originality and individuality, as well as being, in this royal example, a splendid piece of Australian image-building.

Jenny Kee brought the jokey jumper into the royal limelight with her koala bear sweater for Princess Diana. This simplified version of the sweater is worked in stocking stitch, in a Fair Isle pattern according to the chart and plain sleeves. The grey Koala bear motif is teamed with scarlet, yellow and bright navy.

Size: Chest 105cm (42in). Length 70cm (28in). Sleeve length 45.5cm (18in).

Yarn: Aran-weight knitting wool.
MY: 14 × 50g balls Navy.
A: 2 × 50g balls Red.
B: 2 × 50g balls Grey.
C: small quantity Yellow.

Needles: 4½mm (no. 7) and 5½mm (no. 5).

Tension: 35 sts knitted in st.st on 5½mm (no. 5) ndls to 20cm (8in) square.

Back

With 4½mm (no. 7) ndls and MY cast on 69 sts.
Work 18 rows in K1, P1 rib inc 23 sts evenly on last row (92 sts).
Change to 5½mm (no. 5) ndls and cont in st.st.*
Work 96 rows. Place markers at each end of last row to mark beg of armholes.
Work 42 rows.

SHAPE SHOULDERS
Cast off 10 sts at the beg of next 2 rows.
Cast off 9 sts at the beg of next 4 rows.
Cast off remaining 36 sts.

Front

Work as back to *. Work 4 rows st.st in MY only. Commence Fair Isle, following either the chart or the written instructions as you prefer. Use separate lengths of yarn for each section of colour, joining in and breaking off as required. Do not weave yarn across back of work. Cross over yarns at back of work at each colour change.
If you are following the chart, work 7 sts in MY at each side of the chart. Read the knit rows from right to left, the purl rows from left to right.
Row 5 and every following odd row knit. Row 6 and every following even row, purl.
Row 5 (first row of chart): 34MY, 20A, 38MY.
Row 6: 38MY, 20A, 34MY.
Row 7: 33MY, 22A, 37MY.
Row 8: 36MY, 23A, 33MY.
Row 9: 33MY, 24A, 35MY.
Row 10: 35MY, 25A, 32MY.
Row 11: 32MY, 26A, 34MY.
Row 12: 33MY, 27A, 32MY.
Row 13: 15MY, 1A, 15MY, 30A, 31MY.
Row 14: 30MY, 14A, 6B, 11A, 15MY, 1A, 15MY.
Row 15: 15MY, 2A, 14MY, 8A, 12B, 12A, 29MY.
Row 16: 28MY, 11A, 16B, 7A, 13MY, 2A, 15MY.
Row 17: 14MY, 3A, 13MY, 5A, 20B, 10A, 27MY.
Row 18: 26MY, 9A, 23B, 4A, 13MY, 3A, 14MY.
Row 19: 14MY, 3A, 12MY, 4A, 26B, 8A, 25MY.
Row 20: 24MY, 8A, 28B, 3A, 12MY, 4A, 13MY.

Row 21: 13MY, 4A, 12MY, 2A, 30B, 8A, 23MY.
Row 22: 22MY, 9A, 30B, 2A, 12MY, 4A, 13MY.
Row 23: 12MY, 5A, 12MY, 1A, 32B, 8A, 22MY.
Row 24: 21MY, 9A, 33B, 13MY, 4A, 12MY.
Row 25: 12MY, 4A, 13MY, 34B, 9A, 20MY.
Row 26: 20MY, 9A, 35B, 12MY, 4A, 12MY.
Row 27: 12MY, 4A, 12MY, 36B, 9A, 19MY.
Row 28: 19MY, 9A, 36B, 12MY, 4A, 12MY.
Row 29: 12MY, 4A, 11MY, 3B, 1A, 1B, 2A, 31B, 9A, 18MY.
Row 30: 18MY, 9A, 32B, 1A, 1B, 2A, 2B, 11MY, 4A, 12MY.
Row 31: 12MY, 4A, 11MY, 6A, 32B, 9A, 18MY.
Row 32: 17MY, 9A, 34B, 5A, 11MY, 5A, 11MY.
Row 33: 11MY, 5A, 11MY, 5A, 34B, 9A, 17MY.
Row 34: 16MY, 10A, 35B, 4A, 11MY, 5A, 11MY.
Row 35: 11MY, 5A, 11MY, 4A, 36B, 9A, 16MY.
Row 36: 15MY, 10A, 36B, 4A, 11MY, 6A, 10MY.
Row 37: 10MY, 6A, 11MY, 4A, 36B, 10A, 15MY.
Row 38: 14MY, 10A, 38B, 3A, 11MY, 7A, 9MY.
Row 39: 9MY, 7A, 11MY, 3A, 38B, 1MY, 9A, 14MY.
Row 40: 13MY, 9A, 2MY, 38B, 3A, 11MY, 8A, 8MY.
Row 41: 9MY, 7A, 11MY, 3A, 38B, 3MY, 8A, 13MY.
Row 42: 12MY, 8A, 4MY, 38B, 3A, 11MY, 6A, 10MY.
Row 43: 8MY, 1A, 2MY, 6A, 10MY, 3A, 39B, 3MY, 8A, 12MY.
Row 44: 11MY, 8A, 4MY, 26B, 1A, 12B, 3A, 10MY, 9A, 8MY.
Row 45: 8MY, 9A, 10MY, 4A, 10B, 3A, 25B, 4MY, 8A, 11MY.
Row 46: 10MY, 8A, 5MY, 26B, 3A, 9B, 4A, 10MY, 9A, 8MY.
Row 47: 8MY, 10A, 9MY, 5A, 7B, 3A, 27B, 5MY, 8A, 10MY.
Row 48: 11MY, 6A, 6MY, 28B, 4A, 4B, 6A, 9MY, 10A, 8MY.
Row 49: 7MY, 11A, 9MY, 13A, 29B, 6MY, 5A, 12MY.
Row 50: 12MY, 4A, 7MY, 30B, 12A, 8MY, 12A, 7MY.
Row 51: 7MY, 12A, 8MY, 12A, 30B, 7MY, 3A, 13MY.
Row 52: 13MY, 2A, 8MY, 30B, 12A, 8MY, 12A, 7MY.
Row 53: 7MY, 13A, 7MY, 13A, 29B, 9MY, 1A, 13MY.
Row 54: 23MY, 27B, 5A, 4B, 6A, 7MY, 13A, 7MY.
Row 55: 7MY, 13A, 7MY, 2A, 10B, 4A, 26B, 23MY.
Row 56: 23MY, 25B, 3A, 14B, 7MY, 13A, 7MY.
Row 57: 7MY, 12A, 6MY, 17B, 1A, 26B, 23MY.
Row 58: 24MY, 40B, 10MY, 11A, 7MY.
Row 59: 7MY, 10A, 10MY, 41B, 24MY.
Row 60: 24MY, 43B, 7MY, 11A, 7MY.
Row 61: 7MY, 13A, 8MY, 40B, 24MY.
Row 62: 24MY, 41B, 7MY, 13A, 7MY.
Row 63: 7MY, 14A, 5MY, 42B, 24MY.
Row 64: 25MY, 42B, 4MY, 14A, 7MY.
Row 65: 7MY, 14A, 4MY, 2B, 5A, 35B, 25MY.
Row 66: 25MY, 33B, 7A, 6MY, 14A, 7MY.
Row 67: 7MY, 14A, 6MY, 8A, 32B, 25MY.
Row 68: 26MY, 30B, 10A, 5MY, 14A, 7MY.
Row 69: 7MY, 14A, 5MY, 12A, 28B, 26MY.
Row 70: 26MY, 26B, 14A, 5MY, 13A, 8MY.
Row 71: 8MY, 14A, 4MY, 12A, 1B, 3A, 24B, 26MY.
Row 72: 26MY, 22B, 3A, 3B, 12A, 4MY, 14A, 8MY.
Row 73: 8MY, 14A, 3MY, 13A, 5B, 2A, 21B, 26MY.
Row 74: 27MY, 27B, 13A, 3MY, 13A, 9MY.

Row 75: 9MY, 13A, 3MY, 12A, 28B, 27MY.
Row 76: 28MY, 27B, 12A, 3MY, 13A, 9MY.
Row 77: 10MY, 12A, 2MY, 13A, 27B, 28MY.
Row 78: 28MY, 27B, 13A, 2MY, 12A, 10MY.
Row 79: 10MY, 11A, 3MY, 13A, 26B, 29MY.
Row 80: 29MY, 26B, 13A, 3MY, 10A, 11MY.
Row 81: 12MY, 9A, 3MY, 13A, 26B, 29MY.
Row 82: 27MY, 19B, 1A, 9B, 13A, 3MY, 7A, 13MY.
Row 83: 14MY, 6A, 3MY, 13A, 8B, 4A, 18B, 26MY.
Row 84: 25MY, 18B, 6A, 7B, 13A, 3MY, 6A, 14MY.
Row 85: 15MY, 4A, 3MY, 14A, 6B, 5A, 21B, 24MY.
Row 86: 24MY, 24B, 4A, 4B, 14A, 3MY, 3A, 16MY.
Row 87: 17MY, 3A, 2MY, 14A, 32B, 24MY.
Row 88: 23MY, 20B, 2A, 12B, 12A, 2MY, 2A, 19MY.
Row 89: 20MY, 1A, 2MY, 11A, 12B, 4A, 19B, 23MY.
Row 90: 22MY, 20B, 5A, 11B, 10A, 24MY.
Row 91: 23MY, 10A, 12B, 6A, 19B, 22MY.
Row 92: 22MY, 14B, 3A, 2B, 7A, 11B, 11A, 22MY.
Row 93: 21MY, 11A, 12B, 7A, 2B, 3A, 15B, 21MY.
Row 94: 21MY, 15B, 3A, 2B, 7A, 12B, 11A, 21MY.
Row 95: 21MY, 11A, 12B, 7A, 20B, 21MY.
Row 96: 21MY, 20B, 6A, 12B, 12A, 21MY (Place markers at each end of row).
Row 97: 21MY, 11A, 8B, 3A, 2B, 6A, 20B, 21MY.
Row 98: 21MY, 20B, 6A, 2B, 3A, 9B, 11A, 20MY.
Row 99: 20MY, 11A, 9B, 3A, 3B, 5A, 20B, 21MY.
Row 100: 22MY, 20B, 4A, 16B, 10A, 20MY.
Row 101: 20MY, 10A, 17B, 3A, 20B, 22MY.
Row 102: 22MY, 40B, 10A, 20MY.
Row 103: 19MY, 11A, 39B, 23MY.
Row 104: 13MY, 5C, 5MY, 10B, 1MY, 28B, 11A, 19MY.
Row 105: 19MY, 11A, 27B, 5MY, 6B, 4MY, 9C, 11MY.
Row 106: 10MY, 11C, 15MY, 26B, 11A, 19MY.
Row 107: 19MY, 11A, 24B, 16MY, 13C, 9MY.
Row 108: 8MY, 15C, 23MY, 16B, 11A, 19MY.
Row 109: 20MY, 10A, 15B, 24MY, 15C, 8MY.
Row 110: 7MY, 17C, 24MY, 13B, 11A, 20MY.
Row 111: 19MY, 13A, 11B, 25MY, 17C, 7MY.
Row 112: 7MY, 17C, 26MY, 9B, 14A, 19MY.
Row 113: 18MY, 16A, 6B, 28MY, 17C, 7MY.
Row 114: 7MY, 17C, 33MY, 17A, 18MY.
Row 115: 20MY, 15A, 33MY, 17C, 7MY.
Row 116: 8MY, 15C, 35MY, 12A, 22MY.
Row 117: 25MY, 9A, 35MY, 15C, 8MY.
Row 118: 9MY, 13C, 37MY, 5A, 28MY.
Row 119: 31MY, 2A, 38MY, 11C, 10MY.
Row 120: 11MY, 9C, 72MY.
Row 121: 74MY, 5C, 13MY.
Cont in MY only. Purl 1 row.

SHAPE NECK
Next row: K39, turn. Leave remaining sts on spare needle. Dec 1 st at neck edge on every row until 28 sts remain. Work 4 rows without shaping.

SHAPE SHOULDER
Cast off 10 sts at the beg of the next row. Purl 1 row.
Cast off 9 sts at the beg of the next row. Purl 1 row.
Cast off remaining 9 sts.
Return to sts left on spare needle. Cast off centre 14 sts, knit to end.

Dec 1 st at neck edge only on every row until 28 sts remain.
Work 5 rows without shaping.

SHAPE SHOULDER
Cast off 10 sts at the beg of the next row. Knit 1 row.
Cast off 9 sts at the beg of the next row. Knit 1 row.
Cast off remaining 9 sts.

Sleeves

With 4½mm (no. 7) ndls and MY cast on 31 sts. Work rib as Back, inc 6 sts evenly on last row. Change to 5½mm (no. 5) ndls and cont in st.st inc 1 st at each end of 5th and every following 6th row until 13 inc rows have been worked. (63 sts).
Cont until work measures 45.5cm (18in), or length required.
Cast off loosely.

Finishing

Sew in all ends securely. Press work lightly on wrong side, omitting ribs. Backstitch right shoulder seam.

NECKBAND
With right side of work facing, using 4½mm (no. 7) ndls and MY, pick up and knit 19 sts side neck, 12 sts centre neck, 19 sts side neck, 36 sts back neck (86 sts).
Work 24 rows K1, P1 rib. Cast off loosely.
Backstitch left shoulder seam and top of sleeves between markers. Flat sew ends of neckband together, fold in half to inside and slip sew down.
Flat sew ribs, backstitch side and sleeve seams. Press seams.

Jenny Kee and Jan Ayres

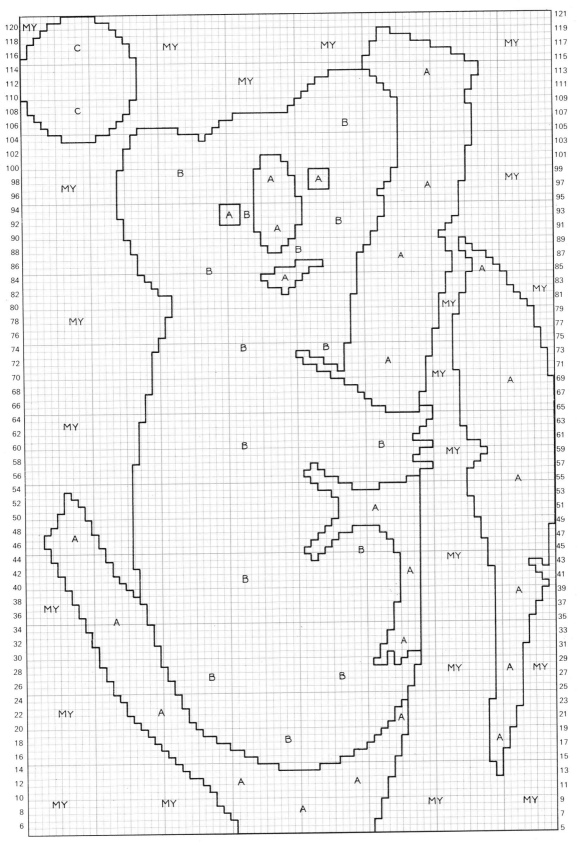

Work 7 sts MY each side of chart

Artwork: Open Weave Sweater and Paisley Patterned Mohair Sweater

[For Open Weave Sweater see photograph opposite. For Paisley Sweater see colour photograph opposite page 64]

The idea of decorating a sweater – especially with beading, sequins and paillettes – was the way that designers in the thirties came to terms with the new demand for sophisticated sportswear. In particular the American designer Mainbocher (the man who dressed the Duchess of Windsor) used the homely knitted cardigan, encrusted with lavish jewelled embroidery at the neck, as part of the new chic he imported from Paris to America in the post-war period. The high fashion for the beaded sweater found a distorted mirror image in the make-do-and-mend decorations sewed on to ancient sweaters in wartime Britain.

Fantastically decorated knitwear, often on the simplest body shapes, is the speciality of Artwork, whose design label aptly suggests their skill. Jane Foster and Patrick Gottelier met at art college, where they put their energies first into making welded clothes, then into Science Fiction costumes for the theatre. While Patrick tried to build a regular career in the display department of Marks and Spencer, Jane went on to work at the costume department of the BBC, where she was able to study the history of dress – a subject that her mother teaches at art school.

When Jane and Patrick decided to set up a creative knitting business together in 1977, they thought in terms of historical themes. To this day, neither of them can knit, but they have a series of knitters working from their sketches to create the effects they want. 'Our knitwear is to do with shape and texture, rather than stitch effects,' explains Jane. 'I find that I have to start a collection by thinking of a theme. Otherwise I would find the designing difficult.'

These past themes have included necklets of coloured beading to recreate Egyptian collars, lurex knitted up loosely into a 'chain mail' for the Mediaeval collection and pieces of beaten metal decorating the knitting of their celtic sweaters.

Their discreetly decorated evening sweater (see colour photograph opposite page 64) has tiny pearl beads illuminating the paisley motifs that glow like coloured jewels on the fluffy black mohair. The stripy Artwork linen and cotton summer sweater (opposite) is in a different mood.

'I spend a lot of time in the V and A library, looking at books and studying textiles,' explains Jane. 'For the Egyptian collection, I went to the British Museum and actually drew from the mummies to get the patterns right. Of course we don't want our things to look like historical costumes, and we are now moving away from the beading and getting more involved with the yarns. Decoration is less important when you can get interesting yarns.'

Artwork started marketing its own yarns in 1981 and since then they have expanded the wholesale side of their business, with 80 per cent of their knits going overseas to America, Italy, Paris and Japan. 'My favourite sweaters were the very early ones we did based on famous painters, recreating Picasso and Miro in intarsia knitting,' says Jane. 'But our most copied sweater was the simple cotton-knit summer sweater with a scribble pattern in black and white. You still see that around today.'

Open Weave Sweater

Artwork's designers like to create surface texture and interest. They believe too in the summer sweater made in simple sporty shapes. Their stringy sweater in mixed sugared almond pastel yarns uses cotton and viscose with linen and cotton. The open weave pattern is knitted in a double loop stitch from a double rib with a full body shape and raglan sleeve.

Sizes: To fit bust 81–86.5/91.5–96.5cm (32–34/36–38). Body length 34.5/37cm (13½/14½in) to underarm. Sleeve length 40.5/42cm (16/16½in) to underarm.

Yarn:
MY: 450g Mixed Pastels cotton/viscose.
A: 250g White linen/cotton.

Yarn is available in kit form from Artwork, 103 Bermondsey Street, London SE1.

Needles: 3¼mm (no. 10) and 5mm (no. 6).

Tension: 18 sts and 26 rows knitted in st.st on 5mm (no. 6) ndls to 10cm (4in) square.

Back and front

Using 3¼mm (no. 10) ndls and A, cast on 70/74 sts.
Row 1: * K2, P2, rep from * to last 2 sts, K2.
Row 2: * P2, K2, rep from * to last 2 sts, P2.
Rep these two rows until work measures 8cm (3¼in) ending with row 1.
Next row: As row 2, increasing 10/12 sts evenly across the row (80/86 sts).
Changing to 5mm (no. 6) ndls begin pattern, as follows:
Row 1: With A, K1, * K2 tog, rep from * to last st, K1.
Row 2: With MY, K1, * K into next st winding yarn twice around the ndl, pick up the thread between this st and the next st and knit it in the same way, rep from * to last st, K1.
Row 3: With MY, K to end dropping off thee extra loops.
Row 4: With A, K1, P to last st, K1.
These four rows form the pattern.
Continue in pattern until work measures 34.5/37cm (13½/14½in), ending with row 4.
N.B. Measure work when it is hanging from the ndl.
Mark each end of last row to denote beginning of armhole shaping.

SHAPE ARMHOLES
(Right side facing)
Work rows 1 to 4 inclusive of pattern again.
Next row: Sl 1, K2 tog, PSSO, pattern to last 3 sts, K3 tog.
Keeping pattern correct, work 3 more rows.
Rep these last 4 rows until 42 sts remain.
With A, K 2 rows.
Cast off loosely.

Sleeves

Using 3¼mm (no. 10) ndls and A, cast on 38/42 sts.
Work 7cm (2¾in) in rib as for back ending with row 1.

Next row: As row 2, increasing 12 sts evenly across the row (50/54 sts). Change to 5mm (no. 6) ndls and work in pattern as for back, increasing 2 sts at each end of the 9th and every 8th row until 74/78 sts (increase by working twice into the first 2 and last 2 sts).
Keeping pattern correct continue straight until work measures 40.5/42cm (16/16½in) ending with row 4 of pattern. (Mark each end of last row to denote beginning of shaping).

SHAPE SLEEVE TOP
(Right side facing)
Next row: Sl 1, K2 tog, PSSO, pattern to last 3 sts, K3 tog.
Keeping pattern correct, work 3 rows straight.
Rep last 4 rows 3/4 times more.
Next row: Sl 1, K2 tog, PSSO, pattern to last 3 sts, K3 tog.
Work 2 rows straight.
Next row: Sl 1, P2 tog, PSSO, pattern to last 3 sts, P3 tog.
Rep last 4 rows until 4 sts remain.
Next row: With A (P2 tog) twice.
Next row: K2 tog.
Fasten off.

Finishing

Join raglan seams, being careful not to pull the stitches too tight.
Join side seams and sleeve seams.

Paisley Patterned Mohair Sweater

Fantastically decorated knitwear is Artwork's speciality. Their fluffy black mohair sweater has Paisley motifs outlined in pearl beads. It is knitted from a double rib in stocking stitch with raglan shoulders and a roll collar. The motifs are in four jewel colours decorated with beads.

Sizes: To fit bust 86–89/91.5–94cm (34–35/36–37in). Body length 34/36.5cm (13½/14½in) to underarm. Sleeve length 44cm (17½in) to underarm.

Yarn: Mohair.
MY: 275g Black.
A: 25g Peacock Green.
B: 25g Old Gold.
C: 25g Red.
D: 25g Purple.
Yarn is available in kit form from Artwork. 103 Bermondsey Street, London, SE1.

Needles: 5mm (no. 6); 5½mm (no. 5); 6½mm (no. 3).

Tension: 15 sts and 19 rows knitted in st.st on 5½mm (no. 5) ndls to 10cm (4in) square.

Notions: 200 × 5mm (¼in) round pearl beads.

Note: It may be necessary to use fuse wire to thread beads. Only use as many beads as are needed for each motif. When working from chart begin at bottom right-hand corner and continue in st.st beginning with a K row.

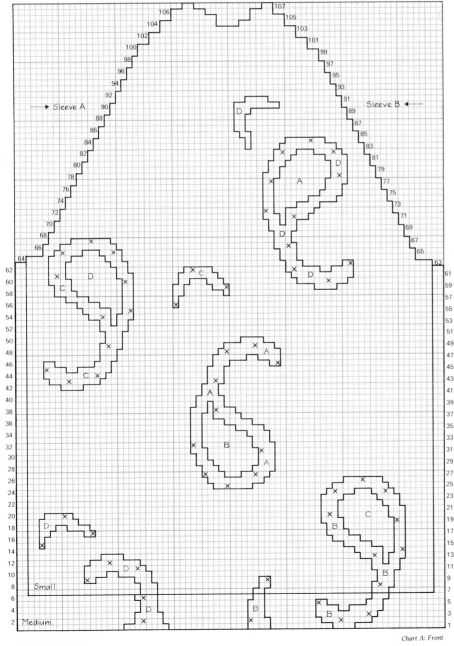

Chart A: Front

X = position of beads

Back and front

Using 5mm (no. 6) ndls, cast on 62 sts.
Row 1: * K2, P2, rep from * to last 2 sts, K2.
Row 2: * P2, K2; rep from * to last 2 sts, P2.
Rep last 2 rows until work measures 10cm (4in) ending with row 1.
Next row: Rib, increasing 10/14 sts evenly across row (72/76 sts). Change to 5½mm (no. 5) ndls and work from chart A for front, B for back, beg at bottom right-hand corner with a K row.

Sleeves

Using 5mm (no. 6) ndls, cast on 26 sts.
Work 9cm (3½in) in K2, P2, rib as for back.
Next row: Rib, increasing 4/8 sts evenly across row (30/34 sts).
Change to 5½mm (no. 5) ndls and work from charts C and D beg at bottom right-hand corner.

Collar

Join raglan seams, leaving left back seam open.
Using 5mm (no. 6) ndls, pick up 80 sts around neck including back neck and front sts.
Work 7.5cm (3in) in K2, P2, rib.
Change to 6½mm (no. 3) ndls and work a further 10cm (4in) in K2, P2, rib.
Change to 5mm (no. 6) ndls and work a further 4cm (1½in) in K2, P2, rib.
Cast off loosely.

Finishing

Use base yarn. Join collar seam and left back seam. Join side seams and underarm seams.

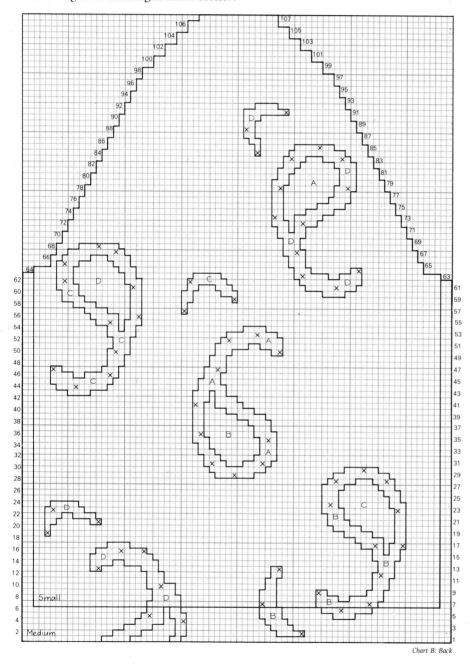

Chart B: Back

108

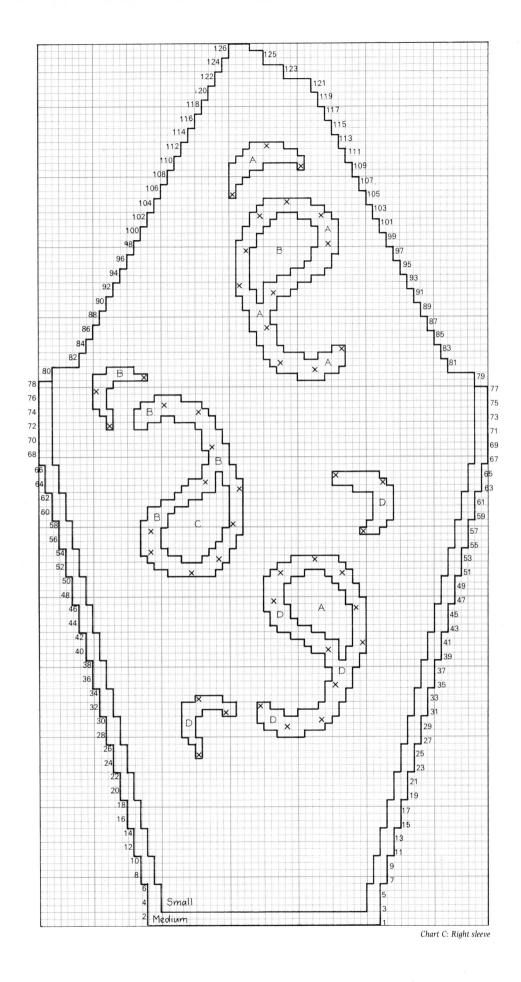

Chart C: Right sleeve

109

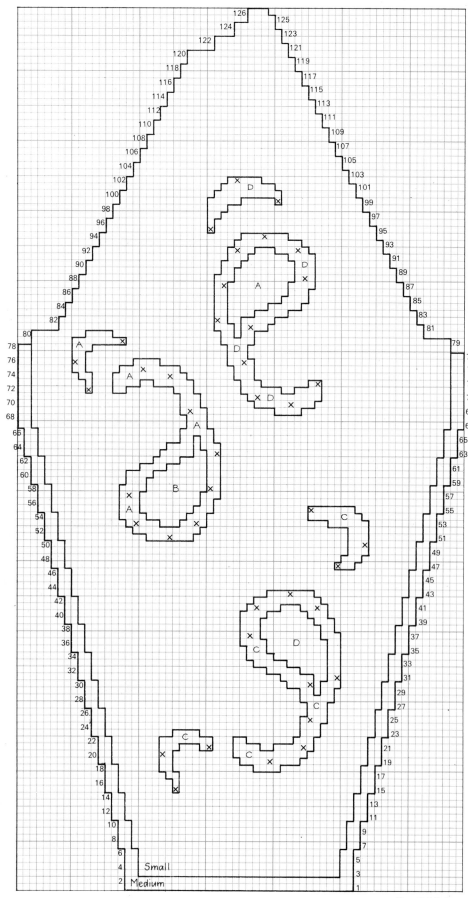

Chart D: Left sleeve

Anne Fewlass: Mediaeval Jacket

The distinction between art and craft in knitting is an awkward one. Without the skill of stitch-making, there is little craft, but equally a garment that is designed to clothe the human body has to be more than a mass of interesting stitches and textures. The British Crafts Council tends to classify 'craft knitters' as those who have extended the art by experimenting with new materials (even plastic, paper or metal can be knitted up), with a painter's palette of colours (often specially hand-dyed yarns) and with unusual finishes and textures.

Anne Fewlass has done all this on the machine. She creates mainly for the machine, producing beautifully finished, original and individual knits, mostly for private commissions. Multi-faceted bead tassels, tails and trims of fur and hand-painted buttons decorate her panelled jackets and richly coloured sweaters.

The carefully contrived clutter – pale pine, patterned rugs, Victorian fireplace and art deco artefacts – that fills her home, does not suggest the theme of her knitting, which is Mediaeval. Trumpet sleeves with insets of colour and texture in a Renaissance slashed effect, pageboy tunics and Florentine colours all suggest historic references. The full sleeved jacket (overleaf) that she designed for Laines Couture in this book emphasises her favourite theme.

'I have always had a feeling for Mediaeval clothes,' she says. 'I like their sense of richness and especially the big sleeves. I think that clothes should be theatrical. I am not interested in knitted classics like Fair Isle. To me they have no sense of drama.'

Anne Fewlass is affected by colour, which she often draws from antique or Eastern textiles. But at other times she will unconsciously draw inspiration from her surroundings. 'I like to have nice things round me in the workroom, because they give me visual input,' she says. 'Yet one day when I was working a tension sample I had picked a series of browns. And when I looked up I saw a dead aspidistra on the window sill and I realised that I had absorbed the exact brown of its leaves into my knitting.'

Anne's background was in fashion design and she says that fashion, and not knitting is her passion. 'I would say that I am really interested in the shape of clothes. They just happen to be made in knitting,' she explains.

She is also passionate about workmanship, finishing her knitting off with the care of a couturier and backing her zips and fastenings with silk. Her patterns are worked out for the machine, although she knows a lot too about the craft of hand knitting: 'I would say that if you can't hand knit well, you won't be able to machine knit properly – or at least to make anything creative.'

Anne Fewlass has always had a feeling for Mediaeval clothes. Her flared, trumpet sleeved jacket with coloured inserts is decorated with beaded tassels. It is knitted in stocking stitch using the contrast yarns double and working the body in one piece from the centre front opening. The sleeves are also worked round with the inserts gathered into the cuff edge.

Size: One size. Length, shoulder to hem, 67cm (26½in). Underarm seam 48cm (19in). Total width round body at underarm 102cm (40in).

Yarn: MY: Laines Plassard Musarde: 12 balls Cranberry.
Contrast 1: Laines Plassard Espiegle.
    1A: 2 balls (21) Grape.
    1B: 2 balls (30) Lichen.
    1C: 2 balls (23) Lilac.
    1D: 2 balls (22) Lavender.
    1E: 1 ball (28) Cornflower.
    1F: 1 ball (26) Sage.
Contrast 2: Laines Tiber Lumi-Tweed: 3 balls (786).
Yarn available from Laines Couture, 20 Bedford Street, London WC2.

Needles: 5mm (no. 6); 1 stitch holder.

Tension: 16 sts and 24 rows knitted in st.st. using MY on 5mm (no. 6) ndls to 10cm (4in) square.

Notions: Beads for tassle finish (optional).

Special abbreviations: cf = centre front; cb = centre back.

Stitches: Stocking stitch; reverse stocking stitch.

Order of colours: Main Body (right to left front): ABCDEA.
Right sleeve: AFCDEB.
Left sleeve: FDAECB.

Main body

(Knitted in one piece from right cf to cb, reverse shaping to left cf).
Using main yarn cast on 88 sts.
Row 1: K (right side facing).
Row 2: P.

PATTERN FOR BODY INSERTS
(Back, front and sides)
* Change to contrast 2.
Row 3: K.
Change to contrast 1A and work first insert as follows:
Row 4: P72, turn, leaving 16 sts waiting on needle.
Row 5: K1, P71 (right side facing).
Row 6: K66, turn, leaving 6 more sts waiting.
Row 7: K1, P65.
Row 8: P60, turn, leaving 6 more sts waiting. Continue thus on each even numbered row.
Row 9: K1, P59.
Row 10: K54.
Row 11: K1, P53.
Row 12: K48.
Row 13: K1, P47.
Row 14: K42.
Row 15: K1, P41.
Row 16: K36.
Row 17: K1, P35.
Row 18: K30.
Row 19: K1, P29.
Row 20: K24.
Row 21: K1, P23.
Row 22: K18.
Row 23: K1, P17.
Row 24: K12.
Row 25: K1, P11.

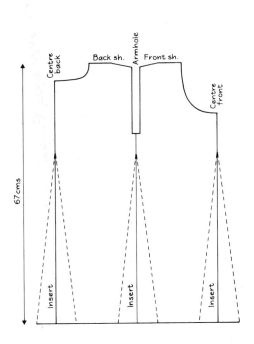

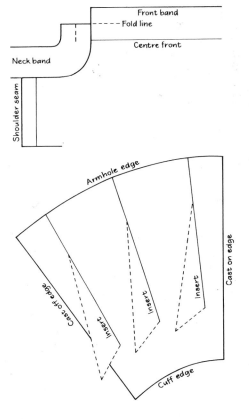

Row 26: K6.
Row 27: K1, P5.
Change to contrast 2.
P 1 row over full 88 sts.
K 1 row over full 88 sts.
Change to contrast 1B.
Row 1: P6 (back work facing).
Row 2: P6.
Row 3: K6, P6.
Row 4: P12.
Row 5: K12, P6.
Row 6: P18.
Row 7: K18, P6.
Row 8: P24.
Row 9: K24, P6.
Row 10: P30.
Row 11: K30, P6.
Row 12: P36.
Row 13: K36, P6.
Row 14: P42.
Row 15: K42, P6.
Row 16: P48.
Row 17: K48, P6.
Row 18: P54.
Row 19: K54, P6.
Row 20: P60.
Row 21: K60, P6.
Row 22: P66.
Row 23: K66, P6.
Row 24: P72.
Change to contrast 2.
P 1 row over full 88 sts.*
From * to * is shaping for 1 full insert (body only).

SHAPE NECK EDGE
Change to main yarn (keep to st.st).
Row 1: K.
Row 2: P.
With right side facing inc 1 st at neck edge every 2 rows 4 times (92 sts). Inc 1 st at neck edge every row 8 times (100 sts).
Cast on 8 sts at neck edge (108 sts).

SHAPE SHOULDER
Keeping to st.st for 30 rows dec 1 st at shoulder edge on rows 15, 20 and 25 (105 sts).

SHAPE ARMHOLE
With right side facing, cast off 23 sts, work to end.
At armhole edge dec 1 st every row 4 times (78 sts).
Work 2 rows keeping to st.st.

Work 2nd insert as for cf over 72 sts using contrast 2, 1C 1D.
Change to main yarn working in st.st and reverse armhole and shoulder shaping (108 sts).

SHAPE BACK NECK
Cast off 4 sts. Work to end.
At neck edge dec 2 sts over next 4 rows (102 sts). Work in st.st for 13 rows.

Work cb insert using contrast 2, 1E, 1A.
Complete the main body by reversing shaping to left centre front.

Right sleeve
Using main yarn cast on 80 sts.
Row 1: K.
Row 2: P.
Row 3: K60, turn, leaving 20 sts waiting on needle.
Row 4: P60.
Row 5: K48, turn, leaving 12 more sts waiting, and continue thus on all odd numbered rows.
Row 6: P48.
Row 7: K36.
Row 8: P36.
Row 9: K24.
Row 10: P24.
Row 11: K12.
Row 12: P12.
Row 13: K80.
Work in st.st over all sts for 6 rows. With wrong side of sleeve facing, work next 6 rows in st.st over first 20 sts on needle only. These 20 sts are for the cuff.
Break yarn and put these 20 sts on holder. Rejoin main yarn. P remaining 60 sts.

SLEEVE INSERT
Change to contrast yarn 2 (right side facing).
K 1 row.
Change to contrast yarn 1A.
Row 1: P40, turn, leaving 20 sts waiting on needle.
Row 2: K1, P39.
Row 3: K38, turn, leaving 2 more sts waiting on needle.
Row 4: K1, P37.
Row 5: K36, turn, leaving 2 more sts waiting on needle.
Row 6: K1, P35.
Work in this way until no sts left. Change to contrast yarn 2.
Row 1: P60.
Row 1: K60.
Change to contrast 1F.
Reverse above shaping picking up extra 2 sts every K row until 40 sts are being worked.
1 row P.
Change to contrast 2.
1 row P over, 60 sts.
This completes the insert.

** Change to main yarn.
Row 1: K80 picking up the 20 sts from holder.
Work in st.st for 7 more rows.
Right side of work facing.
Row 1: K12, turn, leaving 68 sts waiting on needle.
Row 2: P12.
Row 3: K24, turn leaving 12 more sts waiting on needle and continue thus on each odd numbered row.
Row 4: P24.
Row 5: K36.
Row 6: P36.
Row 7: K48.
Row 8: P48.
Row 9: K60.
Row 10: P60.
Row 11: K48.
Row 12: P48.
Row 13: K36.
Row 14: P36.

Row 15: K24.
Row 16: P24.
Row 17: K12.
Row 18: P12.
Work 8 rows st.st.**
Repeat insert shaping using contrast 2, 1C, 1D.
Change to main yarn.
Repeat from ** to **.
Repeat insert shaping using contrast 2, 1E, 1B.
Change to main yarn.
Shape at shoulder edge from ** to row 10.
1 row K.
1 row P.
Cast off.
Work left sleeve as right sleeve using contrast 1F, D, A, E, C, B.

Edging bands

These are worked by picking up sts with right side of work facing and knitting in st.st for 12 rows beg with a purl row in main yarn, then casting off, using contrast 2, *purlwise.*
Shoulders: pick up 20 sts front and back. Sew tog at R6.
Fold onto right side and sew band.
Armhole: pick up 70 sts.
Centre fronts: pick up 90 sts.
Neck edge: pick up 100 sts to row 6 of cf band.
Hem in 2 pieces: pick up 130 sts to cb and row 6 of cf band.
Cuff: Pick up 40 sts.

Finishing

Use back st for all seam and band finishing, using main yarn.

SLEEVE INSERTS
Working from back: Gather cuff edge of contrast inserts with a running stitch and secure tightly at both ends.
Catch into place.
Sew sleeve seam.
Fold band onto front at cuff pick up edge.
Sew below contrast 2.
Sew armhole band at shoulder edge.
Sew sleeve into armhole at pick up edge of main body.
Fold armhole band and sew.
Sew cf corner together at neck and hem.
Sew neck, cf and hem bands.

TASSELS
1. Contrast 1A, 1C, 1D.
2. Contrast 1B, 1E, 1F.
Using cut lengths of approx 33cm (13in) and 6 strands of each colour, make tassels approx 14cm (5½in) long.

STRINGS
1. Contrast 1A, 1C, 1D.
2. Contrast 1B, 1E, 1F.
Cut lengths approx 60 × 7.5cm (24 × 3in) each colour.
Thread through tassel head and plait.
Thread plait front to back at neck edge and secure with knot.
Bead tassel head optional.

Lumière: Summer Frills

Sweaters for the summer season have extended the fashion boundaries of knitwear. Loose and lacy cotton knits, often made up into simple T-shirt shapes, have the right sporty feel with current clothes. The lightweight sweater certainly has more style than the woolly cardigan that used to cover chilly shoulders in the cool Northern European summers. 'We thought that you could wear the frill-sleeve sweater in winter as well as summer,' says Megumi Ohki, one of the two partners behind the Lumière label. 'You can wear a lacy knit under a dinner suit instead of a dressy shirt,' explains Meg. 'And it is very good for the summer because that type of yarn knits up so crisply and the pattern is very clear.'

Hand-knit designers tend to work in natural fibres, and pure cotton (especially in fresh white or in a natural beige) is most frequently used for the summer sweaters, although pastel colours and even bright shades are now appearing. Because cotton, or that other summer favourite, knitted linen, does not have the give and resilience of woollen yarns, designers use lacy or open work effects to give depth, texture and range to summer knits.

Lumière's lacy cotton jumper (shown here) is shaped using the same system of panels – front, back, side and underarm – as for Lumière's cabled wool and lurex winter sweater (see page 75). There is the same asymmetric hemline to the sweater which is shorter at the front than the back. But the lacy stitch and the chevron frill sewn on down the outside of the sleeve gives a completely different overall effect.

Lumière believe that a lacy cotton knit can be worn on summer days and for winter parties. Their plain boat-necked sweater has an interesting textured stitch, which is echoed in the frill down the outside of the sleeve. The jumper is knitted in separate panels, with the front, back and outer sleeve worked in lacy stitch with plainer side and underarm panels, all joined together with the thonged overstitching. The chevron sleeve strip is sewn on when making up.

Size: one size.

Yarn: 11 × 50g balls 100% cotton Georges Picaud Canelle (available from John Lewis, Oxford Street, London W1).

Needles: 3¼mm (no. 10) and 2¾mm (no. 12).

Tension: 32 sts and 40 rows knitted in st.st on 3¼mm (no. 10) ndls to 10cm (4in) square.

Front panel

Using 3¼mm (no. 10) ndls cast on 134 sts.
Row 1: (K2, P2) to end, K2.
Row 2: P2, (K2, P2) to end.
Repeat these 2 rows until 5cm (2in) have been worked. Now work panel as diagram until piece measures 53cm (20in) including rib, ending with a wrong side row.
Change to 2¾mm (no. 12) ndls and work firmly in rib, as rows 1 and 2, repeating these 2 rows until 5cm (2in) have been worked.
Cast off in rib pattern.

Back panel

Work as for front panel, working until piece measures 58cm (23in) before final rib.
Cast off in rib pattern.

Side panel

(2 the same)
Using 2¾mm (no. 12) ndls cast on 50 sts and work 3 rows in K1, P1 rib.
Change to 3¼mm (no. 10) ndls and work as follows:
Row 1 (right side): K1, P1, K1, P1, * Sl 1, K2, PSSO 2 knit sts, K3. Rep from * to last 4 sts, K1, P1, K1, P1.
Row 2: P1, K1, P1, K1, P4 * yon, P5. Rep from * to last 5 sts, P2, K1, P1, K1.
Row 3: K1, P1, K1, P1, * K3, Sl 1, K2, PSSO 2 knit sts, rep from * to last 4 sts, K1, P1, K1, P1.
Row 4: P1, K1, P1, K1, P1 * yon, P5. Rep from * to last 3 sts, P5, K1, P1, K1.
Work until panel measures 28cm (11in) from cast on, ending with a wrong side row.

DIVIDE FOR ARMHOLE

Next row: work 24 sts in pattern. Cast off 2 sts. Work 24 sts in pattern. (Now work on these 24 sts only.)
Work 15 rows in pattern, decreasing 1 st at centre edge on every row (9 sts).
Work 1 row.
Now decrease 1 st at centre edge on following row and every following alternate row until 2 sts remain. Cast off.

Join yarn to remaining 24 sts and complete to match above.

Sleeves

(Work 2 pieces as below, then work 2 pieces in same manner reversing shaping and patterning to form mirror image.)
Using 2¾mm (no. 12) ndls cast on 36 sts.
Row 1: (K2, P2) to end.
Row 2: (K2, P2) to end.
Repeat these 2 rows until 5cm (2in) have been worked, ending with a right side row.
Next row (wrong side): Increase 15 sts evenly across row (51 sts).
Change to 3¼mm (no. 10) ndls and work as diagram inc 1 st at side seam edge (moss st side) at 7th row and every following 6th row until there are 69 sts in all. Continue in pattern until underarm seam (including rib) measures 45cm (17½in), ending with a right side row.

ARMHOLE SHAPING

Next row: cast off 7 sts. Work in pattern to end.
Work 2 rows.
Decrease 1 st at beginning of next row and every following 4th row (until 58 sts remain).
Work 4 rows.
Decrease 1 st at beginning of next row and every following 5th row until 52 sts remain.
Work 2 rows.
Decrease 1 st at beginning of next row and every following 3rd row until 49 sts remain.
Work 1 row.
Decrease 1 st at beginning of next row and following alternate rows until 46 sts remain.
Now decrease 1 st at shaped edge on every row until 37 sts remain.
Work 1 row.
Cast off.

Chevron sleeve strip

(2 the same)
Using 3¼mm (no. 10) ndls cast on 243 sts.
Work 2 rows knit.
Then work as follows:
Row 1: * K1, yrn to m1, K3, K2 tog (knitwise), SKPO, K3, m1. Rep from * to last st, K1.
Row 2 and alt rows: Purl.
Repeat these 2 rows 4 times more, then work row 1 again.
Next row: decrease 50 sts evenly across row (193 sts).
Change to 2¾mm (no. 12) ndls and firmly work 4 rows in K1, P1 rib.
Cast off in rib pattern.

Finishing

Press all pieces lightly on wrong side using warm iron and damp cloth.
Join shoulders for approx. 5cm (2in), using neat back st.
Join side panels to front and back panels with large over-stitches (giving thonged effect).

Using neat backstitch join top sleeve seam with chevron
strip in between, and underarm.
Join sleeve into armhole using neat back sts.

Moss st. 4 sts.	Leaf panel 7sts.	Bobble st. 5 sts.	Spanish lace pattern 102 sts.	Bobble st. 5 sts.	Leaf panel 7sts.	Moss st. 4 sts.
			Rib			

Front and back panels

Moss st. 2 sts.	Leaf panel 7sts.	Bobble st. 5 sts.	Spanish lace pattern 34 sts.	Purl 3 sts.
			Rib	

Sleeves

STITCH GUIDE
Bobble stitch (worked over 5 sts)
Row 1: P2, make bobble by (P1, K1) twice into next st, then take 2nd, 3rd, 4th sts over first st, P2.
Row 2: K2, P1, K2.
Row 3: P5.
Row 4: as row 2.

Spanish lace pattern (worked over 34 sts)
Rows 1, 5, 9: * K3, K2 tog, K4, m1, P2, (K2, yrn to m1, SKPO) 3 times, P2, m1, K4, SKPO, K3.*
Rows 2, 6, 10: * P2, P2 tog tbl, P4, m1, P1, K2, (P2, m1, P2 tog) 3 times, K2, P1, m1, P4, P2 tog, P2.*
Rows 3, 7, 11: * K1, K2 tog, K4, m1, K2, P2, (K2, m1, SKPO) 3 times, P2, K2, m1, K4, SKPO, K1.*
Rows 4, 8, 12: * P2 tog tbl, P4, m1, P3, K2, (P2, m1, P2 tog) 3 times, K2, P3, m1, P4, P2 tog.*
Rows 13, 17, 21: * m1, SKPO, K2, m1, SKPO, P2, m1, K4, SKPO, K6, K2 tog, K4, m1, P2, K2, m1, SKPO, K2.*
Rows 14, 18, 22: * m1, P2 tog, P2, m1, P2 tog, K2, P1, m1, P4, P2 tog, P4, P2 tog tbl, P4, m1, P1, K2, P2, m1, P2 tog, P2.*
Rows 15, 19, 23: * m1, SKPO, K2, m1, SKPO, P2, K2, m1, K4, SKPO, K2, K2 tog, K4, m1, K2, P2, K2, m1, SKPO, K2.*
Rows 16, 20, 24: * m1, P2 tog, P2, m1, P2 tog, K2, P3, m1, P4, P2 tog, P2 tog tbl, P4, m1, P3, K2, P2, m1, P2 tog, P2.*

Leaf panel (worked over 7 sts)
Row 1 (right side): P2, (K1, yon) twice, K1, P2.
Row 2: K2, P5, K2.
Row 3: P2, K2, yon, K1, yon, K2, P2.
Row 4: K2, P7, K2.
Row 5: P2, SKPO, K1 (yon, K1) twice, K2 tog, P2.
Row 6: Repeat row 4.
Row 7: P2, SKPO, K3, K2 tog, P2.
Row 8: Repeat row 2.
Row 9: P2, SKPO, K1, K2 tog, P2.
Row 10: K2, P3, K2.
Row 11: P2, yon Sl 2 knitwise, K1, pass 2 Sl sts over, yon, P2.
Row 12: repeat row 10.

Sarah Dallas: Pretty Pearls

The evening sweater is an invention of high fashion and this century. Women who knitted woolly workwear for their menfolk put their finer needles only to making underwear. The earliest pattern books contained light and lacy garments designed to be worn under conventional outer clothes.

Today, the delicate, dressy knitwear in very simple shapes matches the modern mood for relaxed sportswear. Clothing designers take day for night, making up the same trousers, T-shirts, trench coats and anoraks that are made in tough fabrics for day, in pure silks or satins for the evening.

For knitwear to come out at night, it also needs to be made in a luxurious yarn like pure silk or in fine cashmere, or to be knitted in lacy stitches, or to have its surface decorated with beading and embroidery.

'I enjoy the handwork of slotting through ribbons and sewing on pearls. I suppose it is a hangover from my college days,' says Sarah Dallas. On page 80 you can see her wearing the ethereal evening sweater photographed opposite.

The pretty knit is a British story, something that fits in with the sweet-toothed fashion style that is favoured for evening. It is also something which, as Sarah says, involves decorative handwork, which is quite separate from the technique of knitting. Flower embroidery or encrustations of beads and sequins can give a fancy effect to the plainest sweater.

But the best of these special effects are combinations of stitchcraft with decoration – something that Sarah Dallas understands because she teaches the art and craft of knitting.

Sarah Dallas enjoys the handwork of decorating a sweater with ribbons and pearls. Her long-sleeved cream cotton sweater is knitted in an all-over lacy pattern using V and flower openwork motifs. Satin ribbons are slotted vertically through the eyelet holes of the flowers and pearl beads are sewn into the V's by hand.

Sizes: Bust 80/85/90cm (32/34/36in). Actual size 85/90/95cm (34/36/38in).

Yarn: 7/8/8 × 50g balls Sirdar Majestic 4-ply.

Needles: 2¾mm (no. 12); 3¼mm (no. 10).

Tension: 28 sts over st.st on 3¼mm (no. 10) needles to 10cm (4in).

Notions: 7–8 metres satin ribbon 6mm (¼in) wide; approx. 275–300 pearls.

Back

Using 2¾mm (no. 12) needles cast on 106/114/122 sts.
Work 28 rows K1, P1, rib, inc 1 st at end of 28th row (107/115/123 sts).
Change to 3¼mm (no. 10) needles and pattern, as follows.
Row 1: K12/15/19 sts * SKPO, K3, yon, K1, yon, K3, K2 tog, K13, rep from * to last 12/15/19 sts, K.
Row 2 and every alt row: P.
Row 3: K4/7/11 sts, SKPO, yon, K5 * SKPO, K3, yon, K3, yon, K3, K2 tog, K4, SKPO, yon, K5 rep from * to last 0/3/7 sts, K.
Row 5: K3/6/10 sts, SKPO, yon, K1, yon, K2 tog, K2 * SKPO, K3, yon, K5, yon, K3, K2 tog, K2, SKPO, yon, K1, yon, K2 tog, K2, rep from * to last 1/4/8 sts, K.
Row 7: K5/8/12 sts, yon, K2 tog, K2, * SKPO, K3, yon, K7, yon, K3, K2 tog. K3, yon, K2 tog, K2, rep from * to last 2/5/9 sts, K.
Row 9: K8/11/15 sts * SKPO, K3, yon, K9, yon, K3, K2 tog, K5, rep from * to last 3/6/10 sts K.
Row 11: K7/10/14 sts * SKPO, K3, yon, K11, yon, K3, K2 tog, K3, rep from * to last 4/7/11 sts, K.
Row 13: K.
Row 14: P.
These 14 rows form the pattern.
Rep pattern 6 times (7 full patterns in all).

SHAPE ARMHOLE
Keep pattern straight.
Cast off 4 sts at beg of next 2 rows.
Cast off 3 sts at beg of next 2 rows.
Cast off 2 sts at beg of next 2 rows.
Dec 1 st at each end of next and every alt row until 75/81/89 sts **.
Cont straight until armhole measures 20cm (8in) ending after 12th row of pattern.

SHAPE SHOULDERS
Cast off 11/12/14 sts at beg of next 2 rows and 10/12/14 sts at beg of foll 2 rows.
Leave remaining 33 sts on thread for back of neck.

Front

Work as back until **.
Work 12 rows of pattern.

SHAPE LEFT NECK
K32/35/39 sts, turn, dec 1 st at neck edge on every row until 21/24/28 sts remain, keeping pattern straight until the armhole measures same as back, ending after wrong side row.
Shape shoulder: Cast off 10/12/14 sts.
Work 1 row.
Cast off 11/12/14 sts.

SHAPE RIGHT NECK
With right side facing slip 11 sts (neck front) on thread, and rejoin yarn at neck edge to remaining 32/35/39 sts.
Dec 1 st at neck edge every row until 21/24/28 sts remain, keeping pattern straight until the armhole measures same as back, ending after wrong side row.
Work 1 row.
Shape shoulder: Cast off 10/12/14 sts.
Work 1 row.
Cast off 11/12/14 sts.

Sleeves
(2 alike)
Using 2¾mm (no. 12) needles cast on 62/70/78 sts.
Work 28 rows K1, P1 rib inc 1 st at end of last row (63/71/79 sts).
Change to 3¼mm (no. 10) needles and pattern.
Set pattern thus.
Row 1: K14/18/22 sts * SKPO, K3, yon, K1, yon, K3, K2 tog, K13, repeat from * to last 1/5/9 sts. K.
Row 2 and every alt row: P.
Row 3: K6/10/14, SKPO, yon, K5 * SKPO, K3, yon, K3, yon, K3, K2 tog, K4, SKPO, yon, K5, repeat from * to last 2/6/10 sts. K.
Row 5: Inc 1 in 1st st, K4/8/12 sts SKPO, yon, K1, yon, K2 tog, K2, * SKPO, K3, yon, K5, yon, K3, K2 tog, K2, SKPO, yon, K1, yon, K2 tog K2, rep from * to last 3/7/11 sts, K, inc 1 in last st.
Row 7: K8/12/16 sts, K2 tog, K2 * SKPO, K3, yon, K7, yon, K3, K2 tog, K3, yon, K2 tog, K2, rep from * to last 5/9/13 sts, K.
Row 9: K11/15/19 sts * SKPO, K3, yon, K9, yon, K3, K2 tog, K5, rep from * to last 6/10/14 sts, K.
Row 11: Inc 1 in 1st st, K9/13/17 sts, * SKPO, K3, yon, K11, yon, K3, K2 tog, K3, rep from * to last 7/11/15 sts, K, inc 1 in last st.
Row 13: K.
Row 14: P.
Including the increase sts in patt as soon as possible, cont in patt inc 1 st each end of 3rd and every foll 6th row to 71/79/87 sts. Inc each end of every 4th row to 111/119/127 sts.
Cont in patt until work measures 48cm (19in) or required length.

SHAPE ARMHOLES
Cast off 4 sts at beg of next 2 rows.
Cast off 3 sts at beg of next 2 rows.
Dec 1 st at both ends of next and every foll 3rd row until 71/79/87 sts remain.
Cast off 6/7/8 sts at beg of next 8 rows (23 sts).
Cast off.

Finishing

Press, following instructions on ball band.
Join right shoulder seam.

NECK BORDER

With right side facing using 2¾mm (no. 12) needles, beg
at left shoulder pick up and K24 sts down left side of
neck, 11 sts from centre front, 24 sts up right side of
neck, work across the 33 sts at back of neck increasing
4 sts evenly (96 sts).
Work 8 rows K1, P1 rib.
Cast off loosely in rib.
Join left shoulder seam and neck border.

Sew pearls in position and slot ribbon through eyelet
holes as shown in picture.
Join side and sleeve seams.
Gather top of sleeve head, and insert sleeve, adjusting
gathers.
Sew in position.
Press seams.

In her own Fashion

Zandra Rhodes: Mink Trim Sweater and the 'Bubble' Sweater Dress

[For sweater, see photograph opposite. For 'Bubble' Dress, see colour photograph opposite page 80]

Zandra Rhodes calls her strange, extravagant, exceptional clothes 'works of art' dresses. That description applies equally to Zandra herself (see colour photograph). Even at work alone in her small studio, her face will be painted with dots and squiggles in shocking pink and cobalt blue beneath hair that changes colour with the seasons.

At home in her exquisitely decorated London house, she may lounge on her tangerine satin cushions in a simple track suit, but round her neck will be a bold piece of metallic orange jewellery, artistically matched to her burnished lips and two-tone pearlised and gilded finger nails. When she is really on show at museums, art galleries or on promotional trips, Zandra lives absolutely the style of her fantasy creations.

Zandra Rhodes started her fashion career as a textile designer, when she studied at the influential Royal College of Art in the seminal sixties. To understand her clothes, you have to grasp that every facet of them is an original creation: she will print on to silk chiffon her own pattern in ten different and carefully chosen colours, make it into a concertina of pleats and edge its hand-scissored hem with tiny seed pearls, than scatter its bodice with crystal drops. Thirty-five people (the creative core college-trained students like herself) now help her with this detailed work. 'We are one of the few companies in the world that survives on making expensive dresses, as opposed to being supported by ready-to-wear,' says Zandra Rhodes. 'My business and my staff really do exist on special order dresses.'

But there is more to Zandra Rhodes than just the Cinderella ball gowns which are photographed on glossy and glamorous customers. 'I sometimes find it upsetting,' she says 'that I go to a great deal of trouble to produce an all-round collection and no-one ever talks about the daywear side. It's always very easy to photograph fancy dress.'

Her knits are for every day, and they are an important, if unsung, part of her collections. (Now she is even designing in cashmere for an old-established British firm.) The knits are done by machine, but conceived, like the fairytale dresses, with meticulous attention to detail. The woollies are fantastically pleated, encrusted with tiny pearls, trimmed with fur or feathers and always made in the generously curving body shapes that are hallmarks of the Rhodes style. Even the apparently simple cream sweater (facing page) has a cleverly twisted pleat neck and bugle sleeves.

Zandra's basic working clothes may be an artist's smock and jeans (and she designs those too), but she likes wearing her own knits. 'I especially like them for winter in New York,' says Zandra, who is a superstar designer in the States. 'It's only when I am in America when I wear my knit designs all the time for promotional trips that I am able to evaluate and criticise my clothes as functional garments.'

The hand-knit sweater dress that she designed for this book, banded in her favourite 'Indian' pink, is in the bubble shape – wide at the shoulders and narrowing down at the hips – that is as much her signature as the puffball evening gowns. She wears it in her exotic bedroom in the colour plate opposite page 80. 'I first brought out the Bubble in 1978,' she says. 'I know the date because one of my customers in Houston has just brought one of those first dresses back to me and asked me to copy it. Sometimes I think it is wonderful to create a new shape that stays in fashion for years. At other times, I feel that I should always be doing something new. But the Bubble lends itself to new variations in knit or in fabric because the basic line is so strong.'

Zandra Rhodes has strong ideas about shape, colour, texture and about the flowers and plants that sprout in odd corners, blossom in her basement area and burst in full bloom – especially the graceful white lilies that she made into her best-known textile print. The lily print and her equally famous zig-zag are on the fabrics that swag and swathe her lofty London house, but she has yet to try to create those fantastic printed effects in knitting.

Mink Trim Sweater

Zandra Rhodes draws on the curve of the body and uses fantastic decorations on all her designs – like this soft cream sweater with gathered sleeves trimmed with mink tails. It is knitted in four-ply in an all-over ribbed pattern with a fold-over neck frill that gives a twist effect.

Size: to fit bust 80–90cm (32–36in). Length: 68cm (27in).

Yarn: 12 × 50g balls Lister Lee Motoravia 4-ply.

Needles: 2¾mm (no. 12) and 3¾mm (no. 9).

Tension: 36 sts and 40 rows knitted over pattern on 3¾mm (no. 9) ndls to 10cm (4in) square.

Notions: Mink trim.

Special abbreviation: K1B = Knit into stitch on row below.

Back and front
(2 alike)
Using 2¾mm (no. 12) ndls cast on 151 sts and work in K1, P1 rib for 9cm (3½in) increasing 30 sts evenly across last row.
Change to 3¾mm (no. 9) ndls and pattern as follows:
Row 1: P1, * K3, P1, repeat from * to end.
Row 2: * K1, P3 repeat from * to last st, K1.
Cont straight until work measures 59cm (23½in).

SHAPE NECK
Pattern 60 sts, put next 61 sts onto spare needle, pattern to end.
Next row: Pattern 60 sts, pattern across 61 sts on spare needle, pattern to end.
Leaving the central 61 sts on spare needle, cont straight on each side until work measures 68cm (27in). Cast off in pattern.

Sleeves
Using 2¾mm (no. 12) ndls cast on 72 sts and work in K1, P1 rib for 9cm (3½in). Change to 3¾mm (no. 9) ndls and work in pattern as before increasing 1 st at each end of every other row to 180 sts. Cast off.

Neckband
Using 2¾mm (no. 12) ndls and with right side of work facing pick up and knit 61 sts from front of neck and work in st.st for 2.5cm (1in). Cast off.
Pick up and knit 61 sts from back of neck and work to match front.

Neck frills
Using 3¾mm (no. 9) ndls cast on 16 sts and work foundation row in K1, P1 rib.
Now work 8cm (3in) rib as follows, * K1B, P1, repeat from * to end of row.
Cast off. Pick up and knit 33 sts along the long side and work in rib as Back for 13cm (5in).
Cast off. Work 7 more oblongs.

Finishing
Fold neckband in half and stitch down to wrong side of work. Join neckband seams.
Fold sleeve in half and leaving centre 15cm (6in) unstitched, set in sleeve giving 25cm (10in) seams each side of point of shoulder. Fold the 15cm section in half and neatly stitch together to give an 8cm (3in) seam.
Attach to point of shoulder with mink trim.
Repeat with second sleeve.
Join side and sleeve seams.
Attach neck frills as illustrated.

The 'Bubble' Sweater Dress

Zandra Rhodes invented the 'bubble' shape that she uses for a short black sweater dress with three contrasting stripes of her favourite shades of pink. The back and front with drop-shoulder sleeves are knitted in two identical pieces in stocking stitch with the embossed striped pattern from waist to shoulder line. The neckband and sleeve edges are worked on circular needles in double rib.

Size: 80 to 90cm (32 to 36in). Length approx. 1m (40in).

Yarn: Lister-Lee Motoravia 4-ply.
MY: 14 balls Black.
A: 1 ball Mulberry.
B: 1 ball Violet.
C: 1 ball Pink.

Needles: 3¼mm (no. 10) and 2¾mm (no. 12) and a 2¾mm (no. 12) circular needle.

Tension: 14 sts and 18 rows knitted in st.st on 3¼mm (no. 10) ndls to 10cm (4in) square.

Back and front
(2 pieces alike)
Using 2¾mm (no. 12) needles and MY, cast on 134 sts and work in rib as follows for 18cm (7in).
Row 1: K2, * P2, K2, rep from * to end.
Row 2: P2, * K2, P2, rep from * to end.
Change to 3¼mm (no. 10) needles and continue in st.st until work measures 53cm (21in) from commencement.

SLEEVE INCREASES
Row 1 (right side facing): Cast on 38 sts, then K these sts and complete the row.
Row 2: Cast on 38 sts, P these sts, and then complete the row (210 sts).
Work 2 rows st.st. Now commence embossed stripe pattern as follows, which is worked in st.st throughout:
(Right side facing) work 4 rows using A.
Pick up row: change to MY. With right-hand needle pick up loop of first row of yarn A, place on left-hand needle and K this loop and first st on left hand needle together. Repeat across remainder of row. Continue in MY for 9cm (3½in) ending with P row.
Repeat stripe as above using B.
Work further 9cm (3½in) in MY.
Repeat stripe as above using C.
Now continue working stripes in the same sequence (i.e. A, B, C) working the following lengths in between stripes in MY:
9cm (3½in); 5cm (2in); 4cm (1½in) twice; 2cm (1in) three times; 1cm (½in) three times; 2 rows twice.
Work 2 rows plain.
Cast off 66 sts, put centre 78 sts onto holder, cast off rem 66 sts.

Neckband
(Right side facing)
Using 2¾mm (no. 12) circular needle, K across 78 sts on both front and back (156 sts).
Work in K2, P2 rib for 23cm (9in).
Cast off *loosely* in rib.
Fold neckband to inside and stitch down.

Sleeve edgings
(2 alike)
Join side and shoulder seams with neat backstitch.
Using 2¾mm (no. 12) circular needle, with right side facing, pick up and knit 180 sts around sleeve opening.
Work 25cm (10in) in K2, P2 rib, cast off loosely in rib, fold edging to inside and stitch down.